Web Hosting

About the Author

Carl Burnham is a web developer, hosting consultant, and a specialist in analyzing Internet-related trends and technologies. He co-wrote *Ace the Technical Interview, Fourth Edition*.

Web Hosting

CARL **BURNHAM**

Osborne/**McGraw-Hill**
New York   Chicago   San Francisco   Lisbon
London   Madrid   Mexico City   Milan
New Delhi   San Juan   Seoul   Singapore
Sydney   Toronto

Osborne/**McGraw-Hill**
2600 Tenth Street
Berkeley, California 94710
U.S.A.

To arrange bulk purchase discounts for sales promotions, premiums, or fund raisers, please contact Osborne/**McGraw-Hill** at the above address. For information on translations or book distributors outside the U.S.A., please see the International Contact Information page immediately following the index of this book.

Web Hosting

1234567890 CUS CUS 01987654321

ISBN 0-07-2132795

Publisher
  Brandon A. Nordin
Vice President & Associate Publisher
  Scott Rogers
Acquisitions Editor
  Francis Kelly
Acquisitions Coordinator
  Alexander Corona
Technical Editor
  Peter Mokros
Copy Editor
  Rachel Lopez
Proofreader
  Carroll Proffitt

Indexer
  Jack Lewis
Computer Designers
  Carie Abrew, Tara Davis
Illustrator
  Michael Mueller
Series Design
  Peter F. Hancik
Cover Design
  Greg Scott
Cover Illustration
  Mick Wiggins

This book was composed with Corel VENTURA™ Publisher.

AT A GLANCE

CONTENTS

Part II

Marketing

Part III

Customer Service

Part IV

Web Hosting Services

Part V

Infrastructure and Security Considerations

Part VI

Advanced Hosting Markets

ACKNOWLEDGMENTS

I wish to thank my wife, Rhonda, for her love, patience, and graphical assistance through this writing process. To my parents, for giving me many gifts, including persistence. To my friend Tommy, for words of encouragement and to companies and individuals who provided assistance. And especially to the staff of Osborne McGraw-Hill that helped to make this book possible.

PART 1

Starting a Web Hosting Business

CHAPTER 1

The Changing World
of Web Hosting

If we did all the things we are capable of doing, we would literally astound ourselves.

—Thomas Edison

In the expanding web hosting market, the information technology industry has come far from the early days of simply providing server spacing for customers to view static HTML pages and to access files online. The Internet, now an integral part of conducting business, provides many areas in which web hosts can specialize such as shared hosting, co-location hosting, managed 24/7 enterprise services, e-commerce, or application hosting for businesses.

TRENDS IN WEB HOSTING AND THE INTERNET

Innovative technology continues to be introduced at a record pace as hardware, software, and infrastructure advancements increasingly make the Internet available on portable devices. These include wireless devices such as PDAs and cellular phones, streaming media, e-commerce, Java, and XML applications. Other devices such as web phones, Internet-only terminals, and television-based web appliances are becoming more popular, with web phones leading the way. Custom content delivery through niche portals holds promise, and will continue to drive the wireless market.

For web hosts, a key factor in gaining an early market presence will be harnessing wireless application protocol (WAP) technologies by partnering with key market players and content providers. Web hosts are exploring ways to provide value-added service plans to assist businesses with modifying site content to reach the wireless market. By 2003 wireless networks will be greatly enhanced worldwide, which will make web browsing a standard feature on most wireless devices. According to Cahners In-Stat Group (www.instat.com), by 2004 these wireless devices will account for more than 37 million units sold, compared to 2 million in 1999. This technology will be discussed later in this book, beginning in Chapter 4.

As the surge of innovation continues and brick-and-mortar businesses venture onto the Web for the first time, opportunities to capture new markets arise. Existing sites with basic brochure-type content are seeking to add e-commerce capabilities. According to Forrester Research (www.forrester.com), in a 2000 study of 2,500 global users with web sites, 62 percent chose to outsource their web sites, compared to 44 percent in 1998. Those responding cited key factors such as adding e-commerce capabilities, lack of internal expertise, cost savings, and reliability of host, as shown in Figure 1-1. It is interesting to note, given the breaches of security that have occurred at leading web sites, that security did not appear as a consideration in the 2000 results. In a similar survey completed in 1998, security was cited as a concern by 14 percent of the 22 companies that responded.

Several companies with high-visibility sites were concerned that their hosts would not have the capabilities required to fully support their needs. This presents excellent opportunities for hosts that specialize in applications hosting, managed hosting, and enterprise hosting to pursue market opportunities. In addition to offering IT expertise, consultants, web designers, and IT professionals can partner with web hosts to resell hosting services as a value-added solution for their clients.

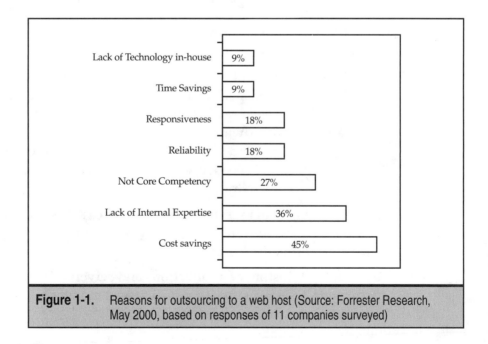

Figure 1-1.   Reasons for outsourcing to a web host (Source: Forrester Research, May 2000, based on responses of 11 companies surveyed)

Businesses have revamped their marketing strategies and core business models to be centrally focused on the Web. Business fortunes are being won and lost on the Internet as investors demand that even startup companies show immediate and profitable results. The challenges for businesses will be to base offerings around core business principles, and to outsource functions that are not central to the business (such as web hosting). Within the web hosting industry, firms that continue to base their hosting services on price alone will not survive, as the trend leads toward a commodity market; especially for low-end shared hosting. Instant access to information has accelerated the rate of change, touching all facets of daily life and resulting in increased demand for IT professionals with a wide range of technical skill levels. According to most industry analysts, within the next four years, web hosts will find it more difficult, as they compete to fill network administrator, systems administrator, and application development programmer positions. Web hosts that have the vision to focus on core specialties, partnering where needed, and to be true value-added business consultants instead of order takers will profit immensely in the next phase of the Internet's growth. Some of the value-added web services in hot demand include the following:

▼ **Performance monitoring**   The web hosting service gauges the level of activity on servers, optimizing where needed.

■ **Distributed content**   Through capacity upon demand, web sites can plan for special one-time events and variable traffic needs. Special online events often require immediate availability of additional bandwidth to accommodate increased visitors . Capacity on demand enables a web host to rev up additional bandwidth as it is needed so the web site is always available as it receives extra traffic.

■ **Streaming media services**   These services support audio and video, which requires a high level of bandwidth to display properly.

■ **Managed hosting of applications and servers**   Features include customized server management, monitoring of applications, and network integration.

- ■ **Security**   Web hosts can better protect customer data through a combination of hardware and software technology, ongoing monitoring, and security policies.

- ▲ **Load balancing**   Load balancing distributes processing or applications among multiple computers within a network, which prevents some servers from operating at capacity whereas others are barely used. This is shown in Figure 1-2.

Throughout this book we will be exploring ways that web hosts can provide these and other web services as they move to become business and integration partners with their customers. Within this chapter, we will first take a brief look at how the Internet began, the markets for web hosts and related markets, and how some companies are meeting the needs of clients today.

PIONEERING A MARKET

The first traces of what is now the Internet began with ARPA (Advanced Research Projects Agency), which was part of the U.S. Department of Defense (DoD), in 1969. Early research into network computing, funded through the DoD, led to the creation of many new technologies, including telephone lines used for network connectivity. The chief contractor for ARPANET was BBN (Bolt Beranek and Newman, Inc.). BBN was the creator of many innovative Internet technologies that exist today, including the router, the modem, the @ sign in e-mail, and distributed packet switching. BBN also was instrumental in the creation of other networks including BBN Planet, the first Internet Service Provider. BBN was sold to GTE, and now is Genuity.

During the high point of ARPANET's popularity, the NSF (National Science Foundation) developed the NSFNET, which linked four supercomputers at different locations. NSFNET provided regional backbone connectivity both for the public sector and research facilities through these multiple supercomputer centers. This network led to other trial networks, and eventually to ARPANET, which was a compilation of interconnected computer networks. The four original nodes of ARPANET included the University of California Santa Barbara,

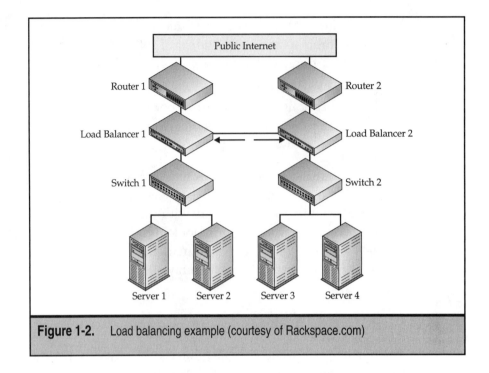

Figure 1-2. Load balancing example (courtesy of Rackspace.com)

UCLA, the University of Utah, and SRI International. ARPANET proved successful in the public sector and was used until 1989.

Issued around 1969, RFCs (Requests for Comments) detailed networking protocols and communications notes that later emerged into Internet standards. In 1988 T1 links (at 1.544 Mbps) were introduced, greatly enhancing speed over previous 56 Kbps linkages. By 1991 the NSFNET become available to the private sector and was enhanced to T3 links (at 45 Mbps). During this time other networks were forming and needed to mutually connect with each other; ISPs (Internet Service Providers) emerged to provide this connectivity. The very first web browser, shown in Figure 1-3, was designed by Tim Berners-Lee, a CERN scientist, in 1989. The browser would be called *World Wide Web*, which soon would mean so much more.

By 1993 personal web sites appeared with some semblance of graphical content, which look like the Stone Age compared to today. During the same year search engines such as Altavista, Inktomi, Yahoo!, WebCrawler, and Excite emerged; these still are the predominate

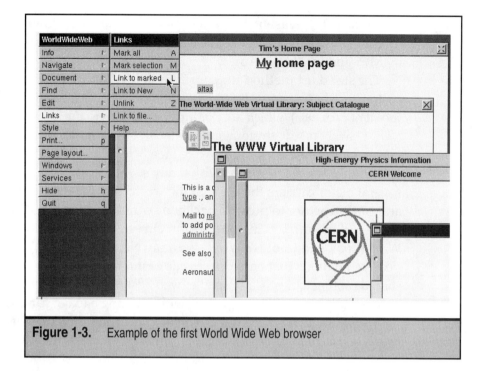

Figure 1-3.   Example of the first World Wide Web browser

vehicles for Internet research today. This made it necessary for web sites to have different types of content to generate the most hits by the search engines. Bulletin board services such as those offered by Prodigy and America Online were introduced, followed by the offering of public Internet access beginning in 1995 with the introduction of the web browser. Once it introduced Internet Explorer, Microsoft took the lead in the browser market.

The National Science Foundation Network (NSFNET) commissioned Sprint to provide a connectivity framework for the public and private sectors throughout the world. Before NSFNET's discontinuation in 1995, several commercial Internet carriers, along with Sprint, were awarded status as NAPs (Network Access Points) to provide Internet connectivity through regional exchange backbone locations. The NAPs were Ameritech (Chicago, Illinois), PacBell (San Francisco, California), MFS Datanet (Washington, D.C.), and Sprint (Pennsauken, New Jersey). MFS Datanet, now commonly referred to as MAE-EAST, is located in Tyson's Corner, Virginia. MAE-EAST makes use of a gigaswitch and has more than 33 connections, with funding provided by U.S. federal agencies. MAE-WEST also is operated by MFS and by NASA Ames.

The standard method for connectivity that emerged was for customers to gain access through small Internet service provider POPs (point of presence), which are dial-up connections to the high-speed carrier backbones, with storage made available for static pages to display information. These early efforts were mostly text based and primitive in appearance when compared with today's web sites. There now are several major carriers throughout the world that have the bandwidth and infrastructure to provide backbone connectivity points for ISPs. Some of these carriers include Sprint, Qwest, UUNET, AT&T, GTE, WorldCom, and Cable & Wireless. Many NAPs utilize sophisticated peering methods that enhance speeds of interconnectivity through shared routing tables. Many smaller web hosting firms are using partner arrangements with ISPs for peering without using a major carrier.

The National Science Foundation also awarded projects that led to broad infrastructure developments. One such project, the InterNIC (Internet Network Information Center), was entrusted with domain name registration services and assigning domains (using .com, .net, .edu, .org, .mil, and .gov) with a corresponding Internet Protocol numerical address. The InterNIC project originally was overseen by Network Solutions, AT&T, and General Atomics. Through the InterNIC domain registration process, applicants completed templates for each domain, which had to include at least two active, independent DNS (Domain Name System servers) as part of the submittal process.

In June 1999 the U.S. government split up the InterNIC and allowed other entities to handle domain name registrations, although the InterNIC (now referred to as Network Solutions) remains a leading domain registration service. Other online registration services now compete in this market, including Register.com and OpenSRS.org. Domain registration services are covered in greater detail in Chapter 8. Nonprofit corporation ICANN (Internet Corporation for Assigned Names and Numbers) has been designated by the U.S. government to maintain the Internet's domain name system. ICANN (http://www.icann.org) also accredits domain registrars, which can register top-level domain names either directly or by reseller arrangements.

The heightened traffic demands for more bandwidth continue to escalate infrastructure costs for main carriers and providers of Internet access as more cross-connects, SONET multiplexers, and other equipment are purchased. New optical switching technology, now being fully utilized by carriers, promises to substantially reduce new equipment outlays, and greatly reduce personnel and operating costs for carriers. This will provide higher bandwidth services for web hosts and rapid bandwidth on demand will be available, providing opportunities for mutual partnerships. This new technology is discussed further in Chapter 16.

THE GROWING WEB HOSTING MARKET

The overall number of ISPs increased to 7,785 in 2000 from 5,775 in 1999, according to Cahners In-Stat Group—a 35 percent increase within one year. Projected out to the year 2004, the market research firm anticipates that the combined annual growth rate for ISP revenues will be 25.7 percent. Within the broadband market, which primarily includes cable and DSL modem access, revenue is anticipated to grow 77 percent by 2004. By 2004 the revenues from broadband access are expected to increase to $13.3 billion from the current level of $1 billion.

There are an estimated 10,000 companies providing a wide range of web hosting services. The types of web hosting services continue to expand to meet the needs of business and consumer markets. In Chapter 2, we will explore the main categories of web hosts in detail. As shown in Figure 1-4, the U.S. market is expected to grow from $1.4 billion in 1999 to $10.6 billion by 2002. Analysts estimate that by 2004 it will reach $19.8 billion.

ISPs are defined as either owners and maintainers of their own networks or as resellers and consultants that resell ISP services. ISPs primarily provide a range of Internet connectivity services. As with web hosting, the market for ISPs continues to gravitate toward the business market. For the year 2001 only an 8 percent annual growth rate is anticipated within the consumer market for ISPs, a 50 percent reduction from previous years. Because ISPs are focused on providing

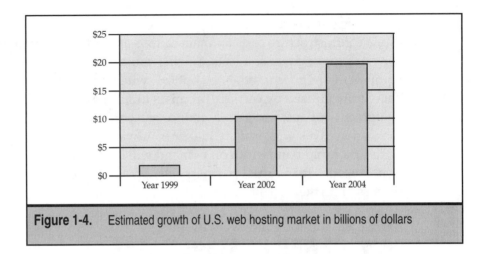

Figure 1-4.   Estimated growth of U.S. web hosting market in billions of dollars

Internet connectivity services, they are increasingly looking for ways to provide value-added web hosting services that go beyond entry-level shared hosting plans. Some are gaining access to more advanced hosting specialties, such as managed services and application hosting, through partnerships with web hosts. The most common method for larger ISPs has been acquisitions and mergers with web hosting companies that already have the technical expertise in house.

NOTE: Nearly 30 percent of revenues generated by ISPs in the business market are from web hosting.

Internet usage worldwide continues to grow as it expands into new markets. As shown in Figure 1-5, it is estimated to reach 377 million users by 2003, from 250 million in 2000. The biggest percentage increase (in 1999) was in South America, with a 165 percent increase. By 2005 it is estimated that 68 percent of all Internet users will be logging on from outside the U.S. and Canada (this was already almost 50 percent in 1999) and 75 percent of the U.S. population will be online, as shown in Figure 1-6. With the increase of online users, web hosts seeking to attract global markets must consider including multiple language translation in their web sites and services.

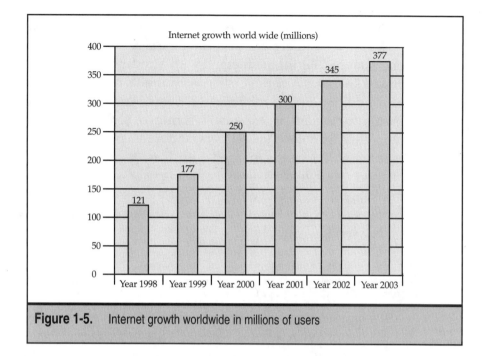

Figure 1-5.   Internet growth worldwide in millions of users

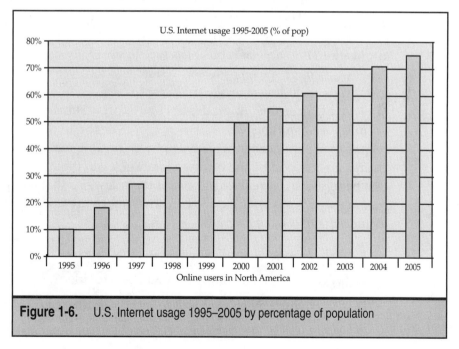

Figure 1-6.   U.S. Internet usage 1995–2005 by percentage of population

Source for Figures 1-6 is CommerceNet (**http://www.commerce.net**)

Mergers abound throughout the Internet industry as companies seek to grab market share and combine services under one name. As one example, EarthLink merged with Mindspring to form one of the largest ISPs after America Online, with annual revenues of $914 million (during 1999) and 4.3 million subscribers. America Online remains by far the leading ISP, with annual revenues of $6.9 billion (during 1999), more than 25 million subscribers, and a 14.5 percent share of the ISP market. AOL recently merged with Time Warner in a $30 billion all-stock arrangement to take advantage of each company's many market properties, and online and offline resources. This trend will continue; especially for web hosts as they attempt to increase the range of web services they offer.

APPLICATION SERVICE PROVIDERS

ASPs (application service providers) provide managed hosting of specific application services, which enables businesses to use enterprise software securely through the Internet on an agreed-upon monthly pricing plan. The software that is hosted by the ASP can be word processing, groupware, productivity, accounting, or other business application, the same as a business would normally use, except that it is online through a web browser. A business receives several benefits from ASPs, including access to the latest software, without the obligation of recurring licensing, upgrade, or IT support and management costs for in-house handling. The ASP is responsible for all of the functions related to the application. This type of web hosting niche has not been clearly understood by the business market, even though substantial cost benefits can be realized. Some of the questions that companies or existing web hosts will want to consider before pursuing this market include the following:

▼ What range of applications will be offered?

■ What level of customization will be provided?

■ What will be the setup and monthly service fees charged?

■ What will be the network infrastructure or data center facilities?

■   What will be the customer support and security policies?

▲   How will security be implemented?

The majority of ASPs do not have their own data center facilities to securely house web servers. ASPs must develop close partnerships with ISPs and carriers that have data centers, or build their own (an expensive proposition) to provide a guarantee of service, which is built into most ASP agreements and defined as a service level agreement. Additionally, ISPs have a large customer base where co-marketing campaigns could focus on specific application needs that partner ASPs fulfill. ISPs typically lack the high-end application specialties that ASPs have. These types of partnering opportunities are discussed in further detail in Chapter 14. To capture a share of the ASP market, ISPs must ramp up their data centers to handle the dynamic traffic demands of businesses in a physically secure 24/7 environment. Internal applications expertise also will be a requisite as businesses look to realize the substantial savings from outsourcing their in-house applications to ASPs.

According to Cahners In-Stat Group, by 2004 more than 3 million small companies will be using ASPs, likely subscribing to them through an Internet carrier or broadband connectivity provider. Internet carriers and providers will benefit by having a specialized range of services to offer. Depending on the agreements, a possible advantage for ASPs could be in having ready access to an Internet carrier or provider's database to conduct coordinated sales campaigns. Many companies that decide to pursue the ASP market select applications that the company is already experienced in, such as e-mail, groupware, or office applications, instead of supporting intensive applications that require a high level of specialized IT personnel involvement. ASPs also are evolving toward providing a multitude of services through the wireless market, such as with Qwest Cyber.Solutions.

As with the overall market, ASP expertise is increasingly acquired through mergers. During 2000 the telecommunications giant WorldCom purchased Internet service provider Intermedia Communications to gain access to Digex Inc. (which is a subsidiary). Digex specializes in ASP and managed web hosting services. Digex will benefit from the merger by having access to a major Internet backbone provider.

Other major backbone carriers that have entered the ASP market include Qwest, which has data centers and provides a range of ASP services through its subsidiary Qwest Cyber.Solutions.

Within the ASP market, the applications being hosted are being led by e-mail services, messaging, and groupware (60 percent), as shown in Figure 1-7. These applications are obvious, given the widespread usage of e-mail as a standard medium for communications. Many ASPs get started by providing services within these areas. Other applications noted here include e-commerce (37 percent), accounting (37 percent), training (36 percent), and customer service (30 percent) according to Zona Research.

For many businesses e-commerce is a critical path toward realizing the potential profitability of the Internet. Online business accounts for 30 percent of all business revenues. By 2003 more than 49 percent of small businesses are predicted to have e-commerce capability. As businesses apply the Internet to handle more of their internal and external operations, the shift to ASPs will escalate (see Figure 1-8).

As web hosts are required to ramp up sites quickly and provide more sophisticated products, many are partnering with managed-

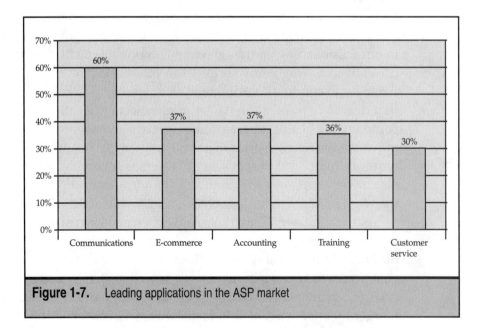

Figure 1-7.   Leading applications in the ASP market

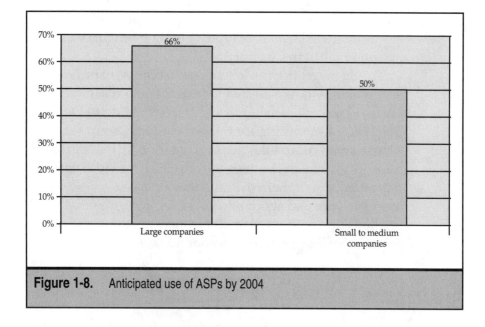

Figure 1-8.   Anticipated use of ASPs by 2004

service hosts (such as SiteRock, Loudcloud, and Luminate), which enable services such as comprehensive 24/7 real-time monitoring, site security, and redundancy. According to the Intermedia Group (www.imgevents.com), Loudcloud customers save an average 87.3 percent by outsourcing IT services. The In-Stat Group anticipates that Internet providers will focus on becoming "business service providers." This is the natural progression of a provider offering enhanced services beyond simple connectivity, through partnerships with specialized application and managed hosting firms.

As spending for web-related services surpasses hardware purchases, traditional computer manufacturers, including Dell, Micron, Compaq, and IBM also are entering the web hosting market. Dell has partnered with Interliant to provide web hosting services. In 2000 IBM leased co-location space from AT&T and Equinix data centers to provide web services. IBM also is building centers in partnership with Internet backbone provider Qwest, in return for 25 percent usage of spacing in each facility. In meeting the high-end needs for fully scalable and redundant hosting, companies such as Exodus, Genuity, and Verio are providing managed hosting services to ASPs and corporations within highly secure data centers throughout the world. Services include 24/7 technical support, extensive network monitoring, and hardware scalability. These types of hosting services will be discussed in further detail in Chapter 15.

For the web host, the key to profitability will be how well they can consult with businesses to help them to reach their business goals— especially small businesses. According to Director of Markets & Computing for Cahners In-Stat Group Kneko Burney, "These small companies are looking for a virtual partner that can not only give them the tools they need to expand online, but more importantly give them the guidance to do it successfully. This means it's not just about eBusiness services; it's about building relationships with your small business customers and offering services flexible enough to accommodate their diverse needs."

SUMMARY

As has been discussed, there are many factors that contribute to a high demand for web hosting. The Internet is providing sweeping changes to businesses and consumers, providing refreshing opportunities, innovations, and challenges to IT professionals. As the Internet continues to expand, new opportunities emerge for Internet businesses. As you will see in the next chapter, there are many categories of hosting plans that are providing added value and filling business niches through specialization or strategic partnering outside the organization to gain market advantages. In many cases a web host will provide a combination of these services, either in-house or through partnerships. The plans discussed in the next chapter include shared, dedicated, co-location, reseller, template, specialized platform, application, and high scalability hosting.

CHAPTER 2

Types of Web Hosting Plans

In response to the unprecedented growth of the Internet and e-commerce, and business demand, sophisticated hosting plans continue to evolve. Web hosting providers, consultants, and systems integrators seek the competitive edge through specialization and win-win partnerships. Businesses are keenly aware of the many advantages that e-commerce and an Internet marketing presence provide on a global scale. By 2003, business and consumer spending on the Internet is estimated to be more than $3.2 trillion. By 2004 some analysts predict that e-commerce will account for 20 percent of the U.S. economy. More traditional brick-and-mortar businesses are especially in need of specialized web expertise, as they lack the in-house IT skills, infrastructure, or the capability to attract high-demand Internet professionals to drive an online e-commerce presence that augments their physical business locations.

Competitive market factors also contribute to the growing trend. Smart businesses are using the Web to stay in personal touch with their customers, incorporating e-commerce into their businesses, developing targeted marketing campaigns, and advertising online in combination with traditional marketing avenues. The Web has proven that companies that are purely Internet based rarely survive; especially if they are not built around core business values. There are no magic overnight success formulas. It requires a combination of approaches, including both online and offline marketing, to keep a company's brand name in front of customers. A web host's job should be to take on more of a consulting role for their customers, to assist them with realistically planning or augmenting their online web presence.

Businesses are seeing the many advantages that outsourcing their web hosting provides compared to the infrastructure and high personnel requirements of handling web services themselves. Chief among these concerns is 24/7 web server management and support, fault-tolerant and redundant power systems, hardware and software security, regimented system backups, and application and e-commerce specialization.

NOTE: By 2004 web hosts will derive 91 percent of all revenues from e-commerce–enabled web sites, driving up an estimated $18 billion in revenues, according to Forrester Research.

The small business market (those with fewer than 100 employees) accounts for 95 percent of all U.S. companies and employs about half of the U.S. workforce. By 2004, 65 percent of large businesses, 83 percent of mid-sized businesses, and more than 99 percent of small businesses are expected to have a web presence that is hosted, according to Forrester Research. By 2003 it is estimated that 49 percent of small businesses will have e-commerce capability, up from 34 percent in 2000.

With the growth of opportunities in the market, web hosts need to offer higher quality services that take on the role of business consultation as well as web site hosting. This can enable businesses to become more effective on the Web by reducing their infrastructure IT costs through outsourcing and concentrate more on pursuing their core business objectives. According to analyst Jeanne Schaaf at Forrester Research, web hosting will grow to $19.8 billion by the end of 2004, up from $1.4 billion at the end of 1999, as shown in Figure 2-1. Putting this into market perspective, that is a 1,300% rate of increase over a five-year period.

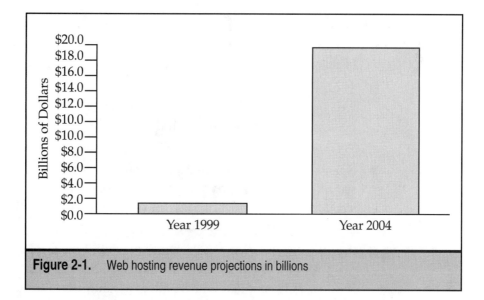

Figure 2-1.   Web hosting revenue projections in billions

CHOOSING THE TYPE OF HOSTING TO PROVIDE

Given this rate of growth, IT professionals with varying technical backgrounds have keen interests in entering new web hosting markets and forming partnerships with existing players to develop a comprehensive suite of services. Just what kinds of web hosting companies are out there and in what niche market areas? What are the characteristics of these?

The main types of web hosts can be loosely organized into the following general categories:

▼ **Shared hosting**   Customer web sites share space on the same physical web servers.

■ **Dedicated hosting**   Involves allocation of a specific web server for use by one customer only, for one or several of that customer's web sites.

■ **Co-location hosting**   The customer houses its web server within a web host provider's secure data center or facility.

■ **Reseller hosting**   Usually a web host provides storage at a discount to web consultants (which can include web designers, developers, or systems integration firms), who then resell the storage as a service or add-on to complement their other range of services that can include web site design or programming.

■ **Template hosting**   Customer creates a web site through a web browser using standard templates from the template hosting web site; usually with the host's logo viewable on the web pages hosted.

■ **Specialized platform hosting**   A customer will require a specific platform for dynamic pages to be generated or to support a specific technology for custom development such as JSP, ASP, or ColdFusion.

■ **Application hosting**   (Also called application service providers, or ASPs) Involves the managed hosting of software services and is popular with small- to medium-sized businesses that want controlled hosting of enterprise software applications securely through the Internet or a VPN (Virtual Private Network).

- ■ **Managed-services hosting**   Includes the management of a wide range of value-added IT services that ensure that a web site (or host) is performing effectively.

- ▲ **High-scalability hosting**   In the upper tier of hosting plans, a customer will require a highly scalable environment to respond to rapidly changing site traffic needs.

Many larger web hosting companies and direct providers have a mixture of plans that encompass several of these categories.

When you decide which hosting markets to focus on, you must consider several core variables, including in-house expertise and infrastructure, market conditions, competition, current trends, and industry partnerships. When you want to gain entry or expand into some of these related hosting markets, you should ask yourself some basic questions, including:

- ▼ What potential markets are emerging within this niche area of hosting?

- ■ Who is the competition? Are they profiting in the market? Is the timing right for providing the type of web hosting services you are considering?

- ■ What competitive advantages can my company provide that are not being met in the industry?

- ■ Is expertise available in-house?

- ■ What are the potential drawbacks? Do the advantages outweigh the disadvantages?

- ▲ What partnership opportunities are available to reduce the level of risk and complement my existing core business?

The remainder of this chapter is dedicated to describing the most common types of hosting plans available so you can determine which is right for your business and your particular market.

SHARED HOSTING

In *shared hosting*, customer web sites share space on the same physical web servers. At this level of hosting, the customer web sites typically are static, meaning the site contents are manually uploaded to a web server through FTP (File Transfer Protocol) or a similar method. Sometimes web pages can be dynamic—page content is generated on the fly through server-side scripting or a back-end database (this will vary, according to what a web host allows within a shared plan).

Static pages often are the equivalent of customer marketing advertisements, which is the reason shared hosting is popular with small to medium-sized businesses whose primary goal is to establish a marketing presence on the Web. Depending on the web host, a shared plan might include a few hundred to a thousand different customers using storage space on each individual server. For IT professionals who want to gain entry into the hosting market, shared hosting is attractive, because the costs of entry are low through reseller or partner arrangements with existing web hosts.

NOTE: According to Forrester Research, shared hosting is expected to double in the next five years, to $890 million, as shown in Figure 2-2.

The standard range of services provided by web hosts varies, with the most common being a cgi-bin directory, FTP, or administrative web access for making updates, e-mail services, domain registration and parking services, and web site design and programming services. These services are discussed in further detail in Chapter 8. Web server spacing plans for a client typically range from ten to one hundred megabytes of storage, with monthly costs ranging from $19 to several hundred dollars per month, depending on the optional services selected (refer to Chapter 9 for more information).

Shared hosting plans are further defined by the level of monthly data transfer permitted, which depends on which plan level the customer selects. Data transfer is defined as the actual files (HTML or XML pages, applets, images, audio files, and so on) that a web server transfers as a response to a web browser request. The average monthly range for data transfers can vary widely from approximately 500 megabytes (20,000 page views) to 5 gigabytes

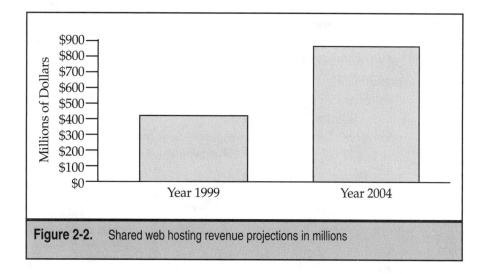

Figure 2-2.   Shared web hosting revenue projections in millions

(200,000 page views). It is misleading for you to list your data transfer as being unlimited, when in actuality there are limits that your systems physically allow.

For clients not looking for a unique domain name to professionally identify themselves in the marketplace, many web hosts provide an alternative, lower-cost method, which allows the use of spacing as a subdirectory extension to the web host's domain name. For example, suppose Triangle Associates decides to have its web site hosted in this way with HostingResolve. Its URL would be listed as http://www.hostingresolve.com/hosting/triangle/index.html instead of www.triangle.com. The client is not required to register a domain name through Network Solutions, Register.com, OpenSRS, or other domain name registration service. This initially was the method used by internet service providers (ISPs) to provide storage to their customers as an add-on service to their dial-up accounts, within a subfolder of the ISP's web address.

A similar method to listing this type of account is to point to the subdirectory in the address before the domain name, instead of www. In this example, Triangle Associates's URL would be http://hosting.hostingresolve.com/triangle/index.html. This type of plan usually does not include the full functions available with a regular, shared hosting plan and is geared toward personal or nonprofit organizations.

The number of web sites that are stored per server can vary significantly, depending on how sites are managed and aggregated on each physical server. Newer technology, called *virtual hosting*, provides a more scalable method to theoretically store up to 5,000 domain names per server. The obvious advantage to this form of shared hosting is improved potential profit margins for web host providers. The drawbacks include development costs and a higher level of IT expertise required than a routine shared hosting plan.

Two of the largest web hosting providers, XO Communications (formerly Concentric Networks) and Verio each have developed virtual hosting platform solutions for their clients and reseller markets. Verio acquired iServer, which was the first virtual server product. Other companies have addressed these needs by developing and packaging virtual server products for web hosts on different platforms. These include Ensim, Sphera, and Systemsfusion. Ensim was the first to market with its ServerXchange product, released in October 1999.

Verio (home.verio.com) is reported to be the world's largest web host, with an estimated 7 percent share of the market. The company's primary niche market includes small to mid-range companies. Services include Internet access, VPNs (Virtual Private Networks), and e-commerce solutions. Verio now is a part of NTT, a Japanese telecommunications firm.

XO Communications (www.xo.com) provides a similar range of services, including shared, dedicated, and co-location hosting solutions. The company utilizes an ATM-based network, with an OC-3, OC-12, and OC-48 backbone and provides Internet access services. These types of network backbones are discussed in detail in Chapter 10. As shared hosting is increasingly a commodity item, client support will become more of an issue, as web hosts venture away from providing business-hour technical telephone support. The trend is to provide technical support online through FAQ pages, Q&A support pages, and tracking-ticket submittal forms to log client problems instead of providing direct customer support. The downsides of this are the feedback might not relate to the problem at hand and the client might not be able to get in touch with the web host provider in a timely manner. A more popular alternative–instant chat and help services–works well for providing real-time customer service.

Customer service and responsiveness are becoming an increasing requirement for a web host. This subject is discussed in further detail in Chapter 6. Consultants, integrators, and resellers are filling this support need by providing the web site design and software specialization and partnering with web hosts that have the support and data center infrastructure to fulfill the various needs of their clients.

Verio is an example of this customer service model. Verio has more than 5,000 resellers providing direct web site software support to more than 340,000 clients, with Verio handling any hardware or network issues that arise. The client contacts the reseller directly for support issues; the reseller determines whether hardware or network issues require the involvement of the host provider. Verio's reseller program is a key contributing factor to its status as one of the largest web hosts in the industry. Bringing together a comprehensive suite of solutions as a result of industry partnerships, reseller agreements, and affiliations will become standard as the market matures. This form of partnering has multiple benefits, and will be covered more in the following section on reseller hosting and throughout this book.

Examples of companies that are involved within the shared hosting market include

▼ **XO Communications**   http://www.xo.com

■ **Verio**   http://www.verio.com

▲ **Digex**   http://www.digex.com

As a customer's needs increase, requiring more dynamic page content, enhanced security, a greater share of bandwidth (due to site traffic increases beyond a shared hosting plan's limits), and system scalability, an upgrade to a *dedicated* or *co-located* solution becomes necessary. Unlike a shared plan, these plans do not share server space with other customers for security and performance reasons, and provide a greater range of hosting features.

DEDICATED HOSTING

Dedicated hosting, a newer form of hosting, allocates a specific web server for use by only one client, for one site or multiple web sites.

Dedicated hosting enables a customer to host multiple sites from one server. The advantages for the customer include more flexibility, software configuration options, capability to handle greater site traffic, and more scalable bandwidth than available with shared hosting solutions. These factors are especially important to high-traffic sites. In some cases clients are allowed root-level directory access. Dedicated hosting plans typically start at $100 per month and can range up to $5,000 per month for high-end e-commerce or streamed content web sites with multiple servers. The monthly range for data transfers averages 5 gigabytes (200,000 page views).

Typically, a web host provides a guarantee of server uptime, such as 99.9 percent, within a service level agreement (SLA). SLA agreements are discussed in further detail in Chapter 6. Be careful to back up whatever percentage you guarantee with the appropriate level of hardware and software, infrastructure, a security plan, and backup procedures. Some clients specify financial penalties or refunds within an SLA agreement in case the web host does not perform as agreed upon. To uphold this level of service, you need written procedures that cover issues such as uploading files, hosting plan parameters, server spacing, amount of bandwidth usage allowed before incurring additional charges, limit acceptable server-side usage to specific technologies, bill payments, and acceptable content usage.

Some web hosts, such as Alabanza (www.alabanza.com), prohibit site content that consists entirely of pornographic or derogatory material, based on legal and ethical standards. You also should have a written policy that removes any liability of the web host as applies to site content. Consult with an attorney when preparing or modifying written procedures that apply to client usage of your services to ensure that your company is fully protected under current laws.

It is always good insurance for a web host to have ready access to multiple providers to ensure redundancy and availability. If your provider has critical traffic problems, you can re-route your traffic through another provider and keep clients' web sites fully operational. Better yet, if the web host is situated within the same building complex, you can be directly connected to the Internet backbone provider. Many web hosts have lost customers and received negative media and Internet exposure from not being responsive when problems were first experienced. In ensuring a high level of customer satisfaction, web hosts such as Rackspace keep individual customer server profiles and provide 24/7 online technical support. When a customer needs new servers, it can be configured and online within a 24-hour period once an order is placed. For customers who need additional web server resources for a specific timeframe—for example if a company is conducting an online contest promotion or needs additional resources for an e-commerce site during the holidays—Rackspace can provide services on a monthly basis.

Examples of companies involved within the dedicated market include

- ▼ **Rackspace**   http://www.rackspace.com

- ■ **Interland**   http://www.interland.net

- ■ **Globix**   http://www.globix.com

- ▲ **Verio**   http://www.verio.com

CO-LOCATION HOSTING

In *co-location hosting* the client houses its web server within a web host provider's secure data center or facility. This form of hosting is popular with small- to large-sized businesses that want control over their web servers within a 24/7 secure environment connected through a major backbone provider without having the infrastructure costs, security issues, or maintenance costs for a data center. Many web hosts that provide co-location services are moving toward providing dedicated and applications hosting services. Still, according to Forrester Research, co-location hosting is expected to double in the next five years to $1 billion, as shown in Figure 2.3.

The standard range of services provided by co-location plans includes 24/7 server monitoring, multiple Tier 1 backbones for scalable bandwidth, and staff on hand to handle server maintenance, housed within a climate-controlled and physically secure data center. Options

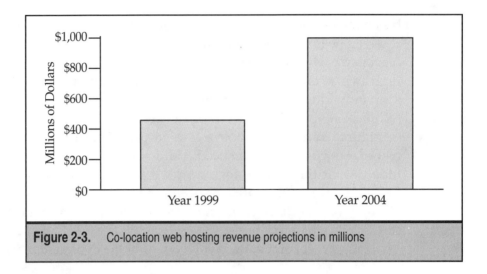

Figure 2-3. Co-location web hosting revenue projections in millions

should be available to include providing alternate energy sources (such as diesel-powered generators), power cycling, and tape backup services.

Co-location plans are further defined by the level of allowable monthly data transfer available (which is measured in megabits per second) and depend on which plan level the customer selects. Co-location plans typically range from $500 to $3,000 per month ($16 to $96 per day) for physically placing a web server within a 24/7 data center facility, in addition to bandwidth fees. Spacing typically is available in rack or cage increments (one-fourth, one-half, or full), with costs averaging up to $200 per square foot. A data center usually is located near a high-technology area where primary Tier 1 Internet backbones are located such as Atlanta, Boston, Baltimore, Chicago, Dallas, Los Angeles, New York, San Francisco, or other major cities throughout the world.

Large companies that provide backbone carrier services also are involved within the co-location market, including UUNet (www.uunet.com). UUNet provides a unique 100 percent uptime guarantee for co-location and other mid- to high-range hosting services, through an SLA with its customers. If services go below the level agreed in the SLA, the customer's account will receive a credit for that month. Genuity (www.genuity.com) provides an online map of its ATM-based hosting infrastructure that details its backbone and the location of its data center operations.

Here are some examples of companies involved within the co-location market:

▼   **UUNet**   www.uunet.com

■   **Genuity**   www.genuity.com

■   **Level 3**   www.level3.com

■   **Exodus**   www.exodus.com

▲   **IBM**   www.ibm.com

RESELLER HOSTING

In *reseller hosting* a web host provides storage at a discount to web consultants (including web designers, developers, or integration firms), who then resell the storage as a service or add-on to complement their other range of services, which might include web site design or programming. Reseller accounts provide the reseller with a virtual hosting package, with the incremental spacing provided for the purpose of reselling to clients at a markup. This type of plan is especially beneficial to consultants who do not have to be concerned with physically maintaining the hardware or the network (unless a web site goes down). The reselling costs are quite marginal; usually assigned to price breaks tied to the number of hosting accounts brought in by the reseller. Reseller plans can be organized in a wide range of different business models. Most common is for resellers to receive a 50 percent discount on the price of a hosting account, that the reseller then sells to the client. Some types of reseller incentive plans available include

▼   **Referrals**   These typically are a one-time payment or given as discounts to other services for providing new business to the web host.

- ■ **Commissions** For new accounts, resellers are provided a variable percentage commission that generally is based on the annual amount of the hosting plan.

- ■ **Discounts** This can include discounts on web hosting plans, marketing items, or special promotions.

- ■ **Virtual plan** The reseller is sold spacing on a web server, with the spacing made available by the reseller to resell. The reseller often is sold space on a dedicated or limited-share server, and allowed to set its own pricing structure and establish its unique branding, similar to some commission plans.

- ▲ **Reseller recruitment** Think of this as multilevel marketing. The reseller recruits other resellers to join the plan, receiving a commission or payment from the web host for the additional business.

The host can make available a reseller-branded site to provide hosting plan details to prospects under the reseller's company name. A reseller typically will be given a control panel, which allows the reseller and its customers to modify their web accounts. The reseller can modify and control access to these control panels based on their clients' needs. Resellers provide a valuable service to web hosts in providing recurring business, and typically are in the form of systems integrators, consultants, web designers, and developers. The arrangement is beneficial to a reseller in allowing them to offer a full suite of business solutions to their clients, without having to worry about network backbone, infrastructure, or maintenance issues.

The reseller typically handles training and technical support issues relating to their client's web site, and will in most cases correspond directly with the web host when technical problems arise, such as server downtime and access. To the reseller's client, the reseller is the host. Web host reseller plans need to clearly delineate what the responsibilities are to the reseller within a mutual agreement. This agreement should also include details of the web hosts' other policies which may exist, including an acceptable site usage policy, a privacy policy, and security policy.

For the web host, billing is normally handled by the reseller in billing for hosting that is resold. In addition, domain registrations and transfers, as well as technical support issues are the mainly the responsibility of the reseller in servicing their customers' hosting needs. The web host may also provide other basic reseller services, including site design templates, control panels, or custom domain name servers which can be listed using the resellers' domain name instead of the web hosts DNS when domain queries are made. Some web hosts even provide resellers with their own toll-free number for co-branded technical support that they can provide to their clients. When the reseller's client calls the number for technical support, the web host uses the reseller's name so the client thinks that the support is coming from the reseller. The control panel account enables the reseller to set up client web site parameters including e-mail, login rights, and scripting functions. The web host can provide anonymous name servers, which help to hide the identity of the web host's servers being used by the reseller.

Recent studies have shown that more funds than ever are being spent on web consultants with a wide variety of backgrounds. During 1998 companies spent $7.8 billion on web consultants, according to IDC. By 2003 that total is expected to increase to $78 billion worldwide, as shown in Figure 2-4. These consultants encompass, among others, web design firms, ad agencies, independent site developers, systems integrators, IT consulting firms, and web hosts directly.

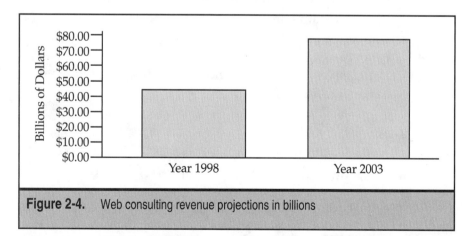

Figure 2-4.   Web consulting revenue projections in billions

As with the other hosting plans discussed, the price range can vary significantly for reselling hosting storage and for web consulting services. Much depends on the level of specialties the client requires for building and maintaining its web site. Initial setup pricing charged by web consultants can vary from several hundred dollars for a static web site to upwards of $1 million for a dynamic, highly interactive web site. A standard e-commerce site that includes shopping carts and credit card processing can average $10,000 to $60,000. An agreed-upon monthly fee includes a hosting space, web site design and development, and routine site updates. Independent consultants, if not affiliated with a firm, typically charge by the hour; a consulting firm usually charges by the project.

TEMPLATE HOSTING

Template hosting is a newer form of hosting that involves a client creating its web site through a web browser using standard templates available from the template hosting web site. Typically, this service is lower in cost than all other hosting plans, although the structured options available to the client limit the design and functional options available. Some plans include free hosting in return for agreeing to the dynamic placement of third-party ads, template hosting logo, or co-branding of content on a web site. The client typically is limited to using an extension of the web host's address instead of its own unique domain name address, which usually is not what businesses want when pursuing a professional image and long-term web presence.

Examples of companies involved within the template-based market include:

- ▼ **Imagecafe**   http://www.imagecafe.com
- ■ **bCentral**   http://www.bcentral.com
- ▲ **Bigstep.com**   http://www.bigstep.com

SPECIALIZED PLATFORM HOSTING

Often a client will require a specific platform for dynamic pages to be generated, or to support a specific technology. Some of the most sought-after web hosts provide support for Java Server Pages (JSP) and servlets, which can operate on most standard web server operating system platforms (UNIX, NT/2000, Solaris, AIX, and so on). Java Server Pages can consist of multiple servlets, which greatly extends the capabilities of a web server.

Many web hosts now are becoming knowledgeable about the speed and reliability advantages provided by JSP. Server appliances such as Intel's family of NetStructure appliance units and Cobalt are being used to power niche functions, similar to slimmed-down servers. These and other technologies are further discussed in Chapter 9. Special platform hosting technologies include, but are by no means limited to the following:

▼ ASP (Active Server Pages)

■ JSP (Java Server Pages) and Java servlets

■ SSI (Server Side Includes)

■ ColdFusion

■ PHP

■ Enterprise JavaBeans

▲ Specific platform APIs (Application Programming Interfaces)

Some web hosts address these specialized platform needs by offering individual hosting plans as part of their overall solutions. Here are some examples of companies providing hosting plans that include some of these specialized platforms:

▼ **Interliant**   http://www.interliant.com (ASP)

■ **WantJava**   http://www.wantjava.com (JSP and Enterprise JavaBeans)

- ■ **XO Communications**   http://www.xo.com (ColdFusion)

- ▲ **NetNation**   http://www.netnation.com (PHP)

APPLICATION HOSTING

Application hosting (also called Application Service Providers or ASP) involves the managed hosting of software services and is popular with small- to medium-sized businesses that want controlled hosting of enterprise software applications (such as word processing, e-mail, groupware, accounting, ERP, and more) securely through the Internet or a VPN. In this way, for a set monthly rental fee, a company can run applications through a web browser and will always be current with the latest software updates. Companies can provide enterprise applications for all of their employees without being concerned with providing in-house installation, technical support, ongoing training, or site licensing software issues. ASPs usually charge a monthly rental fee that can range widely, and can be based on individual employee usage ($1 per use) or a per-month ($25 to $5,000) model. A lot will depend on the level of complexity for the application that is hosted. There also usually is a setup fee.

Other benefits include allowing companies to test new applications before making a long-term software commitment. A business can have a set monthly cost of hosted applications as long as needed and avoid the capital costs of depreciating software purchases. This frees up IT in-house staff from the continual cycle of routine software installation, maintenance, and support to handle the core issues of the business.

Additional customer benefits include:

- ▼ Substantial savings in avoiding IT hardware, software, and licensing expenses

- ■ Faster implementation of applications

- ■ Ease of updating applications

- ■ Ease in adding users to applications

- ■ Easy to understand pricing model

- One source for application training

- One source for application technical support

- Providing a testing environment for new enterprise applications

- Capability to scale quickly to suit enterprise growth needs

▲ Making applications available on nontraditional systems such as wireless devices

The applications that lead the way in this category are messaging and e-mail. Other growing areas include education, e-commerce, accounting, and personnel management. This type of hosting is a central focus of Microsoft's Internet strategy, with the introduction of the Microsoft .NET platform for distributing software through the Web. Microsoft is investing $2 billion per year over a five-year period to develop the technology, which will enable web applications to run in the background among web sites instead of a browser user going to each individual site for information.

The .NET strategy is based on several core technologies, including XML (eXtensible Markup Language), SOAP (Simple Object Access Protocol), Microsoft Visual Basic, and associated web services. The company is aggressively recruiting web developers for the .NET technology, which will involve downloaded components to individual user desktops instead of being server-side driven. Other examples include online subscription-update services such as McAfee, which provides a monthly service whereby companies can check their systems for viruses and update virus signatures through a web browser. As noted in Figure 2-5, according to Gartner Dataquest, the world market for ASPs will increase from $3.6 billion in 2000 to $25.3 billion by 2004.

Many web companies are changing their business focus to an ASP model. B2SB Technologies, which changed its name in 2001 from SmartAge.com, is one such company. The company released an eBusiness Builder application, designed for small- to large-sized businesses, that focuses on front office applications and e-commerce. According to B2SB Technologies CEO Scott Garell, "Despite all its

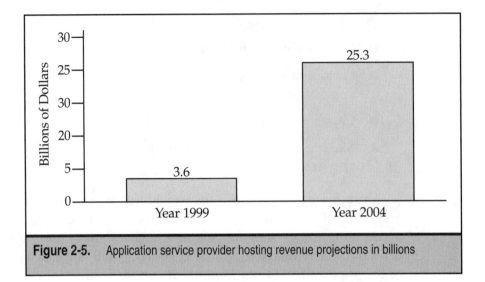

Figure 2-5. Application service provider hosting revenue projections in billions

promise, the Web has failed small businesses. To date, the first chapter of the Web has been to create standalone vertical applications for small businesses. The real win in the next chapter is to bring these applications together to fully share data and maximize return on investment." Large companies also are interested in application hosting because of the many enterprise benefits.

For web hosts considering expanding into ASP markets, the technical expertise, software licensing requirements, and infrastructure are extensive. The first likely consideration will be expanding into a service for which you have trained and specialized IT staff, and providing an add-on service such as a particular database or messaging product. The ASP model presents challenges in the current economic environment and still is not clearly understood by IT professionals or the business community. A company seeking to capture a share of the ASP market must provide potential clients with a clear explanation of the monetary and operational benefits of outsourcing their applications over traditional computing methods that depreciate over time. Businesses, especially upper management, will understand these value-added services. Savings from an enterprise by partnering with an ASP have been reported as high as 70 percent.

An ASP can gain access to new market channels through active partnerships. ASPs are also partnering with ISPs that have a large existing customer base, but lack the application specialties which ASPs bring to the table. ASPs could provide the back-end services, whereas ISPs continue to provide front-end Internet connection services to customers and offer new applications services to customers as add-ons. Through coordinated sales efforts, both could realize increased revenues in new channels.

ISPs such as JumpNet (www.jump.net) have developed partnerships with ASPs that utilize JumpNet's data center's ability to handle storage requirements. "We have some ASPs that are using our data centers, which provide software-related services," says Dewey Coffman, Vice President of Sales and Marketing with JumpNet, "but the majority of our customers are still co-location and dedicated hosting-related.

Other ASPs such as Corio (www.corio.com) use XO Communications (www.xo.com) for all of their data center requirements, and directly provide specialized e-commerce applications and enterprise offerings for their customers. Some of the software applications you can rent from XO include PeopleSoft, SAP, Commerce One, and BroadVision. ASPs will be responsible for all technical support and handle all training for an application, differentiating themselves in a fast-moving market.

NOTE: ASPs such as USinternetworking provide a virtual walkthrough of their data center facilities via their web site, (located at www.usinternetworking.com).

Other ASPs are promoting their successes by highlighting how they have lowered operational costs for existing clients. These types of partnering opportunities available as an ASP are discussed in further detail in Chapter 14. Software companies such as Oracle, with its Business Online ASP service also are providing ASP services.

ASPs must own a secure data center, or have access to one via partnerships or agreements. The data center must have alternate emergency power sources on site, provide standard backup procedures, and have multiple Tier 1 Internet backbone carriers in place. This will allow for scalable bandwidth, which can be specified through an SLA. Many Tier 1 Internet backbones have public peering at the major traffic exchange points and private peering distribution agreements with each other, which enables data packets to be transmitted quickly among providers.

Some of the larger infrastructure providers for ASPs include the following:

▼ **Citrix** http://www.citrix.com

■ **IBM** http://www.ibm.com

▲ **EDS** http://www.eds.com

Examples of companies involved within the ASP market include

▼ **Interliant** http://www.interliant.com

■ **USinternetworking** http://www.usinternetworking.com

■ **Corio** http://www.corio.com

■ **eOnline** http://www.eonlineinc.com

▲ **Qwest CyberSolutions** http://www.qwest.com

MANAGED-SERVICES HOSTING

Managed-services hosting is the management of services that ensure that a web site (or host) is performing effectively. This is a relatively new form of hosting; services can include firewall security, real-time server monitoring, e-commerce services, and content delivery management, typically in partnership with infrastructure providers. Xuma (www.xuma.com) offers e-commerce services that integrate auction bots, tax management, and processing of credit card transactions. One client, CornerHardware.com, was brought online through Xuma's services two months ahead of schedule.

Examples of companies involved within the managed-services market include

▼ **Loudcloud** http://www.loudcloud.com

■ **Xuma** http://www.xuma.com

■ **Sitesmith** http://www.sitesmith.com

■ **InetU** http://www.inetu.com

▲ **SiteRock**   http://www.siterock.com

Companies such as Alabanza (www.alabanza.com) provide a full range of automated and e-commerce hosting services directly to other web hosts. By using BGP (Border Gateway Protocol), the company can provide the optimal bandwidth for its customers among the bandwidth carriers with which it is partnered. BGP is discussed in further detail starting in Chapter 10.

Interliant (www.interliant.com) provides managed services in coordination with Sun Microsystems (www.sun.com), under which both companies market Interliant services. As an Elite Plus member with Sun's iForce initiatives and Service Provider program, Interliant receives preconfigured, rack-mounted, Sun web servers to provide co-llocation and data center services. As with many of the companies mentioned here, Interliant also markets within other hosting models discussed in this chapter.

Services that Rackspace now is providing through a partnership with Appliant (www.appliant.com) includes Lateral Line, which enables customers to monitor how a web site is performing through tracking via a web browser. As states chief executive officer of Rackspace Graham Weston, "Downtime can be catastrophic for an e-business, and with the competition literally only a click away, providing optimal performance and reliability becomes even more crucial. A real-time monitoring system like Lateral Line is indispensable for ensuring user satisfaction."

HIGH-SCALABILITY HOSTING

In the upper tier of hosting plans, a client will require a highly scalable environment to respond to rapidly changing site traffic needs. According to analyst Jeanne Schaaf at Forrester Research, revenues in this area are expected to rise by more than 1,000 percent, to $10.9 billion for fully-managed, outsourced servers and $6.8 billion for high-end custom web hosting services.

Qwest announced a new service in 2000 called e-Solutions, which is targeted at companies that seek to establish multiple e-commerce web sites. Part of the reasoning behind the move is to accommodate customers that Qwest acquired from the company's merger with US West. The plan, the first shared hosting product that Qwest has established, includes an e-commerce catalog for 100 products and up to 20 web pages developed. The e-Solutions plan includes services that are available from various Qwest divisions, including Qwest Cyber Solutions, ASP services in-house, and consulting operations. Besides the e-Solutions plan, Qwest also offers dedicated solutions that start with a 1,000-item catalog with 80 web pages developed, and consulting services hosted on a Sun Microsystems Netra server with iPlanet Web Server.

High-scalability hosting is popular with medium- to large-sized businesses whose primary goal is to ensure that critical e-commerce and server applications are continually operational on the Web. This includes multiple servers or racks housed in a raised-floor data center and clustered together as part of an overall, comprehensive solution. Specialty services that require these services include load balancing, correcting performance bottlenecks, scalability, and real-time traffic monitoring. As with ASPs, the key components are redundancy and support. Some one-time web site events that require such scalability include the Grammy Awards, the Victoria's Secret Webcast, the Olympics, and other major sports events.

There are other technologies that include partnering with content delivery services, such as Akamai Technologies (www.akamai.com). Akamai provides a range of content delivery services, including load balancing solutions, which enables content providers to achieve higher performance when using static content on their web sites. Within the content delivery area alone, it is estimated by analysts to generate $1.1 billion in revenues by the end of 2001, up from $306 million for 2000. These types of technologies are discussed in further detail in Chapter 13.

Plans include multiple sources of backup (including offsite storage), with multiple Tier 1 backbone carriers that have direct access to the Internet in case the primary sources become unavailable. The network includes multiple routers, switches, optimal load balancing and traffic maintenance, firewalls, emergency power sources (diesel generators), and 24/7 technical support to provide the highest level of uptime protection within a highly secure data center.

Methods for automatically monitoring the network, traffic, and servers include software such as HP OpenView, IBM Tivoli, or BMC, to ensure that optimal performance is maintained. High-scalability hosting plans typically range from $50,000 to $1 million per month ($1,612 to $32,258 per day). As the overall market matures, the trend likely will lead smaller web hosts to focus on highly specialized markets. Larger web hosts and carriers, through mergers and partnerships, will provide mega-web services, all under one umbrella.

Examples of companies involved within the high scalability market include:

▼   **NaviSite**   http://www.navisite.com

■   **Globix**   http://www.globix.com

▲   **Qwest**   http://www.qwest.com

SUMMARY

This chapter has shown the wide range of available web hosting services, from shared to high scalability. Throughout this book, we discuss key strategies that web hosts of all sizes can implement to anticipate the needs of their existing and potential clients. By investing in reliable technologies and people, and forging beneficial partnerships, web hosts can provide a full range of value-added Web services to satisfy the needs of the marketplace.

CHAPTER 3

Selecting a Platform and Web Server

This chapter will introduce you to the leading web servers and the platforms on which they run. When developing expertise within a given platform or platforms, much will depend on the range of experience and skill sets of your staff and network infrastructure, and the markets you are seeking to capture.

Here are some basic questions that you will need to ask:

▼ Is in-house staff fully qualified to install and maintain one platform or several?

■ Do you want to specialize in one particular platform, or to be a one-stop shop for the full range of web hosting services?

■ Does your staff have the network administration, troubleshooting, and infrastructure experience necessary to handle problems that arise?

■ Will you have an ongoing education program in place for technical staff to be familiar with the details of newer technologies?

▲ If in-house experience is lacking, are partnerships in place with vendors and other web businesses to accommodate your needs?

Partnerships and alliances are the norm in the industry, as web hosts with varying specialties are combining their talents to capture the market opportunities available. If you are a reseller, developer, or designer and you are not directly providing infrastructure web hosting services, the choice of web host to partner with will include asking some of the same questions that are noted above. In those cases, it will be more feasible to become affiliated with a third-party partner who has the necessary scalable infrastructure and 24x7 qualified data center support needed for a given platform or client.

You also need secure access to a browser administration page, which allows control of individual web site accounts and can manage ODBC database connections, directory access, and users. According to the Gartner Group, some of the most sophisticated web sites that include e-commerce functionality cost more than $1 million to design, with 79 percent of that figure being staff costs.

Many times a customer, whether it is a developer, reseller, or company, will require a specific platform to generate dynamic pages, or utilize a particular technology such as ASP, JSP, or platform-specific APIs. Patches, updates, and maintenance are an ongoing job in administering a given platform, especially in ensuring the utmost security and performance of a web server. Many analysts have reported that up to 70 percent of existing web site domains are not configured properly. Ensure that your staff has the right tools, ongoing education, and resources to meet your clients' needs. A key factor in the wide popularity of the Apache web server is its open-source nature and capability to modify using source code changes.

Commercial web servers running operating systems such as Microsoft Windows NT and Windows 2000 are becoming more popular because of the familiar GUI interface, enhanced scalability (especially Windows 2000), and availability of extended support. Rack-mounted server appliances are relatively simple to install and maintain for many web applications, and are powered by Linux and other Unix-based operating systems. The leading server appliance is Cobalt, with others including eSoft and Whistle Communications. Server appliances are discussed later in this chapter.

If you decide to specialize in and host on just one particular platform, your range of potential customers will be limited; however, your infrastructure costs (including personnel and equipment) will likely be less than if you provide hosting for multiple platforms. If you want to compete in the overall market, many web hosts provide a full range of services, hosted on multiple platforms. There is a wide range of platforms and web servers to choose from within the market, but the focus in this chapter will be on the following popular platforms and web servers:

▼ Unix and Linux running Apache web server

■ Windows NT/2000 running Internet Information Server (IIS)

▲ Server Appliances

MARKET OVERVIEW

Netcraft keeps statistics on the leading web servers and the platforms they operate on (http://www.netcraft.com/survey). Based on HTTP requests made to hostnames, the results are compiled to report on web servers and platforms online. From a December 2000 survey, Netcraft received responses from 25,675,581 sites. The leading web servers noted in Table 3-1 are Apache, Microsoft (primarily consisting of Internet Information Server, followed by Personal Web Server), and iPlanet (which is a combination of web sites that use iPlanet-Enterprise, Netscape servers, and Netsite servers). iPlanet is a collaborative web server package from Netscape and Sun Microsystems that accounts for more than 6 percent of the web server market. Others of note include WebLogic, defined as an application server and Zeus, a Unix-based server that is commercially available. However, as is evident in Figure 3-1, Apache is by far the leader, with more than a 60 percent market share.

Server	Totals	Percent
Apache	15414726	60.04
Microsoft-IIS	5025017	19.57
Netscape-Enterprise	1682737	6.55
WebLogic	890791	3.47
Zeus	676526	2.63
Rapidsite	365807	1.42
thttpd	321944	1.25
tigershark	139300	0.54
AOLserver	125513	0.49
WebSitePro	110681	0.43

Table 3-1. Top Web Servers (as of December 2000)

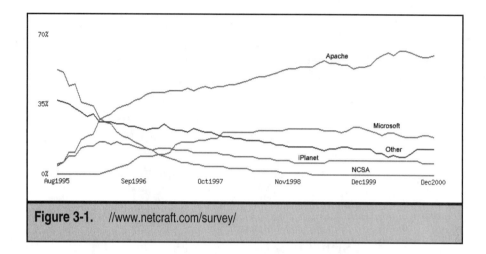

70%

35%

0%

Apache

Microsoft

Other

iPlanet

NCSA

Aug1995   Sep1996   Oct1997   Nov1998   Dec1999   Dec2000

Figure 3-1.   //www.netcraft.com/survey/

Given the widespread popularity of Apache and Microsoft Internet Information Server within the market, the focus for the remainder of the chapter will focus mainly on these two web servers and their respective platforms.

UNIX (OPEN-SOURCE AND COMMERCIAL)

Unix is a proven, multitasking, multiuser operating system that includes network support, a graphical user interface, a development environment, and virtual memory support. Unix has been commercially available for many years, evolving from early implementations that now include versions for AIX, BSD (Berkeley Software Distribution), BSDI, Digital, HP-UX, SCO UNIX, Solaris, Silicon Graphics, and System V. With the wide popularity of the Windows operating system on PCs, Unix also has became available as a low-cost alternative running on Intel-based processors.

There are open-source UNIX varieties that are popular with web hosts, including FreeBSD, NetBSD, OpenBSD, and Linux for PCs. The suggested bare minimum hardware for an Intel-based system running UNIX is a 350 MHz processor with 128 MB of memory (depending on if a dual processor is used, and the type of applications hosted).

Because of the open-source code, reliability, and free nature of its software, this section will primarily focus on open-source flavors of Unix. Of the open-source implementations of Unix, BSD has been available for the longest period of time, beginning at the University of California, Berkeley in the early 1980s. BSD implementations include FreeBSD, BSDI, NetBSD, and OpenBSD. Many developers and web hosts consider BSD implementations to be among the most stable and FreeBSD has the most installations.

Some online resources for BSD implementations can be found at these locations:

▼ **FreeBSD**   http://www.freebsd.org

■ **BSDI**   http://www.bsdi.com

■ **NetBSD**   http://www.netbsd.org

▲ **OpenBSD**   http://www.openbsd.org

Linux

Linux is free of site licensing restrictions; it can operate on popular Intel-based systems and has become quite a popular platform for developers, web hosts, and enterprises. The most popular distributions of Linux include Red Hat, Slackware, Debian, and SuSE. Each includes the same Linux operating system kernel and differs primarily in the options used for installation, documentation, and programs.

According to Netcraft, Red Hat with Apache is used by an estimated 69 percent of Linux users, and many dedicated web hosts and Linux hardware vendors also use Red Hat. Companies such as VA Linux Systems market Linux and FreeBSD as bundled web server offerings. VA Linux also owns SourceForge, said to be the largest open-source development center. Others, such as IBM and Dell, base many of their web server offerings around Linux.

In addition, Cobalt, a leading rack-mounted server appliance, distributes with Red Hat Linux and includes base-level kernel support for Java, with the command line capability to run applets or executables. Competition among distributions of Linux has increased with the release of Red Hat 7.0, which produces binaries that are not compatible with other Linux distributions after compiling. The most popular Linux distributions are listed in Table 3-2.

Further information on these Linux distributions can be found at the following locations:

▼ **Red Hat** http://www.redhat.com

■ **Slackware** http://www.slackware.com

■ **Debian** http://www.debian.com

▲ **SuSE** http://www.suse.com

Apache

The Apache web server (http://www.apache.org/), which also is an open-source product, has long-standing popularity as a highly reliable Unix web server, running on more than 60 percent of existing web sites. Apache began as patches to the NCSA httpd daemon server in 1995, and has evolved to run on most distributions of FreeBSD, OpenBSD, and Linux, and also now runs on Windows NT and Netware 5.x, although the Unix version is by far the most stable. Apache includes 45 modules and 200 directives for its operations,

Linux Distribution	Notable Features
Red Hat	Popular with server appliances, hardware vendors, and web hosts, because of its range of technical support and flexible installation.
Slackware	Simple to install and user friendly.
Debian	More installation options and programs included.
SuSe	Includes SourceForge CompileFarm, which enables developers to create and test applications on different versions of the BSD and Linux operating systems over the Internet.

Table 3-2. Leading Linux Distributions

which takes time to learn. Apache assigns a directory, the DocumentRoot, and stores root directory files there for viewing instead of using the actual root directory (for security purposes). Apache includes support for Java servlets (using the Apache JServ add-on) and other server-side includes, and can be programmed using CGI scripts.

The primary Apache configuration file is httpd.conf. This file includes instructions on how the server will behave, as well as the interrelated components and modules that interact with the server. The configuration file now also contains access and resource configuration information that was previously listed in separate files (access.conf and srm.conf); now all included in one orderly http.conf files. Previous Apache versions had each of these as individual files. The directives in the http.conf configuration file are grouped into three main sections:

▼ Directives that control the operation of the Apache server process—the *global environment*.

■ Directives that define parameters of the *main* or *default* server, which responds to requests that aren't handled by a virtual host, and provides default values for the settings of all virtual hosts.

▲ Virtual host settings, which allow web requests to be sent to different IP addresses or hostnames, yet handled by the same Apache server process.

To make configurations easier, online administration tools are available to manage the httpd.conf file through a GUI. The main one is COMMANCHE (COnfiguration MANager for ApaCHE; others are Linuxconf and Webmin. Some of the recent enhancements to Apache include DSO (Dynamic Shared Object) support, which allows memory to be used more effectively as modules can be loaded at runtime to be used.

A tool now available called apxs, which enables activation and installation of any DSO modules, which are hidden from the user. The mod_proxy module contains numerous improvements for FTP and proxy support. Enhancements to the mod_log_config file now allows for real-time separation of log files for multiple virtual hosts and automatic DNS resolution. The syslog.conf file is useful for security tracking, and for finding out who is accessing the server. It usually is located in the /etc/syslog.conf folder and run as syslogd. The resulting log files are mostly found in a /var/log folder. Of course, your server can be fully customized to store log files wherever you decide. The mime.types configuration file now identifies more than 370 MIME types.

Virtual Hosting

Apache introduced the concept of *virtual hosting*, which has made it possible for shared hosting to be so affordable for web hosts, and is a key factor in the rapid growth of the Internet because of its open-source nature. With virtual hosting, multiple domain names on the same server all point to the same IP address. When each domain name is requested, the associated web pages will be displayed. In the current version of Apache, virtual hosting now is based on the Host: header from a client instead of the main address of the server, which is located in the NameVirtualHost directive and points to virtual file paths on the server.

The NameVirtualHost directive and the associated <VirtualHost> directive each are located in httpd.conf. These directives provide details of each virtual host, and will be listed similar to NameVirtualHost 127.0.0.1:80. The NameVirtualHost directive specifies the IP address of the server, which will be used to resolve virtual host names. For this example, 127.0.0.1 is the IP address of the local machine and 80 is the default HTTP port address. For each virtual machine, different settings within the http.conf file allow each domain name to be associated to the IP address.

The following is a sample virtual host directive:

```
NameVirtualHost 127.0.0.1:80

<VirtualHost 127.0.0.1>
    ServerAdmin webmaster@hostingresolve.first.com
    DocumentRoot /www/hostingresolve.first.com
    ServerName hostingresolve.first.com
```

```
ErrorLog logs/hostingresolve.first-error_log
CustomLog logs/hostingresolve.first.com-access_log common
</VirtualHost>
```

More extensive analysis of virtual host settings are available using the –S command option (refer to http://www.apache.org/docs/vhosts/ for full documentation). Apache logs any errors and file requests on the server. It has the option of storing server log data in three files, an agent_log, referer_log, and access_log. For improved performance, consider putting the log files on a separate disk from where the web server is stored, because these files can expand exponentially if not managed properly. For a more thorough review of log files, packages such as FastStats, Webalizer, and WebTrends are available for Apache, IIS, and other web servers; each provides a detailed graphical representation and analysis of the log files.

Access to directories is controlled by the .htaccess configuration file, which is especially useful for allowing only certain users to have access to specific directories of a web server. Support is available for ISAPI (Internet Server Application Programming Interface) extensions to be used through the mod_isapi module with the Apache for Windows version.

However, there are some differences in the ways in which Apache and Microsoft IIS handle ISAPI. Reading and writing asynchronously is not allowed from a security standpoint as with IIS. Internet Server APIs are loaded and unloaded from memory per request. With IIS, server applications are loaded and remain in memory. When usage becomes too high, they then are unloaded. For PUT and POST requests that HTML pages may contain, Apache limits these types of HTTP requests to 48K to prevent possible DoS (Denial of Service) attacks. The standard IIS implementation does not address this.

WINDOWS NT/2000

Microsoft continues to gain ground as a platform for the web hosting market, because of the GUI Windows interface and corporate brand presence. According to Forrester Research, the portion of the shared web hosting market controlled by Microsoft Windows NT and Windows 2000 will expand from 6 percent in 1998 to 20 percent by 2003. The Windows NT/2000 share of the dedicated web hosting market is anticipated to grow from 29 percent in 1998 up to 45 percent by 2003. Another contributor to the popularity of Windows NT/2000 is the inroads it has made in the business world. Eighty-two percent of corporations have Windows NT installed, according to IDC. This comfort level affects corporate recommendations regarding the preferred web hosting platform to use.

On a cost basis, web hosting with Windows NT/2000 typically is more expensive than Intel-based implementations of Unix such as Linux and FreeBSD because of site licensing and hardware issues. For example, the suggested bare minimum hardware for Windows 2000 Server is a 450MHz processor with 128–256MB of memory (depending on whether it is a dual processor). Also keep in mind that a web site with dynamic content that uses a back-end database will need to have multiple processors with up to 1GB of memory.

Although these requirements seem high, processors and peripherals continue to become more affordable, driven by the market and advances in technology. Most leading web hosts include plans for Windows NT version 4.0 (which has been out since 1996); with more providing Windows 2000 web hosting as word of its stability and robust nature spreads. There are three main servers that Windows 2000 Server offers (the Windows 2000 Professional version is designed to be a workstation only). The main differences can be summarized as follows:

▼ **Windows 2000 Server**   Supports up to 4GB of memory and 4-way SMP (Symmetric Multiprocessing, which refers to the capability for multiple processors to share the same memory, including a single operating system).

■ **Windows 2000 Advanced Server**   Supports up to 8GB of memory, 8-way SMP, load balancing, and 2-node clustering for server farms.

■ **Windows 2000 Datacenter Server**   Supports up to 64GB of memory, 32-way SMP, load balancing, and 4-node *clustering* for high-end server farms. Clustering occurs when two or more CPUs connect together to share system resources and balance the load. Each CPU within a cluster is referred to as a *node*. Clustering usually includes fault tolerance, load balancing, and failover support. Several resources are available online for Microsoft information, including.

- **Microsoft Windows 2000**   http://www.microsoft.com/windows2000

- **Microsoft Support**   http://support.microsoft.com/support/

- ▲ **NT FAQ**   http://www.ntfaq.com

Advantages of Windows 2000

The new server releases of Windows 2000 boast substantial improvements over prior versions of Windows 2000 and Windows NT. On the high end, the Windows 2000 Datacenter Server can handle more than 345 million transactions per day, with support for up to 50 million Active Directory™ objects. At the time of this writing, Microsoft has released a new Windows 2000 server, Application Center 2000, which uses dynamic load balancing (similar in functionality to the Datacenter Server), with support for multiple application servers. Microsoft also has announced several new servers that will be based around its .NET Internet strategy. Windows 2000 also retains the familiar graphical interface from Windows NT 4.

If your current installation uses NT 4.0, you must plan carefully and learn the new operating system naming models before you move to Windows 2000. The Active Directory™ is object based and uses a system called DDNS (Dynamic Domain Name System), which allows synchronized file and directory sharing through LDAP (Lightweight Directory Access Protocol) or HTTP (Hypertext Transfer Protocol). Up to 10 million objects (connected PCs, groups, users, printers, or any network resources) can be associated per domain. Developers can extend the Active Directory™ to create new objects or properties.

Multimaster replication, in which all domains in the same enterprise are equal, is the new technology in place of the previous NT method for maintaining PDCs (Primary Domain Controllers) and BDCs (Backup Domain Controllers). In addition, support is now in place for USB devices and Plug and Play capability, long a standard with Windows 98. The operating system now has Kerberos 5-file encryption authentication capability (very similar to what has been available for years with

UNIX systems). This replaces NTLM from previous NT versions. For encrypted data, backups to tape or other media can be made in an encrypted and secure format.

Public key certificates also are supported within Active Directory™, based on the X.509 standard, which can be used in place of third-party certificate authorities. Fault tolerance with built-in RAID support is a standard feature. With the built-in NTFS 5 file system, you can maintain disk quotas for directories, groups, or users. Each file includes a unique SID identifier, which makes tracking files easy for users. Users can print to a printer through the Internet, a feature that has been available for some time on Unix machines but is not a key feature of interest to web hosts. Windows 2000 has extensive driver support and can work seamlessly with third-party peripherals using a Removable Storage Manager utility.

IIS

The web server that is used by default for Windows NT/2000 is IIS (Internet Information Server), for serving Active Server Pages (ASP), with FTP and Gopher servers included. IIS now is included as part of the Windows 2000 operating system as a service. IIS also bundles Microsoft's web authoring package, FrontPage; NetShow for streaming multimedia; and Index Server for extensive text searching. From a licensing standpoint, IIS allows for unlimited access, if the web site does not involve login authentication. If it does include login authentication, from a licensing standpoint the web site is bound by the number of client licenses you purchase with Windows NT/2000.

Included with Windows 2000, IIS version 5.0 now runs as a service and is merged in with Active Directory™. This is especially useful for Intranet or VPN purposes in sharing of local or remote files and resources through the Internet, depending on the server security policies you set. Within a VPN, authentication is enhanced through the PPTP/L2TP protocol. PPTP (Point-to-Point Tunneling Protocol) is a standard VPN method that uses shared private certificate keys for Internet communications. L2TP (Layer 2 Tunneling Protocol) is a new VPN proposed standard that uses IPSec (IP Security) protocol to support IP address assigning automatically.

Within Windows 2000, you maintain IIS through the Microsoft Management Console (MMC) Internet Service add-in (also referred to as a *snap-in*) or you can manage it with the system management tool. Included with the Windows 2000 Server Resource Kit is a Migration Wizard, which enables you to migrate CGI scripts to ASP coding. In fact, you can migrate web files and applications developed with other web servers (Apache, iPlanet, or others) over to IIS using the utility. There are numerous other add-in utilities that an administrator will want to use. Event Viewer (available through the Component Services add-in) can gauge when problems occur. Performance Monitor can track how server resources are performing.

IIS can be restarted without rebooting the physical computer, in case an application or service stops responding. In most instances, this is because of some memory-related problem, if all coding is correct. You can restart IIS with the Internet Services Manager (ISM); you also can access ISM by selecting Start | Programs | Administrative Tools. Right-click the ISM icon and select to restart IIS, which restarts all Internet Services. You also can reset IIS through the executable file iisreset.exe. Either of these two methods ensures that IIS services are stopped and restarted correctly, which is important because several services are used with IIS.

From ISM you can control the type of Internet service IIS uses on the server (web server or FTP) and the amount of bandwidth that all web sites or other Internet services use on the server. You also can configure additional MIME types for files that need to be interpreted properly through the web (such as Flash animation files, for example). Some additional ISM features include the following:

▼ You can modify server extension options and permissions within the ISM, including the logging of authoring actions.

■ Permissions can be managed manually.

■ SSL (Secure Sockets Layer) security can be enabled.

■ Executables can be uploaded to the server.

▲ You can give certain extensions preference over others to enhance performance. These functions also can be controlled from the MMC.

Of course, within this environment, FrontPage and ASP scripting work well with IIS. You can enable directory browsing to allow users to browse a web site's contents. This also can be enabled through ASP or another server-side component. You can enable JSP and servlet support with a choice of many available third party add-ins. Enabling these and other server-side extensions is discussed more in Chapter 9. If clients (say within an Intranet or VPN) are using the latest browsers to support compression (standard browsers 4.0 and higher), static files now can be compressed by IIS before sending to the browser for viewing, thus improving site responsiveness. For more information on IIS, refer to http://www.microsoft.com/windows2000/technologies/web/default.asp.

Virtual Hosting

For virtual hosting capability first introduced with Windows NT, one network adapter can have multiple IP addresses bound to it (referred to as a *hardware virtual server*), and have an IP address assigned as a virtual domain. Windows 2000 includes a multiple-user domain feature that allows unique namespaces to be assigned to multiple web sites from the same server (this virtual hosting concept originated on the Apache web server). You can manage the amount of processor usage by individual web sites, allowing specific amounts for set periods. You also can control individual site recording of how server resources are being used. Another emerging feature, Windows DNA (Distributed iNternet Architecture), addresses scalability by allowing multiple servers to be clustered together, all using the same IP address.

Additional Resources

If you are currently managing Windows web servers or considering doing so, subscribe to the Microsoft Developer Network (MSDN) which provides access to an extensive library of tools, updates through CD or the web, and advanced previews of emerging Windows technologies.You can find additional information about FrontPage extensions at http://officeupdate.microsoft.com/frontpage/wpp/serk, which is the location of the FrontPage Server

Extensions Resource Kit. FrontPage extensions are discussed in further detail in Chapter 8.

In addition, a free mod_frontpage module for Apache is available, which allows support for FrontPage server extensions. However, support is not available for database ODBC connectivity or for ASP scripting with the module. You can download the module from http://rtr.com/fsupport.

SERVER APPLIANCES

Server appliances are becoming popular with web hosts, because installation and maintenance issues are greatly reduced. The market for server appliances is expected to continue to rise, given these features. Server appliances (shown in Figure 3-2) can be used to provide web

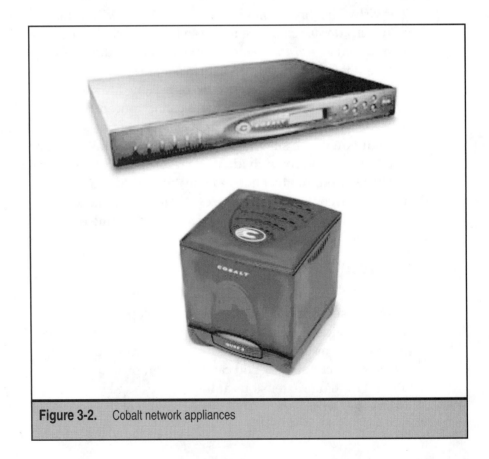

Figure 3-2.   Cobalt network appliances

services, which include content hosting, firewalls, e-mail, and caching applications, and are especially popular with smaller web hosts.

The popularity of server appliances is a result of two factors: their affordability and the fact that little technical expertise is required when compared to a traditional web server. The drawback is the limited scalability for growth, because you typically cannot add new components such as hard drives. Some of the leading vendors include Cobalt Networks (which now is owned by Sun Microsystems) and eSoft. The web server and operating system used is open source, making for low cost of production, yet it is less scalable or upgradeable when compared to a web server. You can find more information about the Cobalt network appliances at http://www.cobaltnet.com.

Typically included with the Cobalt platform are the Apache web server, Linux operating system, Sendmail (an SMTP e-mail server), ProFTPD (an FTP server), CGI, includes support for FrontPage 2000 server extensions, secure encryption, and various Unix tools and utilities. In most cases, initial configuration and maintenance required of an appliance server is done through a browser or GUI menu interface as the preferred method that a customer uses. Typically a customer will not telnet to a Cobalt unit to modify a configuration. In fact, changes are made through a telnet session will void a warranty with Cobalt and most web hosts. However, an administrator should have telnet access through a root shell account. As with other Apache servers, virtual hosting is supported. In fact, each Cobalt RaQ3 unit can accommodate up to 200 virtual domains, with support also for name-based hosting. This is easily configured through the GUI menu. To do this from the Server Management screen, complete the following:

1. Choose Site Management from the Administrator Site.

2. Select Add Virtual Site.

3. Enter configuration data.

4. Select Confirm New Site.

Cobalt Networks now has more than 600 developers involved with creating applications for the Cobalt platform. The leading computer makers in the web server market, including IBM, Dell, Compaq, Sun Microsystems, and Hewlett Packard, also are now designing server appliances targeted to handle specific server needs such as load balancing and memory caching to allow for rapid content delivery. Memory caching in this way enhances page loads and reduces traffic on the network.

Vendors are increasingly designing solutions that are rack mounted and simple to maintain. In 2000, Dell released a line of appliance servers called PowerApp, designed for load balancing. In addition, Dell has introduced a specialized server that handles the unique load balancing requirements of e-commerce web sites. Other vendors such as Network Appliance provide Network-Attached Storage (NAS) solutions that provide highly reliable and scalable rack-mounted storage.

SUMMARY

Deciding on platforms to support will come down to analyzing your available resources, personnel, and infrastructure and creating alliances where needed to arrive at a comprehensive web hosting package to fit all your customers' current and anticipated needs. The next chapter will discuss methods of page design, and techniques that a professional web site must include that apply to a web hosts' own site.

PART II

Marketing

CHAPTER 4

Web Presentation and Design Strategies

There is nothing worse than a sharp image of a fuzzy concept.

—Ansel Adams

The wide reach of the Web has been especially beneficial in enabling smaller firms to compete with the "big boys" on a level playing field. Some early players in the industry capitalized on this. With regard to presentation and design, you must present your web site in a consistent and professional manner. Within this chapter, specific methods will highlight general page design methods and technologies that a professional web site must be aware of, with strategies introduced for working with search engines. By offering affiliate programs, a web host can extend its reach into new markets that otherwise might not be available. According to a survey completed by Forrester Research of web hosting customers, the four major factors involved with selecting a web host are highlighted in Figure 4-1.

Also noted in the survey of concern was the ability of the web host to scale to meet the needs of the client, and the quality of service (or lack thereof) to the client. Your web site should focus on these concerns when attracting new business. What are the intangibles that differentiate your site from the competition? Do you make promises and keep them? This will benefit your site like no other marketing campaign—through positive word of mouth and referrals.

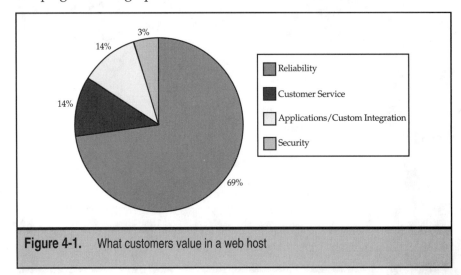

Figure 4-1.   What customers value in a web host

WEB PRESENTATION

Designing a professional web site that is easy to navigate and best represents your web business takes planning. Too many times, a web hosting site's appearance and content are not updated to keep a fresh appearance, with pertinent information throughout. A site is not meant to be created and then stored on a shelf. What will generate the most interest and sales? What information can be told through case studies and customer success stories? How does your site best communicate its strengths, specialized skills, and unique market advantages?

Site Design Basics

When designing your web pages, keep the user and your target market constantly in mind so that information can be located quickly through a sitemap for navigation. Also include search functionality. Users become frustrated when they can't find information they need within a few mouse clicks, or if the site does not include search capabilities.

For pages you design, an overall knowledge of HTML 4.0 tags is necessary, as is JavaScript, even if you are using a web authoring package such as Microsoft FrontPage or Macromedia Dreamweaver. In some cases you will need to tweak coding directly to account for browser version differences and optimal page design, and to include custom programming. Avoid overuse of graphics and animation, because users with connection speeds slower than DSL might have difficulty loading pages. For the beginner wanting to gain more of an overview of basic web technologies, two recommended books are *HTML: A Beginner's Guide* and *JavaScript: A Beginner's Guide,* both published by McGraw-Hill.

"A few years ago, customers would happily sacrifice speed for style," says Vincent Phillips, senior vice president of Charles Schwab eBrokerage, in an interview with Forrester Research. "Nowadays, speed takes precedence…regardless of what designers prefer." Don't get carried away with being so creative in your design that you lose track of what message you are trying to communicate. The old adage remains true: Keep it simple. Make your site crisp and to the point. Attempt to reflect a logical structure and offer clear advantages to using your services. Make it conversational and lead the reader to make an informed choice through the "soft sell" method. Avoid listing trivial information such as your visitor count on a page, or the use of simplistic clipart. It does not provide a professional appearance and makes you look like you designed your pages with a hammer and chisel.

Don't overload a page with images and text. Text can be separated out into small paragraphs for better readability. Internet users typically are impatient, so make the site easy to navigate and fast loading. In general, keep the contents of each page under 50K in size if possible. When designing the content for each page, keep the average connection speeds in mind. (See Figure 4-2.)

Before you design or update your site, draw out on paper or with an imaging package what pages might look like, and ask yourself design questions such as

▼ What type of prospect or client will be viewing pages?

■ Does the layout make sense?

■ Where should the navigation menus be placed?

■ What areas will need changing often?

▲ Should I use frames, buttons, or image maps?

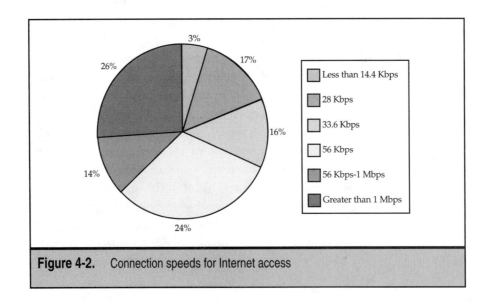

Figure 4-2. Connection speeds for Internet access

When designing your site pages make sure each page includes the following items:

▼ **Page title**   Each page should have an appropriate title for tracking by search engine spiders. Within the actual HTML coding, this can be listed within the header tag section at the beginning of the page, like this:

```
<TITLE>Web Hosting, ASP Guidelines</TITLE>
```

■ **Meta tags**   Each page needs unique meta tags, which describe in about 200 characters what is on the page but are not shown in the actual browser. All meta tags are placed within the header tag section at the beginning of an HTML page and tracked by many search engine spiders. Meta tags are discussed in further detail in the "Search Engine Submittal Tips" section in this chapter. Within the actual HTML coding, this may be listed like this:

```
<META NAME="DESCRIPTION" CONTENT="By outsourcing routine software
to an ASP, you can focus on your key business and reduce costs.">
```

■ **Check spelling**   Within a web authoring package, run a spell check. Also make sure that sentences use the correct grammar, make sense, and flow well together.

■ **Check page size**   Keep in mind the time it takes for each page to load within the web browser, which includes all the HTML, graphics, JavaScript, Java applets, and so on. The contents of a page should be under 50K in size if possible to load in an acceptable time frame.

▲ **Font styles**   Be careful what fonts you use within a page. More elaborate fonts will only slow a page down as it downloads or can even make your content unreadable. Use common fonts that are likely to be installed on the users' systems. These include sans-serif Arial, serif Times, sans-serif Verdana, or serif Garamond fonts. Sans-serif fonts typically are preferred for highlighting text or as a headline because of their larger appearance. Serif fonts are better defined, with curves (called hooks) in characters, and are preferred for text content.

Page Coding

At a minimum, pages should be coded using HTML 4.0 version standards. Most web design packages have a built-in option to test for this. To account for older browsers, use hex value numbers instead of color names when coloring text. An example would be #0000FF to represent blue. If you are using a background image that is tiled for the body of a page, keep it small (one to two pixels). Test your pages on multiple browsers (including Macintosh) and versions to ensure your pages look correct. Navigation should be easy enough for a six-year-old to use. In case of any problems (especially with older version browsers), it is a good idea to provide links to your key site pages, typically added in small print at the bottom of a page. Another good strategy is to avoid using too much Javascript in coding your pages. It will slow them down, as the interpreted code has to be parsed after the page loads.

When designing site pages, always check the coding with an HTML validator. This ensures that pages appear correctly in the different leading browsers. Besides this, when the HTML is correctly formatted, pages are generated faster within the browser. One of the most popular is the CSE HTML validator (www.htmlvalidator.com), which includes the capability to compare pages with the World Wide Web Consortium (W3C) HTML specifications. This feature also is available in many web authoring packages. Validators also are available for XHTML.

Most new software developments are being based around the enhanced flexibility, which XML allows for describing data. XHTML, now a W3C recommendation, is the next version of HTML. It works with 4.0 version and higher browsers, and together with HTML includes XML descriptive tags for page presentation, all within one file.

Images

All images need alt tags added to describe in text what the image is and further describe the page contents. Many search engine spiders also track for this. With alt tags, text-based browsers such as Lynx also can read the description and interpret where the image is on the page. Also, by adding the height and width of every image, the browser will load images faster. DHTML also can be used to represent a text image, which allows a page to load faster when used as background within a table with text overlapping (for 4.x or higher browsers), instead of traditionally using a JPEG or GIF file to display text with an image.

Are you using images as buttons? Keep them short and to the point. For correct appearance across multiple browser versions and for older monitors, save images within your imaging software using the Netscape 216-color safe palette.

JPEG images typically are used for photographs; GIF images are for text, logos, and drawings. For GIF images, to give the impression to the user of loading faster on the page, save the file as interlaced. This will allow it to be seen on the page gradually, instead of making the user wait for it to load completely.

A replacement for the proprietary GIF format is PNG (Portable Network Graphics). PNG is a recommendation of the W3C standards organization; it allows an image to be compressed up to 25 percent better than GIF and makes excellent indexed color images. PNG files are supported by 4.x browsers (except Macintosh) and higher. Most standard imaging packages (Macromedia Fireworks, Paintshop Pro, Adobe Photoshop) now can save image files in PNG format. Find out more about PNG files by going to http://www.w3.org/TR/png.html.

With JPEG images, you can give the impression of the image loading faster by saving the file as interlaced, which will allow it to be viewed on the page gradually as the page loads. To do this, be sure to save the image as a progressive JPEG. JPEG file sizes can be further reduced by image compression so they load faster. For large images, *slice* an image into pieces, putting each image into a coordinated table cell. Slicing can be done through many popular imaging packages such as PaintShop Pro, Adobe PhotoShop, or Macromedia Fireworks.

Links

Nothing is more frustrating to a user than a broken link. Run a link check with your web design package or through one of the online web sites mentioned elsewhere in the chapter. To double check the accuracy of and associated links, some online tools are available:

▼ **Netmechanic** http://www.netmechanic.com/index.htm

■ **Web Site Garage** http://websitegarage.netscape.com/jayde/

▲ **Siteinspector** http://www.siteinspector.com

Tables

The advantages of laying out your page in tables are many; primarily it helps to ensure there are no browser or platform problems with displaying. Tables also help you to lay out your pages in a consistent manner. Laying out pages in tables using pixels and centering them on each page allows for adjustment for larger-sized monitors.

To have a table look the same for different-sized monitors, use percentage instead of pixels for sizing. The approach you take in using either pixels or percentages with tables will depend on what you know about the type of systems your target end users use to view web pages. The most conservative approach is the use of percentages with tables.

Avoid putting too many tables within other tables (called *nesting*). This slows down the page because the browser has to interpret all the tables. If you are using complex tables, add the height and width for each table for faster loading.

Frames

Frames have a bad reputation, mainly because of how they were initially used on the web. Included properly, frames can allow a page to display content from several other pages within frames. Always include the option to allow the reader to view pages outside of a frame. Keep in mind to also include a NOFRAMES tag so search engines can index the page properly for older version browsers that don't know how to handle frames. To make a frame look the same for different sized monitors, use percentages for sizing to compensate for all the spacing in the browser window. The following coding snippet is an example of the <FRAME> tag:

```
<FRAMESET ROW="15,*">
    <FRAME SRC="listing.html">
```

```
<FRAME SRC="main.html">
<NOFRAMES>
<BODY BGCOLOR="#FFFFFF" TEXT="FF0000">
        Body of coding goes here
</BODY>
</NOFRAMES>
</FRAMESET>
```

Relative Links

When linking to other pages that are located within the same web site, it is good policy to use *relative links.* A relative link refers to where the linked page (or graphic, sound, or plug-ins) is in relation to the current page. For example, consider the following relative link on a web page, which is in the plans directory and has the file name listing.html. It would appear in the browser as an underlined text link: <u>Hosting Plans</u>. Within the actual coding of the page, it would appear as follows

```
<a href="plans/listing.html">Hosting Plans</a>
```

instead of the full web site address (the absolute path), such as:

```
<a href="http://www.hostingresolve.com/plans/listing.html">
Hosting Plans</a>
```

This involves less work for the browser, which doesn't have to reload the web site's HTML pages and associated files from the server each time requested, but uses locally cached files that are stored on the user's system.

Display Resolution

Some users still have smaller monitors that can display up to only 640x480 resolution (estimated at 12 percent of monitors). That means that a maximum of 635x380 pixels is the maximum portion of the window that can be used for content. Another factor is the users' equipment or drivers might be out of date. In designing for the standard 800x600 resolution, the maximum portion of the window that can be used is 795x500 pixels.

Browser Versions

Specific versions of different browsers have their own special limitations. Be sure to test pages with different versions of Internet Explorer and Netscape Navigator browsers for any problems. Check out http://www.webreview.com/browsers/browsers.shtml, which lists all the available browsers, versions, and limitations. Consider all types of browsers that are used in the market.

Is it important for content to look correct in 3.x version browsers? Keep in mind that only about 4 percent of the market is still using 3.x version web browsers. Typically, you will want to focus on designing for 4.x or higher version web browsers. Dynamic HTML, or DHTML refers to an interactive page using a combination of HTML, JavaScript, a DOM (Document Object Model), and Cascading Style Sheets (CSS). Although DHTML is supported by browsers 4.x or higher, keep in mind that Internet Explorer and Netscape Navigator still use different implementations.

Microsoft's WebTV accounts for only a small share of the market, but you can check how your pages will appear on WebTV by using WebTV Viewer, shown in Figure 4-3. The screen space for designing to accommodate WebTV browsers is 544x378 pixels. The viewer is available from http://developer.webtv.net/design/tools/viewer/default.htm.

Server Logs

Check your server log files weekly to track where visitors are coming from, and what type and version of browser they are using. You can use this data to modify your site as necessary for older browsers if appropriate, or drop support for older browsers if no users are viewing your page with them. You also can use this data to determine whether to use Cascading Style Sheets, which take advantage of specific browser versions to control font styles and layout of the page. Log files will be discussed in further detail in Chapter 14.

Cascading Style Sheets

Cascading Style Sheets are supported as of Internet Explorer 3.0 and Netscape Navigator 4.0. If you are using Cascading Style

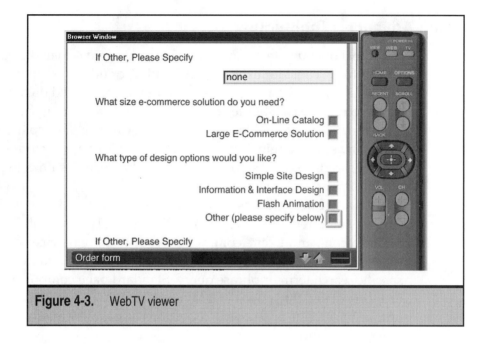

Figure 4-3. WebTV viewer

Sheets, you can verify your pages online from the following URL:
http://www. htmlhelp.com/tools/csscheck/. If you want to ensure
that your fonts appear properly across browsers, don't specify a
font in coding, but allow the browser's defaults to determine which
font to use. If you must specify a font size, use pixels to specify the
size. For printing purposes, design an alternate print page that uses
point sizes so that printed pages can be legibly printed (pixels turn
up too small for legibility when printing).

Staying Current

Keep up with the current standards and conventions of the web
through the World Wide Web Consortium (W3C) at http://www.
w3c.com. The W3C is involved with setting standards for hypertext
and multimedia on the Internet, and emerging standards in XML,
XHTML, and so forth. Always keep an eye on your main competition.
Look at other web hosting and design sites so you can be open to
new design ideas and keep abreast of value-added services and
support programs being offered.

Using Advanced Techniques

If the goal of your site is to provide dynamic content to make pages appear fresh, consider using JSP, ASP, PHP, or other server-side methods. These technologies also can provide advanced database and e-commerce capabilities to power your site and your customer's sites; they are discussed in further detail in Chapter 9. Keep in mind that many search engines cannot track dynamic pages for individual ranking, so also keep a static HTML page that includes links to all of your important site pages.

This also can be addressed by advertising with leading search engines and directories such as Google.com, GoTo.com, Yahoo.com, Mamma.com, and Excite.com, where your hosting services are positioned at the top of search page results that correspond to a specific search term or phrase query. Standard page components can be incorporated into pages and saved as templates, which provide a unique boilerplate appearance to sections of your site and establish brand recognition.

Some of the web authoring packages that allow pages to be saved as templates include Microsoft FrontPage, Macromedia Dreamweaver, and Adobe Pagemill. Microsoft FrontPage is popular for web authoring, especially for designing with Microsoft's server-side scripting technology, ASP. For high-performance authoring, Macromedia has Dreamweaver UltraDev, whereby dynamic pages can be designed to support server behaviors for pages that are based on ASP, JavaScript, VBScript, ColdFusion, or JavaBean coding that runs from the server instead of the client browser. In addition, UltraDev includes the capability to insert pages with live objects, which have multiple server behaviors in web pages to create advanced page components.

Numerous online resources and authoring packages are available to assist with site presentation:

▼ **HTML Help**   http://www.htmlhelp.com

■ **Microsoft FrontPage**   http://www.microsoft.com/frontpage/

▲ **Macromedia Dreamweaver**   http://www.macromedia.com

Using these server-side technologies, a web site can include powerful features for user interaction, database functionality, and dynamic presentation. A good knowledge of most HTML 4.0 tags (for tables, forms, images, and plug-ins) and Javascript still is important, as some of these web authoring packages will not handle all the nuances of smart web page design, browser version differences, or custom programming.

For creating impressive multimedia designs, animations, and movies, Macromedia Flash has become quite popular. There are three types of Flash animation file extensions that are used, ending with .fla, .swf, and .swt. Figure 4-4 shows a sample menu being created within Macromedia Flash. With this menu, you could design a sitemap to allow a user to find their way easily around your site.

Be careful of using Flash for your initial pages. Although Flash is impressive, give the user the option of easily bypassing the front page to navigate straight to where your core web services and

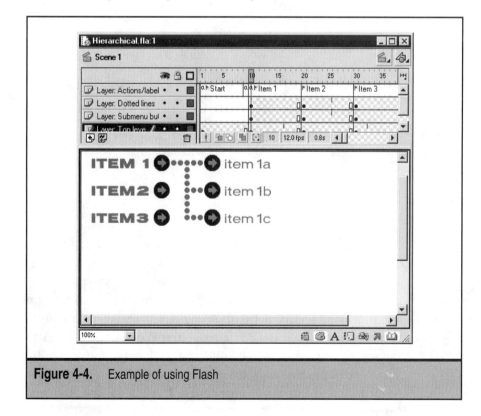

Figure 4-4.   Example of using Flash

products are featured. If you use complex animations that take a long time to load, some users might avoid your web site altogether. A couple of good resources on Flash include *Macromedia Flash 5 Developer's Guide*, by P.S. Woods, and *How To Do Everything with Macromedia Flash 5*, by Bonnie Blake (both Osborne McGraw-Hill).

Wireless Application Protocol Technology

Wireless devices are becoming popular for browsing pages, which are referred to as *microbrowsers*. Consider adding WML (Wireless Markup Language) content for getting your message to all possible audiences. WML is a form of XML that allows web content—including small graphics—to be used through wireless handset devices. Here is an example of what WAP coding looks like for a Nokia series mobile phone:

```
<?xml version="1.0" encoding="ISO-8859-1"?><!DOCTYPE wml PUBLIC
"-//WAPFORUM//DTD WML 1.1//EN" "http://www.wapforum.org//DTD//wml_1.1.xml">
<wml>
<!--Nokia Parser Info: Phone = Nokia
     ; Height = 90; Width = 130; CurrentDeckSize = 38; MaxDeckSize = 1600;
CardsOnEachLine = 5; CardsVerticalGap = 30-->
    <card id="card1" ordered="true" newcontext="false">
    <p align="center"> Web Hosting News </p>
    <p align="left"> NEW Managed Hosting Contact 1-888-555-5555 Today
    for Quote
    </p>
    </card>
</wml>
```

Figure 4-5 shows the results of this code for a Nokia wireless phone.

Remember that XML is case sensitive and requires all tags and attributes to be lowercase, unlike HTML. The coding for the wireless device here can be thought of as an assortment of *cards* and *decks*. Cards can represent text, a menu, or some other type of interaction. Cards are grouped into *decks*, which is the actual WML code sent to a wireless device. The code needs to be within a deck to be sent to a cellular device. The type of phone used determines the width and height dimensions of a card. The actual content sent can request that the user enter information from the keypad. For devices with small interfaces, the

Figure 4-5.   Example wireless message

maximum suggested number of cards in a deck is three. For larger wireless devices, more cards can be used in a deck. Another emerging standard when designing for wireless devices is XHTML-Basic. XHTML-Basic allows pages to be designed without the need to modify especially just for wireless devices. In other words, it can be used with standard browsers as well as with WebTV. Frames and nested tables are not supported, but small images (up to 95 width by 95 height) can be used for display in wireless devices that support images. XHTML-Basic, a W3C recommendation, can be downloaded at http://www.w3.org/TR/xhtml-basic.

More information on designing for wireless devices can be located at:

▼ **WAPForum**   http://www.wapforum.com

■ **XHTML-Basic**   http://www.w3.org/TR/xhtml-basic

■ **Nokia**   http://www.nokia.com

▲ **Ericsson**   http://www.ericsson.com

SEARCH ENGINE SUBMITTAL TIPS

According to an April 2000 RealNames survey, more than 75 percent of web users use search engines to traverse the web; in an average week the frequent Internet user spends 10 hours searching for specific information. To attract potential customers, you must ensure that your site has the best possible ranking in the major search engines so that the most users can find your web site. Methods to help ensure this are highlighted within this chapter. Table 4-1 lists the leading search engines and directories.

Search Engine/Directory and URL	Description
Yahoo! http://www.Yahoo.com Adding URL: http://docs.Yahoo.com/info/suggest/	Yahoo! is the most popular search engine, and is the largest human-generated category guide on the web. Launched in 1994, Yahoo! is the oldest Internet directory. It uses Google (www.google.com) to conduct searches over its 1 million site listings.
MSN Search http://search.msn.com/ Adding URL: http://mediacenter.msn.com/msnsales/home/home.asp	Part of the MSN suite of sites, MSN Search allows users to save search results through Internet Explorer 5.0 browsers. MSN uses LookSmart for directory services and Inktomi for searching.
AOL Search http://search.aol.com/ Adding URL: http://search.aol.com/add.adp	AOL Search provides access to search the web in addition to content from AOL. The primary search source is from the Open Directory (owned by Netscape), which uses volunteer contributions in cataloging the web.

Table 4-1.   Top Ten Ranking of Search Engines and Directories

Search Engine/Directory and URL	Description
Lycos http://www.lycos.com Adding URL: http://home.lycos.com/ addasite.html	Lycos is a directory-based site, which also uses the Open Directory, FAST, and Direct Hit for search results.
Go/Infoseek http://www.go.com Adding URL: Conduct a search from main page.	Go, owned by Disney, is powered by Infoseek, which uses a search algorithm called ESP (Extra Search Precision) search algorithm. It also includes an extensive directory of web sites.
Netscape Search http://search.netscape.com/ Adding URL: http://home.netscape.com/ escapes/search/addsite.html	Netscape Search uses its own database and the Open Directory. It also uses other search engines for results.
Excite http://www.excite.com Adding URL: http://www.excite.com/ info/add_url	Excite, which began in 1995, uses a search index as part of a large portal.
AltaVista http://www.altavista.com Adding URL: http://doc.altavista.com/ addurl/hs~index.html	AltaVista, owned by CMGI, generates search results based on a wide index of the web. It uses the Open Directory and LookSmart for conducting queries.
LookSmart http://www.looksmart.com Adding URL: http://submit.looksmart.com/ info.jhtml	LookSmart is a human-generated guide to web site listings. It also uses Inktomi to generate search responses, and provides search services to other search services.

Table 4-1.   Top Ten Ranking of Search Engines and Directories *(continued)*

Search Engine/Directory and URL	Description
IWon http://www.iwon.com Adding URL: http://www.inktomi.com/ products/search/ pagesubmission.html	IWon, owned by CBS, includes a LookSmart directory guide listing and uses Inktomi for generating search results. The IWon site generates traffic through monetary giveaways.

Table 4-1. Top Ten Ranking of Search Engines and Directories *(continued)*

As displayed in Figure 4-6, the top search engines overlap in their percentage of the market (as of November 2000), because web users frequently use multiple search engines to perform searches.

Several search engines also have partnerships in place with each other through which they use each other's search engines to generate search results (for example, Yahoo! uses Google for its search engine). Other popular search engines include Google, Ask Jeeves, and Hotbot. Google (www.google.com) ranks web sites by their link popularity . Ask Jeeves (www.askjeeves) measures what users select in searches, and is a partner with HotBot. HotBot (www.hotbot.com) includes

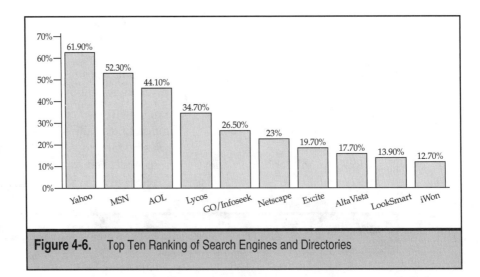

Figure 4-6. Top Ten Ranking of Search Engines and Directories

many custom search functions, and is owned by Lycos. HotBot uses Direct Hit (owned by Ask Jeeves) and Inktomi (a search index company).

Search engines use their own highly intricate algorithms, called *spiders*, which are programs that index web site pages that are accessed, including the links that are listed on the web pages accessed (therefore the term "spider"). Spiders also have been referred to as *robots*; each individual search engine uses its own proprietary method for indexing web pages.

Several factors contribute to a web site gaining a high search engine ranking, including the number of links from other web sites, frequency and usage of specific keywords, and contents of meta tags within site pages. What about instances when you do not want sections of your site tracked by search engines for security or privacy reasons? One common method is to reference a robots.txt file, which is a text file placed in the root directory. An example of the contents of a robots.txt file is as follows:

```
User-agent: *
Disallow: /protected/
```

In this example, all search engine robots will not index this protected directory of your web site. This is considered to be more reliable than using a <META> tag comment in the HEAD section of an HTML page to prevent content from being tracked.

Common Meta Tags

The best way to get spiders to notice your page is by adding information in a meta tag. Meta tags are enclosed by the <META> and </META> tags at the beginning of your page, and provide information about your page. The content of meta tags doesn't display in the user's browser; however, spider programs see this content. Following are some common types of meta tags:

▼ **Description**   This section describes the page contents. An example is

```
<META NAME="DESCRIPTION" CONTENT="By outsourcing routine software
to an ASP, you can focus on your key business and reduce costs.">.
```

- **Keywords** Keywords are used to highlight key phrases, further describing the page contents. For example:

```
<META NAME="KEYWORDS" CONTENT="hosting, applications,
groupware, specialty">
```

- **Author** This tag lists the author of the page, for example:

```
<META NAME="AUTHOR" CONTENT="Carl Burnham">
```

- **Ratings** Different rating services can be listed in this section to provide rating of content. Some of these include RSAC (http://www.rsac.org) and PICS (http://www.classify.org/safesurf/). For example, the following code indicates that the web site that includes this meta tag is safe content for viewing for all ages, and is registered with the noted organization:

```
<META HTTP-EQUIV="PICS-Label" CONTENT='(PICS-1.1
http://www.classify.org/safesurf/" l r (SS~~000 1))'>
```

- **Expiration** This tag gives a date that the page will expire, represented in Central Standard Time. for example;

```
<META HTTP-EQUIV="EXPIRES" CONTENT="Wed, 30 Dec 2000
21:03:28 CST">
```

▲ **Caching** To keep a page from being cached by a browser, add the following:

```
<META HTTP-EQUIV="PRAGMA" CONTENT="NO-CACHE">
```

Besides meta tags, search engine spiders look at specific tags including comments, links, headlines, and hidden forms in HTML pages.

Submitting Your Web Site

Manually submitting a web site to search engines and directories is the best method to use, as mass submittal software often are counterproductive. Search engines are constantly changing the methods used by their spider programs to index web pages, which then are used to generate search results from queries. Search engines are becoming increasingly savvy to mass web site submittal services and meta tag software that attempts to submit a web site to hundreds of search engines at a time, repeatedly using certain key words and meta tags throughout pages.

Some search engines regard this as a form of spamming, especially when resubmitting pages within a certain time period. In some cases, your site can even be blacklisted by a search engine, which results in preventing your site from being listed within search results for the specific search engine. The recommended steps are to manually submit to the leading search engines, and to use the techniques highlighted in this chapter. Another option discussed here is to pay search engines that accept banner or text advertising to receive top listings that is based on specific search phrases whereby your web site will be shown prominently at the top of search results pages.

Remember that many search engines cannot track dynamic pages for ranking. This also includes formats such as ASP, JSP, Java applets, databases, Flash animation, multimedia files, or images that have text as part of the graphic. A search engine cannot index sites that can be accessed only through a registration sign-up or password. One way to address these issues is by having HTML versions of these pages for search engines to locate and index. For the links within these pages, provide the full linkage to the dynamic pages. Make an index page that links the static HTML pages, and submit this central page to search engines to be indexed.

Other methods of getting your site in the top search results on search engines include advertising with key search engines such as Google, GoTo, Yahoo!, and Excite, where banner ads for your hosting services are placed at the top of keyword search result pages that correspond with your hosting specialty or target market. GoTo, with more than 29,000 paid advertisers, has arranged a sizable agreement with America Online to display paid advertising listings in search results on the America Online and Netscape Netcenter search result pages.

A search engine is paid (on a cpm, or cost per thousand) for keyword placement, and also receives revenues from selling lists to advertisers for search phrases used. CPM is the standard rate method for listing of ads, based on per one thousand views. The traditional cpm cost is determined by dividing the cost of an ad by the size of audience (per each thousand). The average rate that search engines are charging is $60 to $80 per cpm. Many web hosts are devoting a sizable amount of their marketing budgets to search engine advertising keyword placement, as search engines are the common method of finding information quickly on the Web.

REGISTRATION AND REVIEW BY WEB HOST RATING SERVICES

Several rating services are on the web to provide directory portals for web hosts to be ranked or listed within various web hosting categories. These services provide for different web hosts to be reviewed to highlight their range of hosting plans available, and to participate in industry message forums. Some of these include Hostcompare.com, Tophosts.com, and SearchASP.com. These web sites also will typically include comparative search features, and accept advertising from web hosts.

A wide range of web host rating service sites are available on the web, including:

▼ **Thelist.com**   http://www.thelist.com

■ **SearchASP**   http://www.searchasp.com

▲ **Recellar.com**   http://www.recellar.com

AFFILIATE PROGRAMS

Affiliate programs provide a lead generation program whereby the web host pays a set amount through an affiliate for leads forwarded or revenues made as a result of the affiliate arrangement. Banners and other promotional advertisements are tracked for qualified *click-throughs* and sales generated from the tracking from other web sites, which accrue payments by the number of times that an ad is clicked. Web hosts can choose to develop their own affiliate programs that track click-throughs from other web sites to the host's page using cookies, scripting, or other methods. Some online services specialize in organizing affiliate programs. Pricing to start an affiliate program might vary widely by program.

Other affiliate business models encourage viewing of banner advertisements through a points program in which a user accrues points, and is awarded coupons and merchandise for looking at affiliate offers. When affiliate merchandise or services are purchased, there usually are more points provided to the user as an incentive. Some of these programs include MyPoints.com, Freeride.com, and Cybergold.com. As with other affiliate programs, web hosts can create their own incentive program in house, providing a payment for a click-throughs plan or referral plan. As with some other parts of the business, the web host can find that in some cases it is more cost effective to outsource these types of services. Partnering arrangements and outsourcing issues are discussed in further detail in Chapter 14.

Some of the more popular affiliate programs include

▼ **Clicktrade.com**   http://www.clicktrade.com

■ **Commission Junction**   http://www.cj.com

▲ **Linkshare**   http://www.linkshare.com

Some of the target web directories available to list your affiliate program once it is established include

▼ **Associate-It**   http://www.associate-it.com

■ **Refer-it.com**   http://www.refer-it.com

▲ **AssociatePrograms.com**   http://www.associateprograms.com

SUMMARY

This chapter discussed some general page design methods and technologies that a professional web site should include, and introduced methods for working with search engines. By offering affiliate and reseller programs, a web host can find new ways to expand into markets that otherwise might not be available. The next chapter will focus on general marketing strategies, including advertising and press releases, that are designed to complement your online web business.

CHAPTER 5

Additional Marketing
Strategies

To attract maximum marketing exposure for your web services, consider your primary target markets. Your marketing approach will vary depending on these markets, and on what type of hosting services you provide, either directly or indirectly. If your services are comprehensive, your marketing approach generally will be all-encompassing. Some initial considerations will be these:

▼   Are you involved with a niche market such as application or managed hosting, or the general market of co-location and shared hosting?

■   What advantages do you offer that differentiate you from the competition in the web hosting industry and the Internet?

■   How are you reaching your target audiences: with a wide or a narrow focus?

■   How are you making your presence known in the offline world as well as on the Internet?

▲   Is there a consistent message for all of your advertising efforts?

Your approach should reflect specific ways that your unique services meet the needs of those key markets and increase brand awareness. As discussed in the previous chapter, careful page design optimized with appropriate tags can get your site indexed properly by the search engines. You also can place selective banner ads with some of the leading ones on a pay-per-click or page ranking basis. This leads to highly targeted traffic based on select key words. Also consider offline marketing approaches. This includes television, radio, newspapers, magazines, and outdoor billboard advertising.

The key to a marketing plan is flexibility and innovation. It will include many market angles and components, which together increase your overall exposure. Also consider market trends in attracting specific niche markets. This chapter discusses general marketing tactics for advertising, press releases, and other made-to-order strategies to complement your online web business.

MEDIA ADVERTISING

In 1999, Internet companies spent an estimated $1.4 billion on advertising, according to Competitive Media Reporting. Most of that money was spent advertising on network television, magazines, cable television, newspapers, and outdoor advertising (in order of money spent, according to Competitive Media Reporting). Other potential markets that are used include radio, direct mail, and telephone book (yellow pages) advertising. Consider using several of these markets in combination, as your budget allows, when establishing name recognition and for attracting new sales.

Effective online and offline advertising campaigns include the components of layout, conception, and execution, which best represent your market specialization and perception of the market to potential customers. Advertising should reflect your unique firm's identity, and should be coordinated with your web site, sales department, in letterheads, correspondence, presentations, and brochures. In some cases, web host consultants and resellers with marketing experience work with clients in providing advertising programs as a natural extension of developing a web site.

Creative eye-catching ads work well for creating positive reinforcement that customers will identify with your service. Seek ways to advertise that further identify and bolster your image and brand based on positive feedback from your customers. Have you conducted surveys with customers to find what they like and dislike about your services? Surveys can uncover hidden details of what you should be bragging about in advertising campaigns and can generate new customer referrals (which are discussed further in Chapter 7). Customer testimonials from these surveys can provide examples of your professional services, whether for shared hosting or high-end hosting.

If your budget can justify it, television offers the opportunity to present your visual advertisement to a potentially large audience, depending on whether you advertise in local or national markets. Your commercial ad is especially effective if placed during a special segment or television program that focuses on computers. If you want to convey the image of a quality product, a commercial should be professionally done by an advertising firm experienced in the market and/or the television field.

According to analysts, prime-time television advertising is the most expensive form of advertising, given the large base of viewers. Consider the largest annual television event: the Super Bowl. A 30-second advertisement cost $2 million in 2000. Typically, local television affiliate advertising can range from $500 to $3,000 to run a 30-second television spot in the prime-time evening hours. Local cable television generally is a more economical avenue for television advertising, with averages ranging from $60 to $90 to run a 30-second television spot in the prime-time evening hours. If a commercial is professionally produced, this cost also must be factored into pricing.

Ads in trade magazines that focus on the computer industry often are used by web hosts. An average four-color ad page for leading computer magazines averages about $60,000. Consider trade magazines that publish and provide coverage by region, in which a four-color ad page averages less than $3,600.

As with magazines, newspaper ads range greatly in price, depending on the size of overall readership, the size of the ad, and where they it is placed. However, newspapers are a more targeted advertising approach than magazines, especially for metropolitan areas, as they run on a daily or weekly basis; they rank just behind television in advertising dollars spent. On average, a 1/4-page, black and white ad can range from $1,500 to $2,500 for a metropolitan newspaper. Unlike other forms of advertising discussed so far, newspaper ads can be modified quickly to account for changes in promotions and other details.

Radio advertising can vary in price and can be a low-cost option best used in combination with other advertising avenues. A typical 60-second radio spot can range from $80 to $180. To be most effective, consider purchasing multiple spots of advertising time on several radio stations to reach the greatest coverage within local markets.

Targeted direct mail campaigns sometimes can generate positive results. Mailing lists average about $125 per 1,000 names and addresses, and $400 for the actual mailing of material (assuming a standard-size letter) for the same number of names and addresses. Another advertising market that often is overlooked is the yellow pages of the telephone book. To get your ad to stand out further, consider placing a color ad, which averages from $700.

Media Mergers

In the trend towards consolidation in the industry, look for more firms to partner with media companies to creatively reach new markets. A perfect example of this is the America Online/ Time Warner $109 billion merger, approved in December 2000. America Online, the largest ISP, is now teamed with Time Warner, the largest media company. Time Warner reaches more than 20 percent of cable homes in the United States and owns TNT, HBO, and CNN; and publishes People and Time magazines. Meanwhile, America Online owns the rights to Netscape Netcenter, has instant messaging services, and currently has 26 million subscribers.

Because a detailed coverage of each form of advertising goes beyond the focus of this book, consult with your local and trade advertising markets when evaluating comparative media ad pricing, giving particular consideration to estimating any creative planning and production costs for an ad. Request an ad kit from specific ad markets that you are interested in, which usually will contain a rate card, a size estimate of viewers or readers, and other sample information.

Consider listing with an online exchange that brings buyers and media sellers together, and enables you to bid for the best advertising price. BuyMedia (http://www.buymedia.com) is one such exchange, and contains an extensive listing of radio and television stations at which advertising time can be negotiated. AdOutlet (http:// www.adoutlet.com) is another exchange offering similar services. Consider all markets in advertising to consistently reinforce brand recognition and prospective sales.

OUTDOOR ADVERTISING

Billboards can provide a powerful media resource, especially for capturing brand recognition in key metropolitan markets, in coordination with web marketing efforts. Monthly billboard spacing can range from $3,000 to $5,000, within these markets. As with any other advertising media, consider the timing and location of billboard advertising. One of the most noteworthy examples of this is Indulge.com, an Internet startup. It placed a billboard in Times Square just before New Year's Eve in 1999, which was viewed by millions of viewers on television and in the area. Although the initial cost ($102 million) was high for a 45-by-40-foot billboard, the company generated substantial new customers and brand recognition. It is estimated that the billboard has been viewed by more than 700 million people, according to Business 2.0 magazine. An online resource for outdoor sign advertising is Sign Web, available by searching at http://www.signweb.com.

Look also at alternative outdoor advertising markets such as vehicle fleet advertising and even aerial banner advertising. Vehicle fleets are becoming popular because of the low costs at less than 70 cents per 1,000 cpm (cost per thousand ad views). The other advantage is the mobility such vehicles provide, especially within metropolitan areas where other media cannot reach.

A vehicle ad can be designed on vinyl self-adhesive "billboards" or paint wrapped on a vehicle directly, as shown in Figure 5-1. An online resource for vehicle fleet advertising is available at http://www.signweb.com/outdoor/cont/outdoor990219.html.

Source: Digital Island

Figure 5-1.   Example of vehicle advertising

PRESS RELEASES

A press release provides another opportunity to establish brand recognition and market exposure by reporting on anything of significance about your company. This can be to announce a new service, partnership, company expansion, or other event. Here are some basic goals to keep in mind:

- ▼ Try to avoid the tendency to be wordy. Consider your audience. Announce the news and why it is important.

- ■ Begin with a news overview; then provide a key executive quote.

- ■ Provide the news release with useful details and timely material to report.

- ■ Include key contact information such as key executives, company phone, fax, and e-mail addresses, physical address, and a specific URL, which provides more information. If news is routinely released to the media, include a press release menu section on your web site.

- ■ Make sure the press release is in the format that is preferred by the news service. For fonts, this will be either Courier or Arial 10-point size.

- ■ Avoid overuse of terms and abbreviations that are only specific to your industry. Make it readable and understandable.

- ■ Include your corporate logo at the top of the page, or on letterhead paper to easily identify your release.

- ▲ Check and re-check for possible misspellings and grammatical errors.

Many Internet companies have received positive (and free) media coverage by making donations to local worthwhile community and charitable concerns. Are you just attending Chamber of Commerce meetings? Allow employees to be involved in a work day to benefit the local community. Your assistance can be listed in your company newsletter and web site, and generate positive media exposure through press releases. How is your web hosting business involved with the surrounding community?

A press release should be no more than one page in length. If you need to send further relevant information, provide a URL for a specific web page. Are you seeking to attract foreign markets? Prepare press releases in other languages, with alternate URLs for information in that language.

In most cases, e-mail will be the preferred method of sending a press release. Keep it simple, without attachments. When sending out e-mails to many recipients, within your e-mail program add e-mail addresses to the BCC (Blind Carbon Copy) field so that the e-mail will list only the contact person's e-mail address in the TO field when received. By following up an e-mail with a telephone call to confirm receipt, you also will increase your chances that the press release will be read by the right person and get the media coverage you are seeking.

If you do not have an existing in-house database of media contacts, or if you do not have a public relations firm to send press releases for you, you can purchase media directory listings that list key contacts, e-mail addresses, and physical addresses. Some directory listings include

▼ **InternetWire**   http://www1.internetwire.com/iwire/home

▲ **Internet News Bureau**   http://www.newsbureau.com

Public relations firms and news release services also can design your press release for a fee. The standard rate is $200 to $250 per page.

You can see an example of a press release on the following page.

INDUSTRY AFFILIATIONS

There are certification standards organizations for web hosts that meet certain established standards. The Web Host Guild provides a seal of approval for web hosting services that meet certification requirements for membership, which includes a direct technical support available (minimum eight hours per day), 30-day money-back

FOR IMMEDIATE RELEASE:

CONTACT: (Make sure this person is accessible by the media.
If not, list others here that can be reached.)
Contact's Name
Company
Telephone
Cellular
Fax
E-mail
Web site:

TITLE OF NEWS RELEASE
City, state, date—(The opening paragraph will contain the basics
of the news item—the "who, what, when, where, and why".)

Body of release—(This will be any appropriate information about
your services or products offered, market advantages, and so forth.
How is this information unique in the market? Use bullets to
emphasize key points here. Within this section you also can include
quotes of research firms, customer testimonials, or key company
executives. Think of what this press release may lead to in exposure
for your service or product—a feature article or an interview.)

For additional information, contact—(List key contacts, with
e-mail, telephone, and fax numbers.)
Summary—(Provide brief summary information about services
or products offered again.)
Company background—(Provide a short overview of the company.)

# # #
(Place at bottom to indicate the end of the Press Release.)

guarantee, daily and weekly backups, and in business at least a year.
Members also are tracked to gauge the performance of their networks.

Web hosting services that are members can use the organization's certification logo, which designates that they meet the criteria for membership. The board of directors has representatives including Interliant, XO Communications, Verio, NetMechanic, Web2010, and Worldwide Internet. The association's web site is available at http://www.whg.org/index.htm.

VeriHost is another web hosting membership organization. Its mission is to ensure high standards throughout the web hosting industry through a rigorous certification process for hosting companies. For membership, candidates must be able to provide at least an e-mail based support system with online self-help customer support, offer 24-hour customer support and one-day account setup and provide proof of network backbone connectivity. Verihost is located at http://www.verihost.com/index.html.

SEMINARS, CONFERENCES, AND TRADE SHOWS

By attending local and regional seminars, conferences, and trade shows (both on- and offline), you can increase your exposure among IT professionals and the business community. Leading annual computer trade shows include Comdex (http://www.comdex.com) and PC Expo (http://www.techxny.com/pc_expo/index.html). Trade show exposition spacing can vary greatly in price, from several thousand to upwards of $1 million. Don't overlook local business trade shows as a more affordable option, to sponsor a booth and promote your web hosting expertise.

Also consider having a company spokesperson be a guest speaker and highlight company solutions, products, and specialized industry knowledge. Check out the Tech Calendar, an online resource calendar for upcoming seminars, conferences, and trade shows, available at http://www.techweb.com/calendar/. Volunteer to be a guest or to sponsor technical talk radio and technology television shows. Several opportunities exist with online industry web news sites, portals, and magazines for interviews; or to be featured as an expert or guest columnist. Submit press releases to these when announcing a new service, partnership, or special incentive program.

ONLINE MARKETING APPROACHES

More online advertising and promotions are being used, with an estimated 5,700 businesses now advertising online. According to a new consumer study released December 2000 by PROMO Magazine and NFO Worldwide, 81 percent of respondents had participated in a promotion in the past six months, mainly influenced by the Internet (60%), print ads (57%), and e-mail (51%). The study was the first of its kind to look into what stimulates (and dampens) consumer participation in promotions. "This data reinforces the idea that the Internet is the ultimate one-to-one marketing and promotion tool," said Kerry J. Smith, group publisher of PROMO Magazine and American Demographics, "providing the ability to develop an ongoing dialogue with customers and potential customers."

E-mail Advertising

E-mail is by far the low-cost winner for getting your company message across. When using e-mail as a marketing tool, make sure it is informative. Avoid sending e-mail as splashy graphics in HTML pages. Not all recipients have a high-speed corporate connection or broadband. Because of how various end user e-mail programs handle e-mail, some might see only garbage when HTML is used. Using large HTML as the format for e-mail can slow down a recipient's e-mail. The safest alternative is to send e-mail as text, with an e-mail link in the body to allow the recipient to receive the file as HTML if they prefer—or better yet, list a web page where related information can be found.

Signatures and vCards

Have all employees include a "signature" with all e-mail sent. Most standard e-mail programs include the capability to add 4 to 5 lines of text automatically at the end of each e-mail message sent. The basic information can include company name, phone number, URL, or e-mail address. This also can be in the form of an attached .vcf file (known as a vCard), as shown in Figure 5-2. This basically is an electronic business card, which is based on established MIME and ISO standards as developed by the Internet Mail Consortium (IMC).

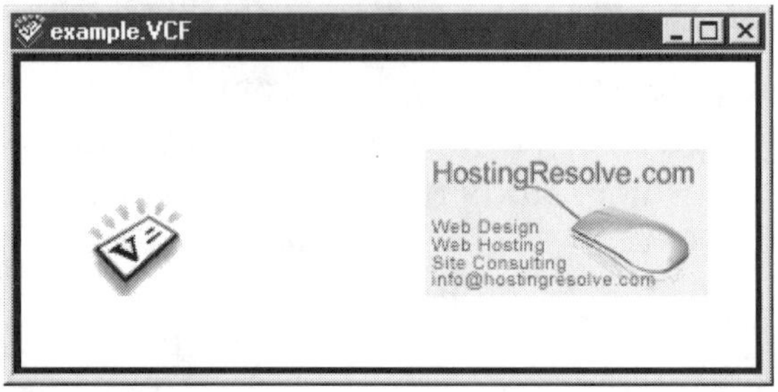

Figure 5-2.   vCard example

A vCard also can include insert options for adding a company logo or photo, and sound (through a .wav file). When using a vCard, keep it simple. A vCard file will be used as an attachment to e-mail, so keep it small—from 1 to 10K. Most standard e-mail programs have .vcf file support capability as well.

Targeted Mailings

Targeted e-mail, as with direct mail campaigns, gets results as long as it is not spam. Everyone hates spam. It clogs up recipient e-mail inboxes, can easily have the opposite effect of what your firm is trying to project. Only use *opt-in* e-mail addresses for sending direct mail. These are lists of individuals and businesses that have requested to receive e-mail within specific subject categories. Targeted e-mail lists generally start from $250 per 1,000 names and addresses. Some online direct e-mail rental lists include

▼ **Electronic Direct Marketing**   http://www.edmarketing.com

▲ **Internet Media Group**   http://www.internetmedia.com

As part of your e-mail marketing campaign, incorporate an informative newsletter that gives basic information about your hosting services along with helpful tips, to build credibility. Distribute the newsletter on a monthly or quarterly basis, and include special pricing incentives for ordering a hosting plan through the newsletter. Include examples of successful web sites that you host. Include a specific e-mail link address in the body of the newsletter that makes it easy for the recipient to opt out (discontinue the newsletter). Within the body of the e-mail, this could be listed as follows:

```
To unsubscribe to our newsletter, send a blank e-mail to:
mailto:leave-newsletterlist@hostingresolve.com
or for AOL users,
<a href="mailto:leave-newsletterlist@hostingresolve.com">AOL Users
Unsubscribe here</a>
```

This also can provide the opt-out option through a CGI script, ASP, or other method if you maintain your subscriber list through a database. The link would look something like this:

```
To unsubscribe, please visit
<http://myhostingresolve.com/list/updated.cgi?l=unsub>
```

By the same token, if the e-mail has been forwarded to another by the recipient, make it easy to subscribe to the newsletter. Within the body of the e-mail, this could be listed as:

```
Reading our newsletter for the first time? To subscribe to our
newsletter, just send a blank e-mail to:
mailto:join-newsletterlist@hostingresolve.com
or for AOL users,
<a href="mailto:join-newsletterlist@hostingresolve.com">AOL Users
Subscribe here</a>
```

This also can be done through a CGI script, ASP, or other method. The link would look something like this:

```
To subscribe, please visit
<http://myhostingresolvenewsletter.com/list/updated.cgi?l=sub>
```

Be creative to establish brand recognition and confidence. Consider having a contest in association with your newsletter and web site (contests are discussed later in this chapter). Announce the contest with web sites, which track contests and freebies. Include in the newsletter a link to a survey or form to be completed, which includes specific questions to determine whether the entrant is a candidate for web hosting.

Make your prospect newsletter separate from the customer newsletter, which should provide more detailed and unique information based on the type of account that the customer has. As with other customer service areas, the key goal in your efforts should be toward building long-term relationships. Customer newsletters will be discussed further in Chapter 6.

Banner Ads

Consider banner advertising as part of a discussion group on a community forum or newsletter, after comparing rates (typically on a cost-per-thousand or flat-rate basis) and the potential audience. Pricing can vary widely, depending on the number of ad views for the market audience. For targeted sites, pricing typically begin from $8,000 per 100,000 views. As part of the ad, offer an incentive, such as no setup fee, an initial month free, a discounted rate, or a contest.

CueCat

Utilize new technologies such as the Digital Convergence CueCat, which allows customers the convenience of connecting to a web site through the CueCat handheld (instead of typing the full web address). The handheld is available free at Radio Shack stores. The device, which is connected through an extension to a computer keyboard port, connects directly to a web site through an Internet browser when a specially marked bar code with a CueCat icon is swiped with the hand device. The code can be included with company brochures, press releases, magazine articles, annual reports, and in newspapers.

You also can connect a television to the device, through a computer and CueCat-provided software, to provide quick access to web content mentioned on CueCat-enabled television programs. Provide your customers with surprise giveaways, such as T-shirts, that include your company URL and logo. This of course provides free advertising for your web hosting business and promotes good will with your customers. Be innovative in your approach. Include a CueCat bar code on the T-shirt or the inside tag that links directly to your main web site when swiped. Also include the code in your printed advertising. Do you send out holiday cards as reminders that you appreciate being able to provide web service to them? If you consider this an unnecessary expense, consider the cost of losing that client.

Contests

Contests can further establish your firms brand recognition, site traffic, and gather qualified leads for future business. Time is valuable. Ask basic questions including name, address, and e-mail address. Try not to include more than four questions that are specific to qualifying the contestant's potential web hosting needs. Allow them to forward information about the contest to other interested parties by including a field for them to list e-mail addresses. Asking for too much information will turn off many customers.

Contests must be tied to a back-end database from the online form for sorting and tracking purposes. Generate enough interest by making the prizes worth the time it takes to fill out your short survey. Have a giveaway contest with a prize of web hosting for six months, a free vacation to Disney World, a mountain bike, a company jacket, or cold hard cash, depending on your promotional budget.

Make it fresh and interesting. It's okay to be human. Add humor by including a cartoon character or mascot to make the contest an interactive and involving experience, to increase traffic to your main web site and encourage entrants to tell others about the contest.

Promote your contest. You have to spread the word. Fortunately, this being the Web, there are plenty of folks to help. More than 250 free web sites, newsgroups, and newsletters tell web surfers where they can find freebies and contests. Use them. Also, spend a little cash to promote. Put high-quality banner ads on the best contest promotion sites. A little money goes a long way with these.

However, keep in mind that contests can't work magic. If you have a mediocre site or if you sell commodity items, the contest won't yield well. If you have a great site and unique products, go ahead, work hard, and build a successful contest.

Some online sources that track contests and freebies include:

▼ **FreeSite**   http://www.thefreesite.com

▲ **Contest Guide**   http://www.contestguide.com

Finally, be sure to post the contest guidelines. As a form of promotional marketing, the guidelines need to cover in detail the specifics and legalities of the contest. Some of these concerns address how the winners' names will be used, a time schedule for the contest, how the information gathered will be used, and state and federal regulations. Specify the number of times each entrant can enter, the age range of the entrant (to prevent minors from entering), how you will select the winners on a random and final basis, an alternate method for registering, and how winners and entrants will be contacted. Include a void clause for areas in which the contest might be prohibited, a detail of prizes, whether cash is an option for prize awards, and how winners will be used in further promotion. When announcing the winners, highlight them in your newsletter and display this prominently via your web site. When awarding a prize to the winner of a contest, include legal specifics for each party, designed to alleviate any unknowns after an award has been made. Make sure that all parameters and guidelines are reviewed by an attorney, because state or local laws might have a bearing on how an agreement needs to be outlined.

Some online sources that provide legal information regarding contests and other incentive programs include

▼ **FindLaw for Business**   http://techdeals.biz.findlaw.com/

■ **LawGuru.com**   http://www.lawguru.com/cgi/bbs/

▲ **Sample Legal Forms**   http://www.halldickler.com

SUMMARY

In formulating a marketing strategy to increase brand awareness, remember to make it unique for your web hosting business and balance it with a flexible marketing plan. As has been discussed, coordinating offline marketing strategies with your web presence will increase your exposure. The next chapter will discuss customer service, the fuel that sustains your business.

PART III

Customer Service

CHAPTER 6

Ensuring Quality Customer Service

No question is so difficult to answer as that to which the answer is obvious.
—*George Bernard Shaw*

Good quality service is noticed. You may have seen it when dining at a good restaurant; the host and waiter remember your name and act genuinely glad to see you. You feel appreciated and special. It is a place you recommend to others for the fine food and service you experience. It is customer-centric, with the focus on servicing the customer in tangible and intangible ways that make their experiences memorable. How can you emulate this with your range of hosting services? This chapter discusses the essentials web hosts need to provide exceptional customer service.

BASIC CUSTOMER SUPPORT

Keeping customers loyal depends on your integrity. Only make promises that you can deliver on in your web hosting business. Without integrity, you are treading water unless you provide a unique product or service that has a monopoly on the market. Some prospects will be on the hosting rebound and are seeking a responsible web host that they can rely on for faster answers to their problems and concerns—one that will respond to an e-mail or telephone call with relevant answers without waiting one day, much less 2 to 3 days; a host that will not continually go down for mysterious reasons, and then deny that anything occurred when questioned.

Your customer's previous host might have had a network that was unbearably slow, or had servers that were being used to capacity, which resulted in reduced web site performance. Others are seeking more value-added perks and expanded services than their existing web host can provide, whether it is being able to use a new server-side technology, access to 24/7 support, enabling their site for e-commerce, or outsource applications. Whatever the reason, by offering quality hosting services for what is promised at a reasonable price, you are likely to attract new customers and keep existing ones for the long term.

Think like the customers. They are looking for the best web hosting value from a business that is credible and trustworthy. Listen to what they are trying to tell you. Some analysts estimate that it costs five times more in advertising, promotion, and personnel expenses to get new customers than to satisfy the existing ones. According to Albert Delorenzi, CTO with Nortel Networks, "Businesses (online) are starting to compete on the basis of their customer relationships— in terms of how well they know each customer. By building strong bonds with their customers, businesses can differentiate themselves and earn customer loyalty." Web hosts need to be mindful of having a creative work environment, where employees are allowed to learn and experience career growth. Too many organizations stifle their employees within narrowly structured job assignments, which always leads to high turnover, low morale—and marginal customer service. This can lead to employee turf protection as an attempt at added job security, especially within larger organizations. The other extreme is assigning tasks to employees that are vague and lacking performance incentive. As the web hosting industry evolves, the problems described are not as common as within more traditional industries. Stock options are fine, but don't use it as the only incentive for working for a company. Stock options also are too unpredictable a reward in today's economic climate—a fact that professionals increasingly realize.

Employees want to work for an organization that they can believe in; one that understands their mission and makes the employee feel like part of the plan. Think of creative ways to promote a teamwork atmosphere in which employees are rewarded and can make their careers thrive through continuing education and advancement opportunities. One company that has proven success with these concepts is America Online. When Bob Pittman became CEO, he gave each senior executive a copy of *The Nordstrom Way,* a book on the legendary achievement of Nordstrom department stores, which focuses on customer service and team concepts. Encourage employees to actively offer input on ways to make their jobs more creative and innovative. Where feasible, allow employees to *telecommute* (work from home). Conduct surveys of your customers to generate valuable feedback on your services, and include a section for the customer to list the key employees or departments that have helped them the most with a problem, complaint, or question (refer to Chapter 7 for examples).

CUSTOMER RELATIONSHIP MANAGEMENT

According to Forrester Research, companies give customers an average of 3.5 ways to reach them. In most cases, the information gathered from sales, marketing, and technical support departments is not shared throughout the company. This is especially common as organizations grow and each department keeps its own records. As a result, customers often get the impression that the organization is impersonal and not responsive to their needs once they become a customer. By organizing customer information into a central *Customer Relationship Management* (*CRM*) database that can be accessed by sales, marketing, management, and technical personnel, your company can be more responsive and anticipate where trends and potential follow-up sales can be generated. CRM can be defined as a customer-centric approach to doing business, with all employees a part of the process. Currently, only 5 percent of businesses are running their operations this way. How are *you* marketing to and servicing your best customers, the top 20 percent that provide the lion's share of your revenues?

The benefits of implementing CRMs are more prompt, personal customer service and improved sales. A CRM includes information garnered from separate sales, marketing, and technical departmental databases. With basic customer account information, employees can conduct a more personal approach to servicing accounts. The additional benefits include an overview of customers' billing history, logs of technical support requests, and web site traffic levels, which can provide a clearer focus for management to offer products of interest to customers and help acquire new customers.

Imagine being able to track individual web site performances and to group them together in categories. You can send an incentive e-mail to targeted customers that individually highlights their increased level of site traffic and how much it is projected to increase based on previous performance, and include a special time-limited incentive for them to upgrade their hosting plan. Within the e-mail, you use the customer's contact name to further personalize its delivery. Within a few days after the e-mail, you can make a telephone call to follow up. This is an example of proactive customer service that is positive, personal, and designed to benefit the customer.

A CRM database can be viewed as a slimmed-down version of a data warehouse (a large database of customer- and company-specific information), which allows real-time information to be shared among employees in all departments. Potential problems can be highlighted for improvement, with detailed marketing analysis included. A fully implemented, company-wide CRM can be expensive and requires much planning. Some of the early adopters of CRM include Dell, Earthlink, Cisco, and Staples.com, according to the Industry Standard magazine (http://www.thestandard.com).

Staples.com attributes sales of $350 million for 2000 to its move to a CRM system. According to Jackie Shoback, Operations Vice President of Staples.com, "I can't imagine running the business and doing what we need to do if we didn't have these tools." Staples.com is one of the top ten most visited retail web sites online. Some companies implement in-house CRM solutions, or outsource to third-party call centers and vendors to keep track of customer preferences and profiles to provide more responsive customer telephone and real-time (online) support. The demand for third-party firms to handle customer service is expanding. By 2004, the world market for CRM-based services is estimated to be $125 billion, according to IDC Research, compared to $23 billion in 2000. Smaller concerns, if they are not outsourcing, many times attempt to modify traditional contact management software to gain a handle on improving customer service. Salesforce.com (http://www.salesforce.com) is an ASP that now enables companies to rent a CRM-based solution that operates online through a standard browser.

Features of the plan include the capability for all company departments to view customer information, track prospects, and make sales forecasts. The plan includes wireless capability and can be geared toward an individual company's unique operations. The pricing model is based at $50 per month, with customers that include Convergent Communications, Siemens, and Time-Warner.

CRM solutions encompass several key components, including the following:

- ▼ Setup costs
- ■ Server basis
- ■ Range of deployment
- ■ Number of licensed users
- ▲ Ongoing support

When preparing for a CRM plan, consider the following goals:

- ▼ Determine what information you need to collect about your customers.
- ■ Categorize customers for organization purposes.
- ■ Determine the best channels, online and offline, to track information.
- ▲ Incorporate a system for management and marketing to review the tools that are used to enhance customer relationships.

Before you implement a CRM solution, you must ensure management and employee buy-in. Some questions here will need to address the following:

- ▼ Is management fully aware of the tangible and non-tangible advantages which CRM provides?
- ■ Is management focusing on improving customer service as a key goal for operations?
- ■ Is the focus of the company on the customer? If not, what is it focused on and why?
- ■ Has input been gathered from employees who will actually be using such a system?
- ▲ Do the employees see how the system will improve their jobs and provide benefits to the company?

Especially with traditional or large-sized companies, implementing a CRM also might involve a change in corporate culture, which can be very difficult to accomplish as new ways of cooperation are needed to share information effectively among departmental areas in a timely manner. Some companies will find this problem insurmountable, as resistance is too great to change any current systems in place. These types of issues must be addressed before you can implement a CRM solution. If your organization faces these potential obstacles, you might need to conduct an audit to gauge whether a CRM would benefit your way of operations. Norkom.com (http://www.norkom.com/global/knowledge_net/CRM_audit/index.jsp), based in Boston, Massachusetts, provides an online resource to allow a company to conduct a free audit, which scores companies on their overall readiness for a CRM solution.

Some general CRM resources available online include

▼ **CRM Forum**   http://www.crm-forum.com

▲ **Search CRM**   http://searchcrm.techtarget.com

Some leading companies that specialize in providing CRM based solutions include

▼ **Siebel**   http://www.siebel.com

■ **Avaya**   http://www.avaya.com

■ **Peoplesoft**   http://www.peoplesoft.com

▲ **Convergys**   http://www.convergys.com

SERVICE LEVEL AGREEMENTS

Providing services is what the Internet is all about; whether for e-commerce, content delivery, e-mail, or other applications. It is important to provide written guarantees to ensure the reliability and quality of those services. In a 1997 survey conducted by ISPs, Inter@ctive Week reported that 33 percent of businesses had service level agreements with their Internet providers. The survey noted that guarantee of availability was important in 94 percent of businesses, with 85 percent stating that they would pay to get this type of guarantee. An SLA is further defined as a guarantee of performance tool, which is individually negotiated through a written contract agreement with the customer paying extra for enhanced levels of service.

SLAs (service level agreements) are used to further define the relationship between a web host and select customers who require a high level of services. SLAs include a written contract agreement, which specifies the expectations for Internet services that are maintained on a continuing basis, to include the following areas:

▼ Reliability and Redundancy

■ Server Throughput and Responsiveness

■ Customer Support

■ Network Security

▲ Performance

Customer service levels are usually clarified within an SLA that is mutually agreed upon at the beginning of the customer relationship. This is especially common with hosting accounts that go beyond the shared hosting level, and can prevent confusion and finger pointing over who gets blamed if something goes wrong. The SLA should define what the responsibilities are, and the level of service and responsiveness that is the customer should expect. This usually involves a higher cost to the customer if a high priority is placed on specific customer service areas (for example, 24-hour technical telephone support or specific written guarantees of high web site availability). The customer should know what to expect.

SLAs are especially common among ISPs and other Internet-based services as a way of demonstrating the level of competitive services available. In planning for an SLA, one factor in deciding on a level of service is how your backbone provider and associated partners have their SLAs organized. If you guarantee a two-hour response time within your SLA, make sure your associated partners and providers should have similar SLA response times specified within their agreements. Some examples of ISP SLAs and guarantees are noted in Table 6-1.

Internet Service Provider	Guarantee	Recourse
Cable & Wireless	Less than 10 minutes downtime per day	One day of free service
Digex	Up to 100 percent uptime (depends on amount of mirroring)	Varies
Frontier Global Center	99.97 percent availability, 1 percent packet loss, 120 ms R/T latency	Service credits
Genuity	Site won't be down more than 15 minutes per day	One day of free service
IBM	Negotiated	Negotiated
MCI WorldCom Advanced Networks	Less than one hour downtime per month	One-day credit for one to four hours of downtime; one-week credit for more than four hours of downtime
Navisite	99.9 percent uptime (including database clustering services, server failover/ mirroring), and 99.9 percent uptime (facility and network infrastructure)	One day of free service
PSINet	100 percent uptime for shared servers; none for dedicated servers	10 percent off monthly bill
Spring	100 percent uptime	Up to 50 percent off monthly bill
TCG Cerfnet (AT&T)	99.5 percent uptime (includes scheduled maintenance)	33 percent of one-day credit for four to seven hours, 59 minutes; 50 percent of one-day credit for eight hours to 11 hours, 59 minutes; 66 percent for 12 hours to 15 hours, 59 minutes; full-day credit for anything above 16 hours

*Source: Giga Information Group, January 1999 (http://www.gigaweb.com)

Table 6-1.   Examples of Internet Service Provider Service Level Agreements

The issue of performance has become an important one with SLAs. Some carriers, such as UUNet (http://www.uunet.com), one of the first ISPs, specify 100 percent availability within their SLA, and go further to specify that *latency* will be no more than 65 milliseconds. Latency is loosely defined as the speed of the connection between two computers on the Internet. The performance of the network is posted and available at UUNet's web site; it provides statistics on how it is performing relative to the SLA and how the customer will be contacted within a set time frame in case of network unavailability. UUNet's agreements specify three main things: the quality of the network (latency), quality of service (100 percent availability), and quality of customer service (notification to customer within set time period should service become unavailable). Packet delivery is specified to average 99 percent or more.

Some hosts will specify an acceptable packet loss during a certain period. This will be the loss that occurs with the initial hop within the network; the average is less than 1 percent over a month's period. The higher the level of web hosting, the more comprehensive an SLA should be; especially to provide the support components that guarantee a 24/7 uptime arrangement. From a customer service standpoint, a customer will be concerned about the following areas to ensure that their web site performs optimally; these should be highlighted within a SLA:

▼ **Reliability and redundancy**   Customers obviously want an optimal level of uptime for their web sites and services and will be interested in how servers are mirrored and backed up, and whether the host is using multiple primary carriers to the Internet backbone. Savvy customers will inquire about what private peering arrangements are in place to optimize traffic flow, and how close your network is to the backbone provider.

■ **Server throughput and responsiveness**   Inadequate servers that are not updated and are not actively managed lead to sluggish and slow response times. An insufficient connection to the Internet itself also can lead to reduced speeds for accessing web sites. In addition, if you do not plan for scalability, a web site might experience sudden bottlenecks in the critical stage of its popularity, which could hamper the effectiveness and serviceability of the web site.

■ **Customer support**   Providing timely and responsive customer support is a key concern in how a host handles questions and addresses questions and problems that might appear. Be accessible and able to address issues in a timely manner.

■ **Network security**   Security breaches where a system is compromised by a hacker, virus, or Trojan continue to be customer concerns. The headlines have noted many leading web sites that have experienced attacks and breaches of security. Critical customer account information, including credit card numbers, has been stolen in some cases. A customer will expect the web host to have an active security plan in place, and will want to be notified immediately if any security breaches are discovered.

▲ **Performance**   Performance tools to ensure compliance include log analysis of applications and server-based monitoring. If you provide specifics regarding percentage availability, furnish the customer with some type of recourse if their web site continues to be down because of the web host or carrier from which Internet backbone services are acquired, or because of a performance-based issue. Some common methods include providing account or billing credits for the next billing period or a free day of service. These also might be used because the web site is experiencing higher traffic levels and a plan upgrade is required.

Monitoring Tools

As application and managed hosting services become more popular, in order for web hosts to abide by SLAs, SLA tools can be used to gauge performance. Software is available that enables web hosts to monitor the network and compare it with the individual parameters of SLAs. Firehunter, one such product offered by Agilent (http://www.agilent.com), provides the ability to monitor network performance against the specifics of SLA agreements and within targeted areas to isolate where potential problems might occur.

This provides added verification that SLAs are being adhered to. You can set baselines that establish standards for accepted performance for individual web sites. A typical report also provides a tracking mechanism for gauging the overall health of a system and how it is responding to user requests (as noted in Figure 6-1).

Through active monitoring over a web browser, Firehunter enables an alarm if a problem occurs that is identified within the specifics of a SLA agreement. A customer can monitor its web site through the browser in real time, gauging such areas as server performance and network responsiveness, and to generate statistical reports. Figure 6-2 shows a report that displays how e-commerce payments are performing viewed in a graphical perspective; for authorized, compared to declined payments, and the total dollar value of authorized compared to declined payments.

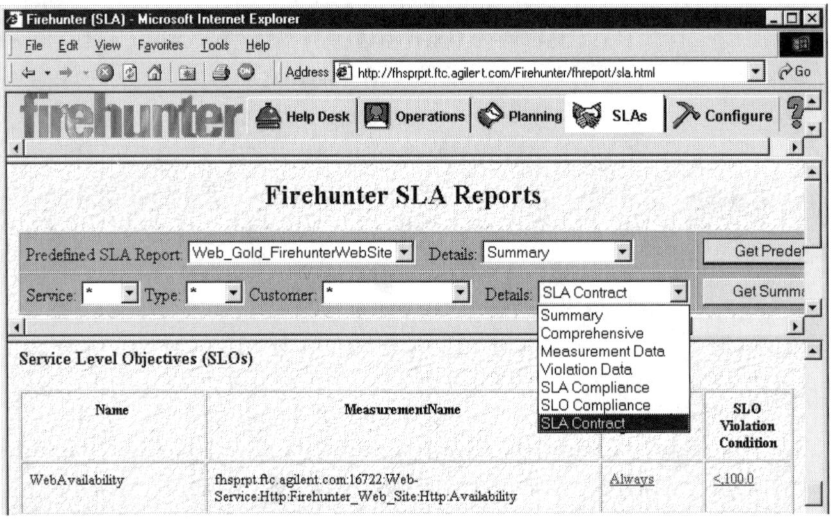

Figure 6-1. Firehunter SLA report options

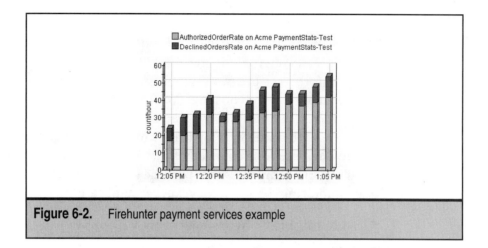

Figure 6-2.   Firehunter payment services example

These types of snapshot views allow customers to visualize and track performance clearly. This can be especially beneficial to gauge the responsiveness of a web site as it generates hits, with the ability to track how certain sections of a web site are performing (see Figure 6-3).

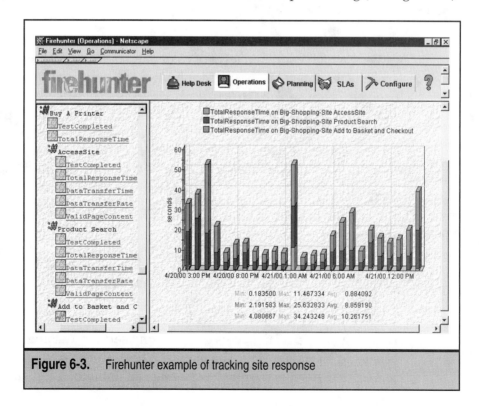

Figure 6-3.   Firehunter example of tracking site response

Some of Agilent's customers include Verio and Qwest. According to Dan Vortherms, Vice President of Product Engineering for Verio, "Firehunter/PRO offers Verio the ability to differentiate our services based on performance guarantees." SLAs also often are specified in relation to an overall web hosting QoS (Quality of Service) standard, which is further identified in Chapter 10. This often will be in coordination with a web host's partners (especially the carriers, which provide backbone connectivity).

Some leading companies that provide software products that include monitoring for service level agreements are

▼ **Agilent** http://www.agilent.com

■ **InfoVista** http://www.infovista.com

■ **Concord Communications** http://www.concord.com

▲ **Micromuse** http://www.micromuse.com

ASPs

ASPs are a relatively new web hosting model that are required to provide a high continual level of customer support. Customers are relying on the ASP to host applications that were previously handled in house. Infrastructure providers are starting to provide niche services to ASPs, such as Cisco's Hosted Applications Initiative and AT&T's ASP EcoSystem, which can allow ASPs to concentrate on what they do best instead of network infrastructure issues. Besides these, the In-Stat Group mentions Sun, IBM, Oracle, and Microsoft as initiating programs in partnership with ASPs.

Managed Hosting

Because of these attempts to address application scalability and infrastructure maintenance issues, an even newer hosting model, *managed services hosting*, is becoming increasingly popular. Managed services hosting includes the management of services, whether it is scaling an application, clustering among servers, caching, load balancing, or monitoring. The managed host provides a specialized service that ensures the efficiency and availability of the customer's

online services. Companies such as Loudcloud (http://www.
loudcloud.com) specialize in these services by providing proprietary
web services through the application of off-the-shelf software, to
ensure 100 percent availability of a web site.

As noted in a study of Loudcloud customers, which focused on
outsourcing of Internet infrastructure, the Intermedia Group found
that the many benefits customers cited included the reduction of costs.
Over a two-year period, customers will save an estimated average of
87.3 percent in capital cost avoidance and associated IT support costs.
These types of avoided costs included

▼ **Operations and IT staff**   System administrators, database
administrators, application server administrators, network
engineers, security engineers, deployment managers, and
24/7 operations support staff

■ **Hardware**   Production server hardware, staging server
hardware, immediate availability network, device replacement
(including Virtual Private Network, Caching DNS Servers,
load balancers, firewalls, and Gigabyte Ethernet Uplink),
high availability storage, tape backup, backup and restore
hardware, routers/switches, and console servers

■ **Software**   Server software, network devices/software,
network management software, systems management
software, intrusion detection software, web visit analysis
software, and backup and restore software

■ **Facilities**   Data center selection, leasing of space, rack space,
and cage setup

▲ **Support costs**   Capacity planning service, application
architecture expertise, database servers architecture expertise,
network architecture expertise, full stack monitoring tools/
processes, configuration management/provisioning
infrastructure, and security log management

Other benefits noted by Loudcloud customers included

▼ **Rapid deployment**   Deployment time was reduced an
average of 9 to 1.

- ■ **Improved quality**   Access to the full range and depth of IT services was more encompassing than that available through in-house resources.

- ■ **Renewed diligence to core business concepts**   Without being preoccupied with handling recurring IT issues, companies were able to center on key goals of their business.

- ▲ **Greater scalability**   Customers were able to better take advantage of market opportunities through systems, which could expand as needs required and for services to be paid for only when used. According to one customer, "Loudcloud is proactive rather than reactive, knowing about problems and potential problems before I do."

Software companies such as Microsoft also are addressing this need. Microsoft has recently introduced Application Center 2000, which provides tools to effectively enable and monitor clustered servers. Application Center 2000 is discussed in further detail in Chapter 15. As the hosting market expands into providing managed-services (more than half of the growth in hosting is predicted for this niche market by 2004) expanded SLAs that cover performance issues will become commonplace as standard components that customers will come to expect.

CUSTOMER NEWSLETTERS

Provide a monthly e-mail or newsletter to customers, designed to provide an overview of your latest web hosting features, highlight enhancements, and provide technical tips to web sites to keep running smoothly. You can make available a similar monthly e-mail or newsletter for prospects who visit your web site to subscribe to, with content focusing on monthly specials, contests, and success stories of satisfied customers. Include easy methods for subscribing and unsubscribing—and abide by them.

The following (Figure 6-4) is an example of an e-mail that directs customers to your online newsletter.

The personal touch goes a long way. Think in terms of your customers and what they want to accomplish through you, their web host. Opportunities abound for you to go beyond the ordinary in providing exceptional service to impress your customers. In doing so, you create confidence in your services, generate referrals, and raise the bar for your competition.

SUMMARY

Providing prompt and responsive customer service, whether it be for billing, sales, or technical support is critical to ensuring a long-term relationship. By focusing on the customer and the recommendations here, a web host can gain competitive advantages. In the next chapter we will discuss surveys and referrals as avenues to gauge customer satisfaction and enhance sales.

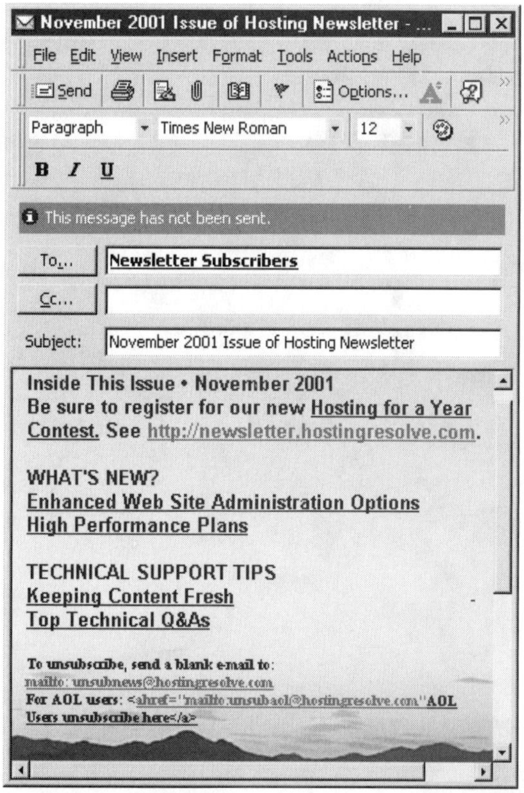

Figure 6-4. E-mail newsletter

CHAPTER 7

How To Gauge Customer Satisfaction

In any conversation, the person who asks questions controls its outcome.

—Anonymous

As highlighted in the previous chapter, the personal touch can go a long way toward keeping customers satisfied and gaining valuable long-term referral business. However, the fact remains that many web hosts are not doing this. According to an October 2000 report by Forrester Research, 48 percent of customers that are using a web host are currently dissatisfied. Most of the complaints centered on the lack of customer service. This is interesting, as 63 percent of small businesses state that the Internet improves customer service.

Customer service can differentiate you from your competition, especially when it is based on respect and appreciation for the customer. Focus on ways to bring more value to the customer. Actively listen to their complaints; they are trying to tell you something. Some of the customer satisfaction methods we will discuss include online surveys and questionnaires, and instant chat customer interaction.

CONDUCTING WIN-WIN SURVEYS

By conducting periodic surveys, being responsive, and staying in contact, you can closely measure your customers' satisfaction. Some of the best sources for revenues are referrals from your own satisfied customers. Through online surveys, a web host can receive valuable feedback about how satisfied clients are with key sections of their business, as noted in Figure 7-1. By conducting surveys on a routine basis, you can gain insight into the areas your business needs to concentrate on further, and discover how to expand the range of products and technical services that you offer.

Provide incentives to customers to complete the survey. If you use a pop-up page, make sure it doesn't continually come up within the browser window every time the main page is visited (this can become very irritating to a prospect or client). This can be gauged using Javascript or cookies.

Take Our Quarterly Customer Survey
Our mission is to provide the best quality web hosting services for your business.
How are we doing? Your input will help us to assist you better.
By submitting a survey, you will receive a one-time $100 credit towards your account. Thank you completing our survey!

What is your domain or service hosted with us? List here

Overall, how would you rate the reliability of your service?

Excellent	Very Good	Good	Poor	Unacceptable
⃝	⃝	⃝	⃝	⃝

How responsive is technical support? Are responses to requests and questions received in a timely manner?

Excellent	Very Good	Good	Poor	Unacceptable
⃝	⃝	⃝	⃝	⃝

How knowledgeable is technical support? Did responses answer questions and

solve problems? Is there an employee who was especially helpful? List name here

Excellent	Very Good	Good	Poor	Unacceptable
⃝	⃝	⃝	⃝	⃝

Are our FAQs, support pages, and how-to sections helpful? Have they answered your questions and solved problems?

Excellent	Very Good	Good	Poor	Unacceptable
⃝	⃝	⃝	⃝	⃝

Next Page Clear

Figure 7-1.   Web hosting survey, page one

A survey also can highlight customers who have individual complaints or problems that they would not otherwise pick up the phone to make you aware of. This provides an opportunity to acknowledge the problem and follow up to avoid losing that account. Holding onto that customer is a lot cheaper than going out and pursuing a new one. By conducting surveys and following up, your customers will know you don't take them for granted, and you appreciate their input and suggestions and act on them. This can be a powerful marketing tool if used effectively.

▼   A survey also can be used to determine how successful a recent promotion or incentive program was in gaining acceptance or awareness of a new product offering. Additionally, once you receive the results you can send out a press release that casts your company in a positive light. The results of a survey also can help to identify potential customers which would make good case studies and testimonials for demonstrating the merits of your specific hosting solutions provided.

Provide a section where the respondent can list specific employees who have been especially helpful with a problem or in answering a question. Find ways to reward these valuable employees or teams through gift certificates, points programs (such as MyPoints or FreeRide), cash, or other incentives.

Encourage respondents to provide referrals to businesses they know are in need of your web hosting services, as noted in Figure 7-2. Initiate a referral program in which you pay an existing customer a one-time fee for each lead that directly results in new web business (for example, an initial 6 percent referral commission based on an annual plan). You can tie this in with an affiliate program in which the customer agrees to display your banner ad on its web site in return for potential referral income. Base the percentage on a gradual scale in relation to the level of the hosting plan that is referred.

Customer surveys can be done on a quarterly or periodic basis as needed. Provide plenty of comment and suggestion areas to glean other information that might help you learn more about the clients' needs and what to offer in the future. Include an incentive for completion of the survey, such as a discount on services, cash incentive, a gift certificate, points program, or a jacket (with your company logo on the back of course), depending on the level and types of accounts that you maintain. Consider providing a site optimization report to all survey respondents. This could include details of pages that contain broken links or errors, or are slow loading. Offer to provide a web site makeover for ten winners through a drawing of survey respondents (in-house or outsource to partner). This in itself could present a niche market, as customer web sites often are not updated, lack dynamic content, or contain an outdated design.

Be sure to notify your customers through e-mail and a client page on your web site about the survey. If you use a pop-up window, use

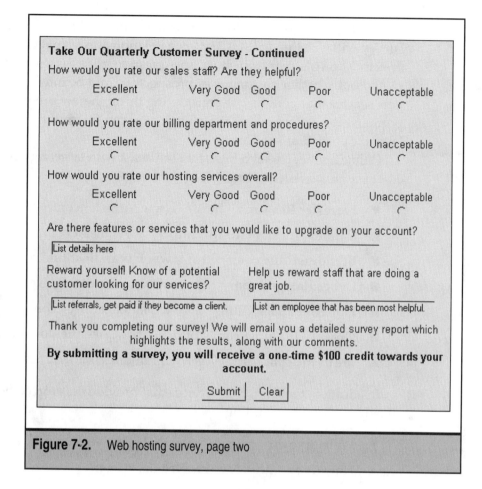

Take Our Quarterly Customer Survey - Continued

How would you rate our sales staff? Are they helpful?

Excellent	Very Good	Good	Poor	Unacceptable
○	○	○	○	○

How would you rate our billing department and procedures?

Excellent	Very Good	Good	Poor	Unacceptable
○	○	○	○	○

How would you rate our hosting services overall?

Excellent	Very Good	Good	Poor	Unacceptable
○	○	○	○	○

Are there features or services that you would like to upgrade on your account?

List details here

Reward yourself! Know of a potential customer looking for our services?

Help us reward staff that are doing a great job.

List referrals, get paid if they become a client.   List an employee that has been most helpful.

Thank you completing our survey! We will email you a detailed survey report which highlights the results, along with our comments.
By submitting a survey, you will receive a one-time $100 credit towards your account.

Submit   Clear

Figure 7-2. Web hosting survey, page two

Javascript or cookies so that it does not come up each time the page is visited. Provide a definite time frame for how long the survey will be conducted, how the information from the survey will be used , a privacy statement if the survey is used for other marketing incentives, and some type of freebie offering to encourage completion of the survey. Privacy issues are discussed in further detail in Chapter 8.

The information gathered in a survey will not be valuable unless it is used to gauge customer satisfaction and make improvements, and for subsequent analysis. The standard method for surveys is to build an HTML multipage form; then use a server-side script (CGI, Perl, PHP, and so forth) that updates a back-end database on a web server.

Services such as Planetfeedback.com enable you to integrate your survey with existing CRM (Customer Relationship Management) systems. You also can add short, one-question polls to your web site to find out whether customers or prospects would be interested in a new service that you may be considering through new programs or partnerships. Before taking the plunge, you can find out the interest level for particular services.

Online market research firms that can assist with targeting customers and specific markets include

▼ **Forrester Research**   http://www.forrester.com

■ **Cahners In-Stat Group**   http://www.instat.com

■ **Brandinstitute.com**   http://www.brandinstitute.com

■ **Cyberdialogue.com**   http://www.cyberdialogue.com

■ **Planetfeedback**   http://www.planetfeedback.com

■ **Greenfieldonline.com**   http://www.greenfieldonline.com

▲ **ithinkinc.com**   http://www.ithinkinc.com

In addition, there are web services that provide outsourced hosting of online surveys, including

▼ **Websurveyor**   http://www.Websurveyor.com

▲ **Netsurvey**   http://www.Netsurvey.com

LISTENING TO CUSTOMERS ONLINE

You can provide customers and prospects with interactive technical and sales support through online chat from third-party providers. Besides the convenience it provides customers, it's much cheaper for companies if their customers go online to find answers rather than phoning a call center or waiting for a response to an e-mail query.

NOTE: By 2002, Forrester projects 87 percent of consumers will use the Internet to answer their questions; telephone inquiries will drop to 13 percent. Standard e-mail (which usually has a delayed response) will fall to 4 percent.

With instant chat server software installed as part of your web site, a customer can click an icon, which then launches a small pop-up window within their web browser to enable an online discussion with your staff. This also provides a visually appealing interface to interact with a customer or prospect. When using an instant chat solution, you must have adequate qualified personnel on hand to handle the contacts or outsource to customer service operations.

According to Forrester Research, 46 companies that offer customer-based outsourcing services reported that it costs an average of:

- ▼ $1.17 per self-service web search (37 percent)
- ■ $33 for a telephone call (54 percent)
- ▲ $9.99 for a regular e-mail (9 percent)

Most instant chat and help services and software give an online support person the flexibility to handle multiple support chats at the same time, which is a big advantage over standard support ticket, e-mail request, and telephone assistance methods. If a support person is not available to handle a support chat online, most solutions provide the built-in capability for the user to send a regular e-mail. Many of these services and software are marketed as ASP solutions. Several examples featured here provide a range of services and software that enable a web host to enhance their online customer service interaction.

Kiwilogic.com

Kiwilogic (http://www.kiwilogic.com) enables you to create *Lingubots*, as shown in Figure 7-3, which are custom help agents that can be added to web sites. Using Kiwilogic's "Lingubot Creator" authoring tool, an

Figure 7-3.   Kiwilogic.com, example agent

agent can have different personality traits in responding to customer inquiries for FAQ pages, instant chat, or other customer service needs.

An intriguing component of an agent is the flexibility to use your own images—whether of a real person or virtual one—when responding to questions that customers might have online. Images can be uploaded to include different personality responses and display a range of different emotions when prospects or customers ask standard questions, as shown in Figure 7-4.

LivePerson.com

LivePerson is found at http://www.liveperson.com. Liveperson consists of a *Customer Interaction Suite*, which includes FAQs (frequently asked questions), e-mail, and live chat interactive capability. According to Mike O'Connor, Manager of Customer Service for ProPay, "We were impressed by the considerable customer insight we've gained from the Knowledge product. LivePerson informs us what questions our customers and prospects are asking and how well we are doing at providing answers." Clients include Neiman Marcus, Ford, and the Franklin Mint.

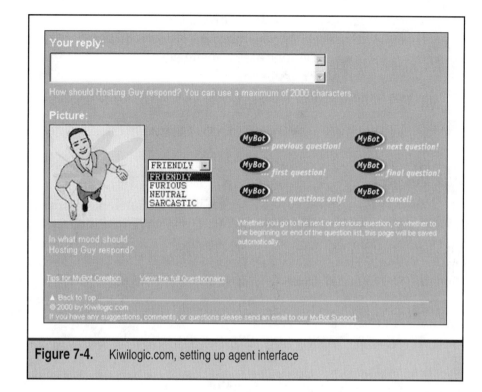

Figure 7-4. Kiwilogic.com, setting up agent interface

RightNow.com

RightNow is located at http://www.rightnow.com. Its services include live chat, e-mail, self-help, surveys, and contract management products. "The ability to create separate interfaces allows us to quickly provide a unique support system for each of our business partners, without having to duplicate our efforts," noted Michael Sperry, Technical Support Engineer, Starfish, about the RightNow service. Clients include WorldCom, Xerox, and Interland.

HumanClick.com

HumanClick is found at http://www.humanclick.com. Its services include live chat, e-mail, self-help, surveys, and contract management products. As noted by Matt Schaefer, with American Wilderness Gear on HumanClick, "By enabling our customers to communicate one on one with our friendly staff, our site now has a 'real people' feel that was previously not possible." Products offered include a basic version, an Express version, and a Pro version, which includes capabilities for greater customization. Clients include WebHostIt.com, HomepageNames.com, and New Balance.

Ask Jeeves

Ask Jeeves (http://www.ask.com) takes a different approach, providing a customer support solution that uses search technology to respond to customer inquiries. It also includes the capability to directly interact with a client online. Ask Jeeves clients include Dell Computer, First Union, and E-Trade. Competitors to Ask Jeeves include eGain, AskIt, Kana, SupportWizard, and Servicesoft, with each focusing within specific target markets. Other companies that provide similar products are noted in the section on CRM in Chapter 6.

OTHER METHODS OF INTERACTION

The Internet provides many different avenues that allow interaction with customers and potential new business. Besides surveys and realtime chats, experiment with different approaches in order to enhance your communication with customers online. You also can provide a monthly newsletter, webcast, or online forum that highlights your services and provides assistance through answering technical questions and tips.

Newsletters

As discussed in Chapter 6, providing a monthly e-mail or newsletter keeps customers informed about your services and provides them with key tips and suggestions that can enhance their web business. Offer tips on how they can promote their online business. Invite them to contribute their own articles, questions, or stories on how their web

site has benefited from your services. Include a focus section to
highlight a different customer web site within each issue. Don't
lose your customers through indifference—that is what you hope
your competition will do.

Using Your Industry Expertise

Another avenue becoming popular, especially for attracting new
customers, is online seminar webcasts that discuss service benefits
and hosting plans during segments. Sponsor an online seminar webcast,
allowing participants to ask questions throughout in demonstrating a
new service or technology. This can be in coordination with a partner
that provides a unique service. One company that has proven successful
with this strategy is Commerce One, a business-to-business Internet
trading exchange that also markets e-commerce applications.

In addition, there are numerous online and offline ways to build
value for your services besides traditional marketing approaches.
Participate in web sites in which an employee can participate as an
expert within a web hosting discussion forum. Volunteer to contribute
an article, or to sponsor an e-mail newsletter or forum that directly
relates to your web hosting business or niche market; you can send
these out to thousands of subscribers. In addition, consider business
and trade magazines, and newspapers. Contribute articles about
web hosting, or volunteer to write an objective column on current
Internet-related issues, with your company and URL listed in
the credits.

Adding Customer Support Pages to Your Site

Throughout your web site, you need to ensure that customer service
is a top priority. Each page should create a positive impression and
theme for your business to convey your unique online presence.
Refer back to Chapter 4 for key tips on page design. Some general
considerations that your web site should have from a customer
service perspective include

▼   Make the page clear and understandable. Avoid using cliché
terms and complex technical explanations.

- Spell out abbreviated terms the first time you use them to avoid any confusion. Consider the difference between ASP (Active Server Pages) and ASP (Application Service Provider).

- Include specific e-mail address links to allow customers with questions to make efficient e-mail contacts within the most suitable departments.

- Provide existing customers with special e-mail addresses and telephone numbers for inquiries or assistance and make these resources available only to them; not to the general public.

- Don't overuse autoresponders for e-mail. Nothing frustrates a potential or existing customer more than receiving boilerplate responses that have nothing to do with their requests.

- If you are using autoresponders, provide prompt follow-up to the initial generic e-mail sent, explaining that a real person will be responding soon. The actual follow-up should be within 24 hours.

- If you are using autoresponders, use scripting or third-party software to include the customer or prospect's name to personalize the e-mail.

- Provide access to customer support and sales inquiries online through chat software or third-party providers such as Liveperson (www.liveperson.com), RightNow (www.rightnow.com), and HumanClick (www.humanclick.com). This method enables customers to make technical queries and handle questions about specific web hosting solutions in real time without holding on the telephone or waiting to receive an e-mail response.

- If you are using instant chat for customer support, ensure that personnel are available to accept chats through their computers online, especially during business hours; otherwise, the tool will not be as effective.

- Consider adding dynamic components to create a more personal read. Include appropriate articles, news feeds, or discussions garnered from a database or server-side script, which personalize the site to specific technical interests.

- Given the market emerging for wireless technologies such as cellular phones and PDA, consider adding coding to your site pages to accommodate for the increasing mobility of web users. Java, XML, and other enabling technologies have made this feasible.

- Assume that the potential customer or prospect knows little about the technology. Include links to pages that clearly define and explain the use of technical terms such as ASP, JSP, managed hosting, and SSL.

- If you are attempting to attract international markets, ensure that alternate pages are available for viewing in multiple languages, and that you have interpreters on staff or a contract basis.

▲ Reward your customers: Provide giveaways, cash incentives, gift certificates, and points programs for completing surveys that provide referrals and valuable feedback for new programs and markets to pursue.

Other areas of your web site that can address the way you interact with customers are your FAQs section, knowledge base, glossary, tutorials, discussion forums, and support how-to pages. Make available technical FAQ pages to cover specific topics of interest to IT administrators, web developers, and resellers. Organize them alphabetically, by subject or category, and with effective search capabilities. Consider having separate FAQ sections that address the technical range level of the customer (beginner, midrange, advanced). A knowledge base is similar to a FAQs page, but answers specific technology topic areas that have been addressed before by prospects and customers. The knowledge base should be understandable for a wide range of customers with varying backgrounds, and should provide links to definitions of technical terms and content; it also should be fully searchable. Microsoft is one web site that quite successfully has used a searchable knowledge base to answer typical support questions and problems with Windows and other Microsoft applications and programs.

You also might consider adding a customer discussion forum that customers can log into on your web hosting site, where questions can be asked of designated employees and customers can share their experiences with other customers. By providing a glossary (see Figure 7-5) of technical terms for the novice in an understandable way, you can provide clients and prospects with a clearer picture of the technology and services that you provide.

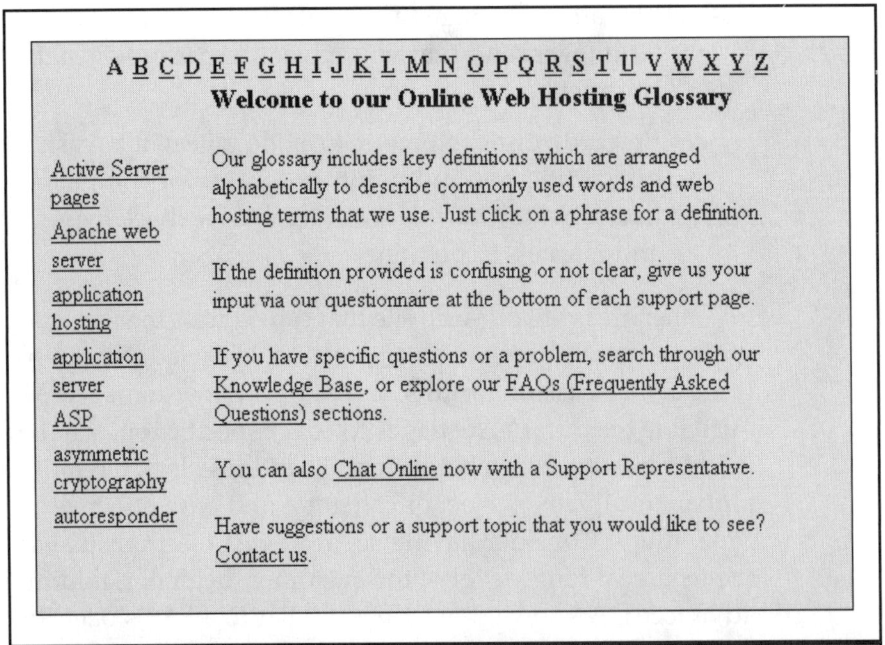

A B C D E F G H I J K L M N O P Q R S T U V W X Y Z
Welcome to our Online Web Hosting Glossary

Active Server pages
Apache web server
application hosting
application server
ASP
asymmetric cryptography
autoresponder

Our glossary includes key definitions which are arranged alphabetically to describe commonly used words and web hosting terms that we use. Just click on a phrase for a definition.

If the definition provided is confusing or not clear, give us your input via our questionnaire at the bottom of each support page.

If you have specific questions or a problem, search through our Knowledge Base, or explore our FAQs (Frequently Asked Questions) sections.

You can also Chat Online now with a Support Representative.

Have suggestions or a support topic that you would like to see? Contact us.

Figure 7-5.   Glossary index

To make sure the explanations make sense, include a brief questionnaire near the bottom of your support pages to gauge whether your material has answered the readers' questions effectively (shown in Figure 7-6). Don't assume that technical terms are clearly understood by prospects and customers.

Based on responses you receive, you can evaluate whether support pages are making sense to clients and serving a vital purpose in helping to solve problems and answer questions. If your material is only frustrating users, they will look elsewhere for answers—likely toward your competitors' services.

SUMMARY

If used effectively, surveys, e-mail, chat, and online support can enhance your customer service and be a cost-effective marketing tool in your quest to provide exceptional service. This will differentiate your web business from others by nurturing a long-term customer relationship. The next chapter will focus on some of the standard range of services that a web host provides.

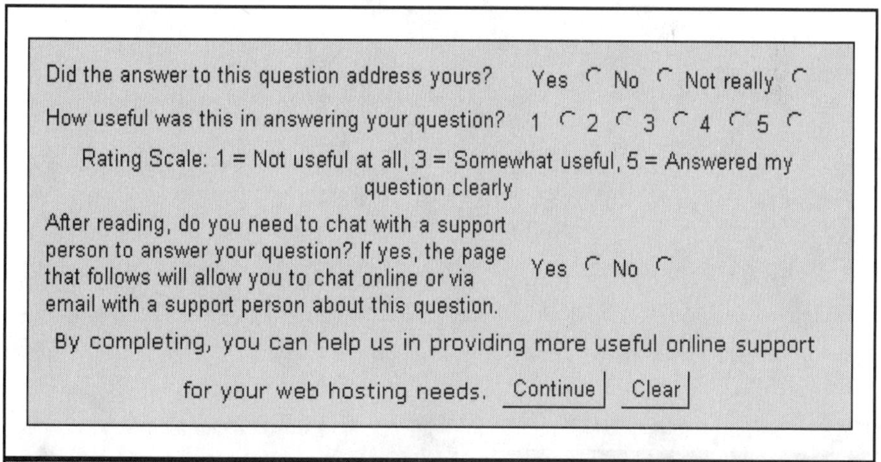

Did the answer to this question address yours?   Yes ⃝ No ⃝ Not really ⃝

How useful was this in answering your question?   1 ⃝ 2 ⃝ 3 ⃝ 4 ⃝ 5 ⃝

Rating Scale: 1 = Not useful at all, 3 = Somewhat useful, 5 = Answered my question clearly

After reading, do you need to chat with a support person to answer your question? If yes, the page that follows will allow you to chat online or via email with a support person about this question.   Yes ⃝ No ⃝

By completing, you can help us in providing more useful online support for your web hosting needs.   Continue   Clear

Figure 7-6. Web page questionnaire

PART IV

Web Hosting Services

CHAPTER 8

Deciding on a Standard Range of Services

Typically, the range of services a web host provides depends on its understanding of market parameters, technical expertise, infrastructure, and the partnerships it has established. Some of the common services for entry-level plans are discussed in this chapter. The following general infrastructure questions can be applied to new or existing web hosts, and help identify the range and caliber of hosting services you and your staff offer:

▼ Does your staff have applicable technical skills in network administration, specific applications development, systems integration, or scripting languages? These combined technical skill sets are the logical areas on which your initial core web hosting services will be based, and you can pursue industry partnerships where your services are lacking to round out your range of services.

■ If you are a small shop or a reseller of hosting services, do you have the necessary skills and hosting support you need? Is support staff available 24/7 to manage the server farm and provide support? Have you tested the quality of support in the middle of the night? Is backup personnel available by pager, telephone, or other method in case primary personnel is unavailable? If the answers here are no, you might want to expand your staff to monitor and maintain your servers around the clock in a secure data center environment, or consider outsourcing to a managed hosting service.

■ Is enough Internet bandwidth available from multiple providers to ensure redundancy in case of outage of one provider? Is it enough to handle current users, and scalable to handle peak server usage and anticipated growth? By designing redundancy with growth in mind, a web host can enhance its range of services and ensure the highest availability of web services to its customers.

■ Does staff actively attend industry expositions and seminars to keep abreast of the latest technology trends? By attending these and subscribing to industry periodicals and online forums, staff can stay current with issues and trends affecting the industry.

■ Is a CRM (customer relationship management) or help desk application in place, including logs of technical support requests and solutions for technical staff to share and reference? As discussed in Chapter 6, if used effectively these types of applications can help a web host find reoccurring problems, provide more effective customer service, and formulate new marketing programs in which customer needs have been clearly identified.

▲ Are security measures in place, such as physical constraints, firewalls, DMZ (demilitarized zones), encryption, disabling certain operating system functions, and monitoring? Are these measures designed to protect servers and data from mischievous employees and external hackers? Does your staff subscribe to security forums and e-mail lists that highlight the latest security breaches and patches available for server platforms? If you are not able to provide these services, consider starting small as a reseller for a web host that does provide them or co-locating within a secure data center that provides them.

These issues are the same criteria that prospects will use to evaluate your services and decide whether they want to host with you. You should routinely review your infrastructure by asking questions such as these; the answers will help you clarify and improve the quality of services you provide. This chapter introduces and describes the various standard services you can provide as a web host, from the basic to the complex.

E-MAIL SERVICES

Most hosts provide a basic level of domain e-mail accounts. This can range from 10 e-mail accounts to an unlimited number for the customer to use and assign to others as needed. These e-mail accounts can be maintained by a web host and usually allow users to check e-mail through a secure web page. Depending on the e-mail software you use, e-mail monitoring features typically include tracking of disk space usage, POP3 and SMTP traffic, spam blocking features, and remote administrative control through a browser; they also include e-mail, fax, or pager forwarding to administrative staff if problems occur, and usually support IMAP4.

IMAP4 enables users to access e-mail from a standard browser and includes administrative functions to control defaults such as the sizing of individual accounts and amount of time to keep old messages before deleting them. Support also might be available for LDAP (Lightweight Directory Access Protocol), a standard directory protocol that has become popular. LDAP can work with TCP/IP to provide easy access to information stored in a directory (such as e-mail address, employee contact name, phone number, and so on).

Web hosts typically modify MX (mail exchanger) records to forward e-mail to domain name addresses. Within the individual zone database record for each account are instructions on where to send outgoing SMTP mail. For example, mail sent to chris@hostingresolve.com actually goes to christzoskyiac@temp.com, which is a user's POP3 account. Another example is e-mail sent to chris@hostingresolve.com instead of to the actual mail server chris@mailserver.hostingresolve.com.

You also can reference IP addresses for redirection. E-mail forwarding of domain e-mail to specified POP3 accounts typically is provided with a hosting account, as is an autoresponder script, which enables e-mail sent to specified domain addresses to automatically generate a response message. If a web host also happens to be an ISP, POP3 e-mail accounts also might be included with a base plan. The most commonly used servers that enable web hosts to provide these types of e-mail services include IMail (www.ipswitch.com), Sendmail (www.sendmail.com), and Microsoft Exchange Server 2000 (www.microsoft.com). Refer to these web sites for further details.

CGI-BIN ACCESS

CGI (Common Gateway Interface) scripting is widely used for server-side programming. In most cases, each hosted account has access to its own private CGI-BIN subdirectory located on a web server, where scripts are stored and given a .cgi extension. CGI scripts usually can run from any location; however, it is recommended that you use the default CGI-BIN directory. Scripts can be written in various interpreted programming languages including Perl, Python, C, TCL, and even

JavaScript, although Perl is the most popular. The BIN part of the directory name originally referred to binary executables, but typically CGI scripts now use Perl scripting.

CGI has long been a standard method for providing server-side functionality. A typical use of CGI is to send forms by e-mail. When a user enters information into a form on a web page and submits it, the data is sent to the server for processing. Once the script processes the data, a message is sent back to the browser confirming receipt.

NOTE: If you are doing design work in which a form is used for submitting information by e-mail, include a standard e-mail link on the web page in case something goes wrong with the CGI script. That way, a user can click the Back button in the browser, use the e-mail link to send the information requested, and notify the Webmaster that something is wrong.

Although CGI is popular, it has several drawbacks. For example, for each request made by a CGI script, another instance of the CGI application has to be created and started. As a site becomes more popular, this can become a serious drain on the server's resources. Many web hosts and developers now are using more efficient server-side technologies instead of CGI, such as Java servlets, which have the full power of the Java language and provide more stability. Java servlets, JSP, and other server-side technologies are discussed in further detail in Chapter 9. CGI is comparatively slower, and is not very secure for e-commerce transactions. CGI scripts have been exploited many times by hackers using known security weaknesses. Security is discussed in detail starting in Chapter 11.

Some online resources for CGI include

▼ **CGI Library at Stanford** http//cgi-lib.stanford.edu/ cgi-lib/

■ **Matt's Script Archive**   http//www.worldwidemart.com/scripts/

■ **CGI Resources**   http//www.cgi-resources.com

▲ **Script Search**   http//www.scriptsearch.com

FTP SERVICES

FTP (File Transfer Protocol) enables customers to upload HTML files, images, and so forth to their hosted sites using FTP software. The web host provides the customer with a user ID and password for accessing his or her account. Some of the most popular FTP client programs include CUTE-FTP and WS_FTP. When launching the program, the user fills in the IP address or domain name, user name, and password assigned by the web host. Once connected, the user can upload files to the web server. FTP also can enable visitors to download files using *anonymous FTP*, which does not require a password. As a security measure, when an anonymous visitor logs in, he or she will be given access only to a specific subdirectory available exclusively for downloading files. Some web hosts prohibit this feature, citing security concerns.

Other methods include using Microsoft FrontPage or Macromedia Dreamweaver, as the FTP method for delivering files. Customers use the FrontPage package instead of FTP for uploading or downloading files. Other methods available through operating systems include the Web Folders feature in Microsoft Windows 98/2000 (if enabled from the My Computer icon) and Fetch (in MacIntosh systems).

DOMAIN SERVICES

One of the primary responsibilities of a web host is providing a place for customers to set up their web sites. As a standard part of providing hosting services, through partnerships with registrars (Network Solutions, Register.com, OpenSRS,and so forth), many companies can offer to go through the application process of registering domain names for their customers (as separate pricing or bundled into the cost of other services). This section discusses the basic services involved, including domain name registration and domain parking, and outlines the standard parameters of basic hosting plans.

Domain Registration

Registrars are organizations such as Network Solutions, Register.com, OpenSRS, and other entities that have exclusive rights to maintain and issue domain names within certain top-level domains (including .com, .net, and .org). The first domain registrar, Network Solutions (previously called InterNIC), began providing top-level domain registrations in 1992 as part of a cooperative arrangement with the National Science Foundation, a U.S. government agency. Beginning in June 1999, the U.S. government opened the registration process to allow open market competition for registering. Since then more than 100 entities have been approved to provide domain registration services, contributing to the rapid rise in the number of domain names that have been registered within the last several years.

The domain registration fee (typically ranging from $20 to $35 per first-year period) is required one year in advance when the domain is registered. When domain names are registered through a registration service, it typically takes at least one business day for the order to be processed. Additional payments are due for the continued usage of the domain name.

To avoid customer confusion it is best to add a script to your web hosting site that enables a web prospect to do a *whois search* to confirm that a particular web site domain name is available. A whois search is a script that can be added to a web page which allows for domain queries to be done to verify the availability of a requested domain name. The scripting instructions to do this are usually provided by a domain registrar service as part of an agreement. Once a domain name is confirmed as available the web prospect can easily sign up and register the domain name through your site pages. You can do this through the specific registrar with which you have an agreement or add your own web script to your pages.

One online resource for a Unix whois client is.cs.colorado.edu in /mirrors/OpenBSD-src/usr.bin/whois. From a Unix machine connected to the Internet, a whois command can query whether a domain name is available. If you're accessing the CORE whois database, and looking for igasifzana.org you would use this command:

```
whois -h whois.corenic.net igasifzana.org
```

Most commercial entitles use the .com domain name. Nonprofit organizations most often use .org. Typically, businesses that provide Internet services use .net, but more general web sites are using .net because of the shortage of .com domain names. Aside from the top domains noted, other domain names include educational (.edu), government (.gov), the military (.mil), international organizations (.int), recent business additions (.biz), and information (.info).

Some registries include database listings for country-specific domains (such as .nz for New Zealand). As shown in Figure 8-1, the United States was by far the leader in the number of web sites registered in 1999. Leading the All Others category were the Netherlands, Sweden, and Taiwan. As of March 2000 the total number of domains registered now totals more than 13.2 million worldwide.

Registries manage domain databases that indicate whether a particular domain name is available for a specific top-level domain extension (for example, newsite.com or newsite.net). When a whois query is made on a name that is already registered, the database will list the registrar for the domain name; the primary and secondary DNS (Domain Name Server); the registered owner of the domain name; and the owner's address, telephone number, e-mail address, and technical contacts. The primary contact can be the party that is registering the domain for the customer.

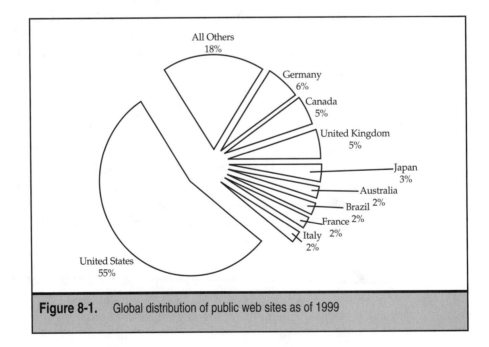

Figure 8-1.   Global distribution of public web sites as of 1999

The primary e-mail address associated with the domain should be provided in case the web site becomes unavailable. In other words, the e-mail address should not be affiliated with the domain being registered. In addition, because database queries are made through the Internet, this e-mail address will be available to telemarketers and e-mail spammers, so many clients use a secondary web e-mail address (for example, an address at hotmail.com or yahoo.com) instead of a real POP3 e-mail address.

A domain name will be assigned to correspond with an IP address during the domain registration process. The names of a primary and a secondary name server are required when registering a domain, and each must be on different network segments as added insurance that at least one will be reachable in case the other is not. Be careful when changing the IP addresses on servers. Ensure that the secondary DNS name server's records are updated to reflect the modified IP addresses. Otherwise, if the primary DNS server becomes unavailable, the secondary server will not be able to resolve names. For each domain hosted use separate zone files that contain specific pointers for that domain.

Once the registration process is complete, web users will be able to access a web site by the domain name instead of the IP address that was assigned for the web site initially. In some cases web hosts will allow customers to forgo the process of registering a domain and charge for storage space as a *third level domain,* in which the domain name points to a subdirectory on a web host's server. For example, http://newcompanysite.hostingresolve.com would be the virtual web address for an account named newcompanysite. This method is most common with ISPs that provide web storage as part of their services. Most businesses want to acquire their own unique domain names.

A domain name also provides a customer with a branded presence specific to its business. The initial land grab for domain names increased substantially in 1999, making it more difficult for businesses to find an appropriate domain name. The sale of registered domain names, especially generic names, became hot properties, and sold for high premiums. For example, business.com was sold in December 1999 for $7.5 million. The domain name registration process also has been the subject of many trademark issues; more than 9,000 names in the .com domain are in legal dispute. Some cases are instances of cybersquatters who purchased unique domain names in bulk to later sell at a premium to companies with similar names. Other instances are the reverse; trademark name owners attempt to take similar-sounding domain names away from legitimate web sites contending that their trademark was infringed upon. These issues will continue to arise until a better process is created.

New domain name extensions have been proposed to address the issue of the lack of domain name addresses, with some scheduled to be available in 2001. These and other new domain name extensions will present many opportunities for web hosts to register domain names. Several online entities have been accepting pre-registrations for these proposed domain names.

Some of the new domain names proposed include

- ▼ **.shop**   Retail businesses selling products or services
- ■ **.firm**   General business web sites
- ■ **.biz**   Business specialty web sites
- ■ **.info**   Information-related web sites
- ■ **.arts**   Entertainment or cultural web sites
- ■ **.nom**   Personal web sites
- ■ **.web**   Entities providing web-based services
- ▲ **.rec**   Recreational web sites

These new domain names have been proposed for review by ICANN (Internet Corporation for Assigned Names and Numbers) and CORE (Internet Council of Registrars). Refer to ICANN's web site for the most recent information at www.icann.com/announcements/icann-pr15may01.htm. CORE has been proposed as the registry operator or partner for the following domain name spaces, which have been submitted for review to ICANN: .health, .museum, .post, .info, .air, and .biz.

Other registrar services, such as BulkRegister.com, are available to partner with, which is a streamlined approach to registering multiple domains for individual accounts. The advantage to registering for the customer is the web host can handle all the details of registering a domain without the customer going through the details of registering a domain name through a third-party service. Some web hosts do not provide this service, leaving it up to the customer to handle the details of registering a domain name. During 1999 a record 4.7 million domain names were registered for the first time, as shown in Figure 8-2. As of March 2000, the cumulative domain name registrations for these three top-level domains had risen to more than 10 million.

Domain Parking

Domain parking enables a customer to associate a domain name (usually registered through the web host) with the web host until content is ready to be added and a site becomes live with actual page content. Typically this also allows the domain name to be redirected to another domain that is already registered with the web host. Some web hosts provide this at no charge; others charge a small one-time or recurring monthly fee.

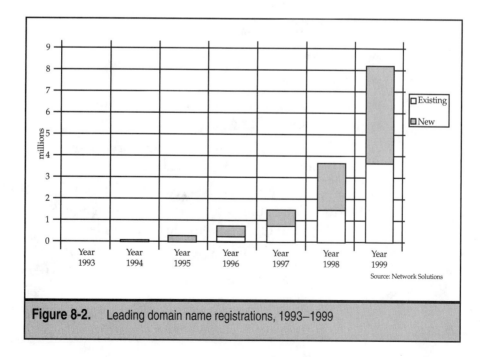

Figure 8-2.   Leading domain name registrations, 1993–1999

Hosting Plan Parameters

Many web hosts provide hosting for multiple platforms, if adequate server resources, capital, technical expertise, and in-house support are available to actively maintain various platforms. The customer makes the final decision on which particular platform best suits its needs. Other hosts will specialize in a single platform or server appliance that has proven reliable (and more cost effective) for its hosting business. As discussed in Chapter 3, server appliances are popular because of their low cost and reliability, and are powered by Linux and Apache. The base plans that web hosts provide can vary significantly with the level of services and platforms, as highlighted in Chapters 2 and 3. The following sections outline examples of entry-level hosting plans that you can provide.

Windows NT/2000 Accounts

Windows NT/2000 entry-level accounts typically include the following features:

▼ Unique web domain address

■ 50MB of disk space

■ Multiple e-mail accounts

■ FTP account

■ Access to a separate CGI-BIN directory for server-side scripting

■ Access to a secure Control Panel to modify account information and access site statistics

■ Support for ASP (Active Server Pages), FrontPage 2000, and Access; optional support available for SQL Server and JSP (and other server-side technologies)

■ High-speed T3 Internet connection

▲ Registration with top search engines

UNIX Accounts

Unix entry-level accounts typically include the following features:

- ▼ Unique web domain address
- ■ 50MB of disk space
- ■ Multiple e-mail accounts
- ■ FTP account
- ■ Access to a separate CGI-BIN directory for server-side scripting
- ■ Access to a secure Control Panel to modify account information and access site statistics
- ■ Support for PHP, mSQL, and MySQL databases (optional support available for FrontPage 2000, SQL Server, ASP, and JSP (and other server-side technologies)
- ■ High-speed T3 Internet connection
- ▲ Registration with top search engines

The following sections highlight some of the most common features that generally are provided with shared hosting accounts. This listing is not meant to be all-inclusive or to represent all types of hosting accounts or options available, but to provide the basis that you can compare with more sophisticated web hosting business models discussed elsewhere in the book.

Storage

The initial storage provided to a customer generally averages from 10 MB (an average of about 300 static web pages) to 100 MB (an average of about 3,000 static pages). The spacing for the customer's archived log files should be separate from the initial storage allocated for the web site. To calculate the number of static pages, assume that each page is roughly 30 K in size. Because of competition in this area, storage amounts vary widely for shared hosting plan accounts. The storage requirements depend on the expectations of the customer. If the customer just needs a static site with seven or eight pages, a low-end shared server solution will do.

Find out what the customer's expectations and intentions are for the site. For e-commerce functionality or if the customer needs back-end databases for a dynamic site, you should recommend a dedicated or more sophisticated hosting solution that provides a server specifically for the customer's scalability needs. The customer is relying on you to explain and recommend the solutions that work best.

Data Transfer

The amount of allowable data transfer per month can range from 5 GB of monthly data transfer (about 165,000 pages served) to 15 GB (495,000 pages served) and higher. This range depends on the pricing models you use, based on average server space usage for customers, market share, and competition. Some web hosts will list this amount as unlimited, which is misleading. Provide clear parameters of what is expected.

Server Uptime

Although server uptime can vary according to host, infrastructure, providers, and acts of God, web hosts typically list their servers as being available more than 99 percent of the time and should include personnel and service to stand behind this guarantee.

WEB SERVICES

Many web hosts provide varying levels of assistance beyond hosting services; others refer the actual site consulting, design, and development work to resellers. This section discusses the web services you can offer to clients.

Web Page Design

A web site includes the initial site layout, image creation (logos, banner ads, rich media, image maps, site navigation), registration with leading search engines, and ongoing updates and maintenance. This also might include custom scripting (server or client), programming, adding dynamic components, application development, integrating with existing customer databases, or other Internet services (search engines, merchant accounts, e-commerce, online forums, and so on).

Resellers often are better suited to provide customers with direct consultations on site design and will have staff that stays abreast of the latest design techniques and technologies. Customers are seeking more from their web sites including the latest technologies for dynamic content and interaction with visitors. The specific agreement for site development services must specify exactly what you will do, what is not covered, and how payments are to be made in return for services.

Microsoft FrontPage Extensions

FrontPage Server Extensions provide functions that are available from the popular web authoring FrontPage package. From a web server, the following server components are installed by default:

▼ FrontPage Server Extensions DLLs and executables

■ ISAPI or CGI components to implement FrontPage Server Extensions functions

■ HTML forms for remote administration through a standard browser

▲ FrontPage Server Administrator and Server Extensions Resource Kit

For the customer to use these extensions, they must be installed (available either on Windows or Unix-based) on the web server. This is a straightforward process. A network administrator launches the installation program, which copies the FrontPage Server Extensions to a directory on the host server. This installs the FrontPage Server Extension DLLs and CGI executables to the directory of each sub-web and virtual server that is specified by the network administrator for the server. The files are installed in the following three directories, which are stored beneath the root of every FrontPage-enabled web site:

```
/_vti_bin/shtml.exe
/_vti_adm/admin.exe
/_vti_aut/author.exe
```

The process might vary slightly, depending on the server platform used. Once installed, an administrator can specify access permissions and remote security. You can find information on FrontPage Server Extensions at http://officeupdate.microsoft.com/frontpage/ wpp/serk/.

CONTROL PANELS

Control panels are a popular tool to provide customers with easy access to their accounts to manage account details, make modifications, protect specific directories, track billing history, enable e-commerce functionality, and add numerous other optional functions. The control panel features that web hosts and vendors provide can vary greatly, and are not offered by all web hosts. Control panels also are sometimes referred to as *site administration pages.* A control panel enables users to access accounts through their browsers from a secure login page, and can add or modify features of their account (see Figure 8-3). Web hosts charge varying prices to add different functions.

Depending on the functions enabled through the control panel interface, resellers typically receive enhanced features that enable them to manage multiple customer site details instead of managing multiple user IDs and passwords. Through the interface, updates can be applied to control many aspects of an account, and the web host can add or modify options in the list at any time.

Control panels are either developed in house by web hosts or purchased as a software package. The Plesk Server Administration (www.plesk.com) provides a streamlined server setup with administration tasks, to allow remote server administration via a standard web browser. CPanel is another package that is available through distributors such as LiquidWeb (www. liquidWeb.com/cp/) and PowerSurge (www.powersurge. net/cp/), which includes more than 82 control panel functions built in. It also has the capability to restart server services as needed.

Some of the more useful features that typically are included with a control panel are

▼ **Account management** This option includes details about the account, including type of hosting plan, the date the plan began, user names, and amount of storage and bandwidth used. It also includes options for upgrading a plan account with greater storage and bandwidth.

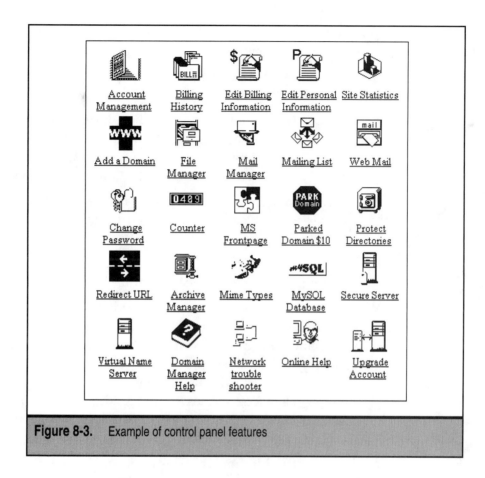

Figure 8-3.   Example of control panel features

- **Change password**   If the customer wants to change a password, he or she can make immediate changes, which modifies their login to the control panel or to FTP.

- **Add domain**   The customer or reseller can easily register additional domain names as needed, without going through a third-party source.

- **Mail manager**   The customer can add domain e-mail accounts, redirect e-mail to other addresses (such as POP3 or web e-mail), delete e-mail accounts, or change passwords.

- **Protect directories**   By password protecting specified directories, general users are prevented from gaining access to directories selected unless they have an assigned user ID and password.

■ **Mime types**   This enables particular programs such as Real Video, Lotus Notes, or PDF files to be used within the site.

■ **Database functionality**   Options here include creating a database, making modifications, running queries, or reading technical support pages for any number of database programs (MySQL, mSQL, Access, SQL Server, Oracle, and so on).

■ **Archive manager**   This option enables the customer to archive specific files for compression, backing up, or for extracting.

■ **Shopping cart**   Options here include creating and managing a shopping cart so the site can organize items for sale.

■ **Secure server**   Instructions are provided here on installing a secure certificate (a form of digital identification) for the site, including registering and purchasing from a certificate authority such as Verisign (www.verisign.com) or Thawte (www.thawte.com). (Earlier version browsers supported only Verisign.) Digital certificates are highly advisable for verification purposes and for conducting secure transactions. Some registrars use certificates when verifying a domain's registered contact.

■ **Network troubleshooter**   This option includes information about the web server hosting a site, host servers that provide specific services, and whether any problems are occurring. This section also can provide a section for advanced users to ping or conduct a traceroute to check a particular server.

▲ **Site statistics**   Optional access might be available to site statistics contained in log files, but in graphical format. Some of the most common packages include Webalizer, FastStats, HitList, and WebTrends, as discussed in Chapter 3. From the statistics generated, a customer can gauge how well a site is performing with search engines, visitor locations, number of visitors, number of page hits, and which sections of a site are the most popular.

Some control panels also provide direct access to FTP or ASCII log files for viewing. Other features include options for mailing lists, Telnet access, and support for viewing of pages in different languages. Many of these optional features are discussed in detail in Chapter 9.

CUSTOMER SERVICE AGREEMENTS

When a customer signs up for a hosting account, the customer should sign an agreement (sometimes called an *acceptable usage policy*). This specifies a code of conduct that prohibits any site content or activity that is illegal, or that could open your hosting business to potential litigation including copyright infringement, pornographic material, excessive spamming, or material blatantly harmful to others. This also will include attempted exploits that are covered in detail in the Computer Fraud and Abuse Act, the Economic Espionage Act, the Electronic Communications Privacy Act, existing export laws, or any applicable state or federal laws in place. Unauthorized use of programs that might have a detrimental performance effect or pose a security risk for web servers also can be covered. These can include gaming; spamming; warez; or instances in which outright flooding, port scans, or Denial of Service attacks are used (security is discussed further in Chapter 11).

Details should include the host's right to remove such content, if necessary, or to terminate or suspend an account, and should include indemnity for any lawsuits that might result from any content in question. Hosting insurance also is becoming available for such instances. Wording should disallow any responsibility for loss of data, other than those specified within service level agreements (SLAs), and the explicit right of the web host to deny or terminate services. The web host might want to include specifics of what is expected from the customer in terms of the basics of maintaining a web site, or should suggest a consultant to the customer if the web host does not provide consultation as an additional service.

There also should be a privacy policy that provides disclosures for how information is gathered and used by a web host. With the recent focus on privacy as a concern on the Internet, your customer's privacy must be guarded at all times. A privacy policy should specify the use of a customer's IP addresses for technical support issues that might arise, and any instances in which cookies are used to remember the customer's last visit to a page. As part of the process of signing up for a user account, the customer must provide contact information, including sensitive credit card information, and a social security number for later identification purposes. The privacy policy should specify that this will be used only for billing purposes and clearly state that the customer's contact information (including physical and e-mail address) will not be sold to a third party for marketing purposes.

If the web host has partnered with another online business for sharing of customer data, that partnership needs to be clearly stated. Some unscrupulous web sites resell customer contact databases, including physical and e-mail addresses to the highest bidder. If a newsletter or other marketing material is mailed or e-mailed to the customer by default, provide a straightforward method for the customer to unsubscribe or update his or her contact information. Encryption and other security methods used for protection of customer information also can be mentioned when providing full disclosure to a customer.

Depending on the type of hosting account the customer initiates, the customer and host can agree on an SLA that addresses negotiated levels of service that the host will provide to ensure continued availability and responsiveness for site or application needs. The agreement should specify that the customer will receive a percentage discount, free month, or other benefit if services are unavailable for a specified length of time. Some downtime is inevitable because administration tasks are required to perform maintenance. This downtime should be scheduled during off hours, and the customer should have full knowledge of what is being done. If a customer has a high-level account, such as a fully managed one, a backup server should be available to continue to maintain services (this should be identified clearly within an SLA for this type of account).

SLA agreements typically are found with more specialized hosting accounts, such as managed hosting or with ASPs (application service providers), although they are available with more basic plans. Monitoring and enhancing servers within an enterprise to ensure that a network is fully scalable is a continual process. Web hosts also should implement multiple backup name servers, backbones, and clustering for critical systems to guarantee availability of services. This also ensures enhanced reliability and redundancy that can be outlined and defined within an SLA. SLAs are discussed in detail in Chapter 6.

IN-HOUSE EXPERTISE

Consider the skill set of your staff when ensuring the performance and reliability of your hosting services. You will need a much higher level of specialized infrastructure skills as you expand from shared hosting to dedicated, and other high-end hosting plans. Ensure that critical technical support areas have adequate coverage to handle ongoing network maintenance and support. A network or security administrator must always be versed on proper maintenance for supported platforms, and should be able to apply security measures and patches where needed.

Your technical support staff must be skilled in technical areas ranging from specific platforms and languages to security issues and industry trends. Staff should attend industry seminars, as well as track patches, updates, and troubleshooting tips using online and offline resources. As part of a team, network administrators must be encouraged to share and rotate administrative tasks, and must have access to the best third-party administrative tools to do their jobs effectively. Addressing these two areas will benefit the company and have a positive impact on morale as employees continue to update and expand their range of technical skills.

Training also includes sharing of technical notes, including network topology diagrams, and troubleshooting tips. Staff should have access to a centralized technical knowledgebase, which can be part of an overall CRM solution. Many web servers have been exploited by hackers because the site's security was not up to date, or hosts lacked ongoing procedures for effective maintenance and updates. This is discussed further in Chapter 11.

Try to hire employees from the best companies who have good references and a wide range of technical skills. Resist the temptation to hire college graduates to handle support and troubleshooting without an experienced mentor to manage and train them. Because of the shortage of qualified IT talent available, you might need to hire contractors, automate, or outsource segments of your operations where appropriate.

RESELLER CONSIDERATIONS

Resellers such as web designers, systems integrators, consultants, and even ASPs have proven that physically maintaining a rack of servers is not required to be successful at providing web hosting services. In many cases, this is to the resellers' advantage, because they can focus on providing value-added services for their clients instead of taking care of infrastructure responsibilities. Through the selection process, a reseller can base its selection of web host on factors that include 24/7 data center quality support, range of platforms supported (Unix and Microsoft), flexibility of hosting plans available, and type of Internet backbone used. The web host should provide a secured control panel area for the reseller to manage individual client web site details such as access to directories, database connectivity, and enabling add-on e-commerce services.

Other areas of interest are whether web servers are backed up every day, the level of server redundancy, whether load balancing is in place, and whether private peering is used to enable faster connections and throughput. The web host gains additional business from these reseller partnerships and can benefit from specialized services the reseller may provide.

Another source of leads that web hosts can offer is a referral program for individuals and businesses. This usually includes a small, one-time commission for referring qualified leads that result in new hosting business. The fee typically ranges from $10 to $25 for a shared hosting account to a percentage of the sale for higher-range accounts (managed, application, co-location, and so forth). Aside from customer referrals, the most effective lead generation method is a referral ad program in which a text link or banner is placed prominently on another web site. The text or banner will contain URL-specific coding that is unique for tracking the referral, typically generated through a server-side script such as ASP, PHP, or JSP. In return for traffic that results in a sale, the referred web site owner is paid the referral. The web host can enable referrals to log into a password- protected page where referral commissions can be tracked, or the host can send an e-mail when a sale is made as a result of the customer signing up through the referral ad. Some resellers start out providing referrals, and then transfer to a reseller program to generate more potential income.

SUMMARY

To stay competitive as a web host, you constantly must review the services you provide and be responsive to customer needs. The range of services you offer depends on your understanding of market parameters, your in-house expertise, your infrastructure, and the partnerships you have established. Many of the more common services discussed here are domain services, storage spacing, e-mail services, CGI-BIN, and FTP access, which are especially prevalent with entry- level plans. Some of these services can be readily handled by in-house personnel; others must be made available through partnerships, resellers, or through outsourcing. More advanced services available with popular server-side technologies will be discussed in the next chapter.

CHAPTER 9

Providing Server-side Functionality

Web hosts are constantly expanding their range of services to be competitive in the Internet marketplace. Your customers want to provide engaging, interactive experiences on their web sites, which many times require secure e-commerce functionality and back-end database connectivity. There are numerous server-side scripting technologies and environments available to meet these and other requirements. You usually will select those technologies your staff is most familiar with and charge more for those services.

These services might include support for Java Server Pages (JSP), Active Server Pages (ASP), the PHP hypertext preprocessor, or other server-side technologies. Often a web host will market these services as add-ons to an existing plan, or within separate plans. The necessary degree of specialization and support might not be available in house, especially for newer technologies; you might need to pursue other channels through partnerships, contracting, or outsourcing. This is especially true for a web host that provides only basic shared hosting services and no others to differentiate itself in the market.

SERVER-SIDE AND CLIENT-SIDE FUNCTIONALITY

Server-side technology, as its name implies, are applications that operate from a web server including CGI scripts, JSP, ASP, SSI, and PHP. In contrast, a client-side application is downloaded and run on a web client (such as a browser or wireless device). Examples of client-side applications include JavaScript coding, DHTML (a combination of scripting, Cascading Style Sheets, and HTML 4.0), a Java applet, Flash animation, or an Adobe PDF file.

As a client-side application, Macromedia Flash (www.macromedia. com) is a vector-based graphics technology, which appeals to a wide audience for displaying streaming movies and graphics. A Flash file when created, can be exported for viewing within web browsers, and will have a .swt or .swf file extension.

There will be instances in which client-side applications are preferred: to reduce the amount of processing done on the server, for displaying content dynamically, and if you do not need to access back-end applications such as a database. Client-side scripting is not hidden as with server-side scripting; users can view the code using Notepad or another text editor. The effectiveness of your client-side application depends on the customer's speed of connection, type of client (the browser or other method used to access a web page), and what the customer's goals are with the web site. There are still browser incompatibilities with the leading browsers and some client-side applications. What appears perfect in one browser or version of a browser might appear skewed in another. In many instances you will need to deploy a combination of scripting methods and approaches.

Some applications and programming languages such as image maps, Visual Basic, and Javascript can operate from either the client or server. Javascript does this by using designated objects to support server-side functionality. For Javascript, the <SERVER> tag is used within HTML to designate to the browser that the coding is based on the server. The technology that traditionally has been used when describing server-side technology is Common Gateway Interface (CGI) programs and scripts, written using either Perl or any programming language. The focus in this chapter will be on server-side technologies that provide functionality and scalability for server-based applications. There is a wide variety of server-side technologies in which web hosts can specialize. An overview of the most popular technologies will be introduced here.

COMMON GATEWAY INTERFACE

CGI has long been used to handle server-side processing for functions such as processing forms, surveys, and guest books. A CGI script commonly uses either the GET or POST method in sending data from the client to the server. The GET method sends the data as part of a URL from the client to the server using an environment variable. The POST method does not use environment variables. The query is sent to the CGI script through a standard input (STDIN). This is more secure, as the data is not sent in clear view as with the GET method, although with POST the data could be cached and later tracked. The GET method also is listed in server log files when you use it, which could be a security problem if an unauthorized user gains access to the server. Following is an example of POST; the query in the URL includes what is being queried after the question mark:

```
http://www.hostingresolve.com/cgi-bin/glossary.pl?Structured_
Query_Language
```

The value for the URL as a result is

```
QUERY_STRING = Structured_Query_Language
```

The GET method attaches a response (such as content that is entered in a form) onto the end of a URL, such as:

```
http://www.hostingresolve.com/formreq.html/firstName=Thomas&
lastName=John&e-mail=jthomas78@hotmail.com
```

As an interpreted language, Perl works well with CGI in accessing environmental variables for standard input and output, and to call other applications. Perl is available for most platforms and is an open-source language. Developed by Larry Wall back in 1987, Perl is an abbreviation for Practical Extraction and Report Language, with files in standard ASCII text format. There now is an Apache module for Perl, mod_perl, which enables Perl scripts to run faster because coding can be written directly to the API of Apache. The first line of a CGI script references the standard paths where server resources are located, such as for locating the Perl interpreter in the /usr/bin/perl directory. In the first line of code this usually is listed as:

```
#!/usr/local/bin/perl.
```

A significant limitation of CGI is that each time the server receives a request from a web user, a separate, external process executes for each request on the server. When many requests are received, this slows down a server and can make it unresponsive. CGI also does not operate within a secure process, as with newer server-side technologies such as a Java servlet.

JAVA SERVER PAGES

Java Server Pages (JSP) is a Java technology created by Sun Microsystems that allows scripting securely from the server side to allow for a dynamic HTML page to be displayed from the server when the page is requested from the client browser. JSP is a key part of the Java 2 Platform Enterprise Edition (J2EE) specification, and allows the extensive features of the Java language to be used. *Tag comments* (Java code scriptlets placed within <%...%> tags) are a part of the HTML file which, when loaded in a browser, will allow dynamic content to be displayed. The tag comments also are referred to as *JSP elements* or *scriptlets.* The current version of JSP includes comprehensive XML support.

When a server that includes a JSP engine comes across a web page with a .jsp extension, it translates the page into a Java servlet; then forwards the dynamic page to the client. The client then views the page as an ordinary HTML file. This translation occurs in the background through the JSP engine, which is an add-on for web servers. The JSP engine compiles the page into a servlet; then into a class file, which forwards the generated HTML to the client. When the JSP is first requested by the client there is a slight delay as this translation first takes place. Subsequent requests for the page will not have any delay.

From the server, the servlet runs within a protected memory space (the Java Virtual Machine) on the server until the page is modified (or the server is reset), and the page is translated and reloaded again. As additional requests are received by a server, if the servlet has already been requested, the server will generate a new memory thread and complete the request. The capability is built in to handle multiple requests seamlessly as part of the server. Support is available for Java servlets in all popular server platforms, so if your site is moved to another platform, Java servlets can be transferred easily. JSP is similar in concept and appearance to ASPs, the Microsoft technology for allowing dynamic content. However, ASP does not have this feature for running within a protected memory space because ASP pages have to be compiled and interpreted each time a client loads the page. ASP also has certain platform limitations.

Advantages of using JSP include

▼ **Code separation and reusability**   For developers, the actual Java code is not part of the HTML that is generated for a JSP page. Because the code is referenced within tags, the process is separated from the HTML. JavaBeans also can be used to further simplify, which encourages code reuse. Web designers can focus on the web page itself and how it appears without being concerned with the details of the Java coding underneath. For high-end programming, JSP also can be used with Enterprise JavaBeans in developing enterprise-wide application solutions. Most vendors that have Enterprise JavaBeans solutions also provide a version of the JSP engine. Enterprise JavaBeans will be discussed in further detail in Chapter 15.

- **Speed**   A servlet runs in a protected space of server memory; not as an external program as with CGI. This results in pages that load quickly and are able to handle multiple requests without taxing and slowing down the server.

- **Platform independence**   The technology is not limited to a specific platform and can be moved to any popular web server platform as needed without modification, as long as a JSP engine is installed for the web server. Many vendors provide JSP engine products for all popular platforms of web servers, which enables JSP pages to be generated from the server using an easy add-on. For a complete listing of web servers that support JSP, refer to the URL at java.sun.com/products/jsp/industry.html.

- **Access to the full power of the Java language**   JSP, through servlets, has access to the extensive Java Application Programming Interfaces (APIs) and core libraries, which provide many possibilities for enabling dynamic web sites, providing database access, developing robust web applications, and even managing server functions such as load balancing. Along with a JSP engine running on the server, you also should install the JSDK (Java Development Kit), version 1.1 or higher.

- ▲ **Security**   A servlet runs as a thread in a small, protected memory space as part of the server. Each subsequent request made of the servlet by other clients is handled securely as a separate thread, instead of an external program being launched each time as with CGI. The Java language also has extensive built-in security features. Further information on the Java language can be found at java.sun.com/docs/books/tutorial/.

The following example provides a simple example of a JSP file that displays the current date in the browser when the JSP page is accessed by a client (with the JSP coding highlighted in bold here):

```
<!DOCTYPE HTML PUBLIC "-//W3C//DTD HTML 4.0 Transitional//EN">
<HTML>
<HEAD>
<TITLE>Current Date</TITLE>
</HEAD>
<BODY>
The current date is:
<% out.println(new java.util.Date()); %>
</BODY>
</HTML>
```

The result is shown in Figure 9-1.

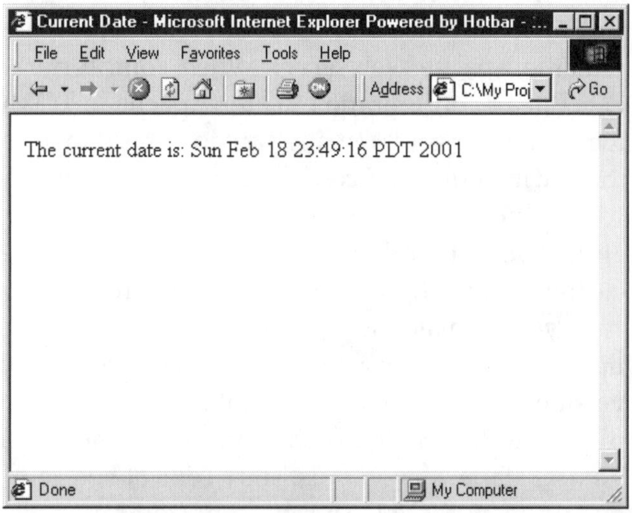

Figure 9-1. Example of JSP in web browser

JSP also can include a scriptlet reference to another file such as <%@ include file="outlet.txt" %>. This will include content from the outlet.txt file when the page is loaded and run through the JSP engine. The file referenced here easily could have been an XML, HTML, or even an ASP file.

Implementing Jakarta Tomcat

Sun Microsystems first developed JSP as Java Web Server, but since has provided JSP to the Apache Group to encourage more rapid development. The Apache Group refers to its JSP product as Jakarta Tomcat, and describes it as a servlet container with a JSP environment. Built completely with Java, Tomcat includes the servlet API version 2.2 and the JSP 1.1–compliant container. A small web server is included with the JSP Tomcat engine and is available for download at http:// jakarta.apache.org. As is, Tomcat can be used as a standalone package for testing and development or as an add-on to web servers such as Apache, IIS, or iPlanet. The main configuration file for Tomcat is server.xml. This file will include the initial configuration for components and define the structure of Tomcat.

The following instructions apply to setting up Tomcat to work with the Apache Web server. When Tomcat starts, it automatically generates a configuration file for Apache in TOMCAT_HOME/conf/ tomcat-apache.conf. Usually you don't need to do anything but include this file in your httpd.conf (by appending Include TOMCAT_HOME/ conf/tomcat-apache.conf). If you have special needs—for example an AJP port other than 8007—you can use this file as a base for your customized configuration and save the results in another file.

If you manage the Apache configuration yourself, you must update it whenever you add a new context. Depending on the version of Apache used, it might require a restart of the server. The file TOMCAT_HOME/conf/tomcat-apache.conf is generated when Tomcat starts, so you must start Tomcat before Apache. Tomcat will overwrite TOMCAT_HOME/conf/tomcat-apache.conf during each startup, so customized configuration should be kept elsewhere. The Apache-Tomcat configuration uses Apache core configuration directives and Jserv (another Apache implementation available for

JSP) unique directives, so it might confuse you at first. There are two things simplifying it:

▼ In general you can distinguish between the two directive families by noting that all the Jserv unique directives start with an ApJServ prefix.

▲ The entire Tomcat-related configuration is concentrated in a single configuration file named tomcat.conf, or the automatically generated tomcat-apache.conf, so you can look at a single file.

Jserv is a Servlet API 2.0–compliant (an earlier version JSP implementation) container that was created to be used with Apache. At the end of the Apache configuration file (httpd.conf) add the following directive:

```
include <full path to the Tomcat configuration file> for example:
include /tome/tomcat/conf/tomcat.conf
```

This will add your Tomcat configuration to Apache, after which you should copy the jserv module (or modules in the Win32 case) to the Apache libexec directory and restart Apache. It now should be able to connect to Tomcat. As previously stated, you need a web server adapter to sit in Apache and redirect requests to Tomcat. For Apache, this adapter is a slightly modified version of mod_jserv. The web host WantJava (http://www.wantjava.com/) was the first servlet and JSP hosting provider to support only the Jakarta Tomcat Servlet Container.

Alternatives to JSP

Web hosts have slowly adopted JSP, because the technology offers powerful benefits to enterprises and web developers. One reason that the technology is slow to catch on might be a lack of technical staff who are familiar with Java. For nonprogrammers, Java takes time to learn. If customers are just concerned with adding basic features, either Server-Side Includes (SSI) or JavaScript will suffice, although this is not the type of customer base that most web hosts want to attract. The profitability lies in providing a full range of web services that businesses want and need, and that allow them to best utilize the Internet as an effective business tool. By studying the servlet API you can learn a lot about the potential uses of JSP. For more detailed information on JSP, see *JSP: The Complete Reference*, by Phillip Hanna (Osborne McGraw-Hill).

You can also get further information on JSP from these sources:

▼ **JSP**   http://java.sun.com/products/jsp

■ **Jakarta Tomcat**   http://jakarta.apache.com

▲ **WantJava**   http://www.wantjava.com

ACTIVE SERVER PAGES

Active Server Pages (ASP) is a Microsoft technology that was developed to allow scripting from the server side, and is widely used by businesses. It enables a dynamic HTML page to be displayed from the server when the page is requested from the client browser. ASP has been integrated with the Microsoft IIS platform as of version 3.0. Internet Information Server is included in Windows 2000 products and available with Microsoft Windows NT 4.0 (for instructions, refer tohttp://www.microsoft.com/NTServer/nts/deployment/planguide / install.asp).

As mentioned in Chapter 3, IIS version 5.0, included with Windows 2000, now runs as a service. To be interpreted properly by IIS as ASP, you must save a page with the extension .asp. When a file with an .asp extension is used, the ASP engine is started. This engine resides in a DLL file called asp.dll that runs in memory along with IIS.

The ASP page includes sections denoted by container tags, which includes VBScript statements by default. These tags are enclosed in <%...%> and interpreted by IIS when the page is loaded. Although the standard scripting language is VBScript, the other common scripting language used by IIS is JScript (Microsoft's implementation of JavaScript, which takes advantage of features within Internet Explorer and IIS). The tag to denote Jscript scripting within a page is <%@ language = jscript%>. This interpretation is carried out internally by IIS through the processing of ASP.All.

Other languages can be supported in IIS through add-ons, including PHP, C++, Javascript, Python, Perl, and JSP. There is no compiling of code, because each page is interpreted and reinterpreted as IIS receives it. JSP pages provide an important advantage over ASP: Java servlets reside in a protected memory space (Java Virtual Machine) on the server. After the first instance of a JSP page, the page does not have to be reinterpreted each time as with ASP.

The following is an example of ASP:

```
<html>
<head><title>Example</title></head>
<body>
<%
for i = 1 to 5
 response.write("<h" & i & ">This is ASP " & I
& "</h" & i & ">")
next
%>
</body>
</html>
```

Figure 9-2 shows the results of this code.

When clients access large ASP scripts using slower access methods such as dialup, you should enable buffering, either from within IIS or by adding the statement <% Response.Buffer = True %> to the ASP pages in question, making page loading faster.

ASP and COM

For the web developer, ASP provides established ways to describe contents that are a part of a page. These are built-in COM (Component Object Model) Windows objects, which can be accessed and reused as needed from within ASP coding and can call other Windows applications. This is referenced as the ASP Object Model, which includes five objects:

▼   **Request**   This object gathers information from the client. It usually includes information from cookies, a user-input form,

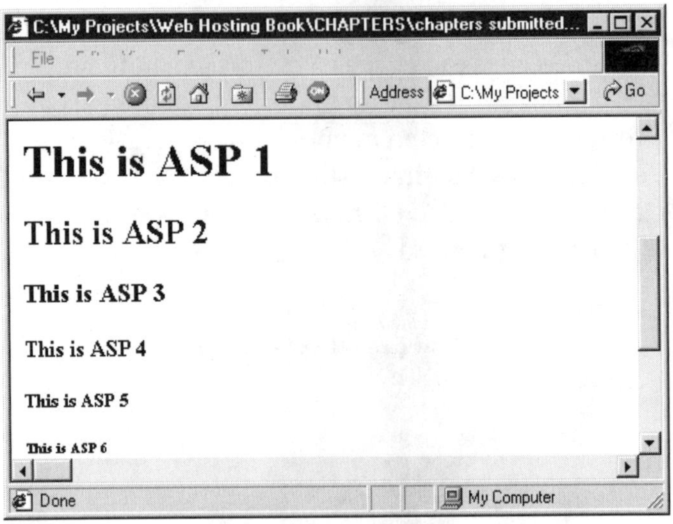

Figure 9-2.   Example of ASP in web browser

or other HTTP request. For example, the following code returns
a string that describes the browser that sent the request:

```
<%Request.ServerVariables("HTTP_USER_AGENT")%>
```

■ **Response**   This object sends information to the client. The
Response object can be used to predetermine how a page is
cached, using a timeout value to indicate when the page is
reloaded from the server, or to send data to the browser or
another file. For example, in the code <%Response.Redirect
"UserUpdate.asp?Name=Mary"%>, a query string is
appended to Response.Redirect to pass the name Mary to the
UserUpdate.asp file. This also could have been done by using
a Session object.

■ **Session**   This object stores information and modifies settings
for the client (during a session). This object contains information
that applies to an individual session when the user is accessing
a page. Session variables tend to be easier to work with than
cookies. The timeout period typically is 20 minutes before a

session is reset if the user has not revisited, at which time the session expires. The following code sets the timeout to 10 minutes:

```
<% Session.Timeout = 10 %>.
```

■ **Application**   This object shares application information with the client. An application object is available for all users; not just individual users. It remains active until the application is stopped or the web server stops responding. There is a lock method available to ensure no two clients can access a variable at one time. If not coded this way, two clients could try to use a variable at the same time. In the example here, the NumVisits variable is prevented from being accessed in this way.

```
<% Application.Lock Application("NumVisits") =
Application("NumVisits") + 1 Application("datLastVisit")
= Now() Application.Unlock %>
```

▲ **Server**   This object accesses IIS properties and methods. This object will initiate ActiveX components, which includes COM and distributed COM.

This example generates a quote that changes each time the page is loaded, with a new quotation used from the newones.txt file in the /Quotes/ virtual directory.

```
<%
 Set NextQuote = Server.CreateObject("MSWC.ContentRotator")
 NextQuote.ChooseContent("/Quotes/Newones.txt")
%>
```

Microsoft also provides interfaces within COM for access to their extensive ADO (Active Data Objects) database-access API. ADO enables you to gain access to and control database objects.

Developing ASP

As with JSP, there are various ways to develop pages for ASP, through the use of popular web development software such as

FrontPage 2000 and Dreamweaver or even with Notepad, if you are doing straight coding. You can test ASP pages before you upload them to a server by installing and running IIS on a local Windows NT or Windows 2000 workstation. If you use Windows 98, you can install Microsoft Personal Web Server (PWS) as an add-on (located on the Windows 98 CD in the add-ons\pws folder) to test ASP.

Vendors other than Microsoft have products that allow ASP to run on other platforms, including

▼ **Chili!Soft** http://www.chilisoft.com

■ **Instant ASP** http://www.instantasp.com

▲ **Apache::ASP** http://www.nodeworks.com/asp/

The Future of ASP

A new ASP technology, ASP+, currently is available as a beta preview and will be a part of Microsoft's overall .NET strategy in developing technology platforms that are focused on the application service provider market. One key advantage that will be included for ASP developers is faster performance. Instead of scripts that are interpreted, programming code and components will be compiled through the MSIL (Microsoft Intermediate Language) into native code. Supported programming languages will include C#, C++, Visual Basic, JScript, and XML. Custom controls can be built through existing ones to form a single file. Further information on the beta preview and ASP+ are located at msdn.microsoft.com/downloads/default.asp?URL=/ code/sample.asp?url=/msdn-files/027/000/976/msdncompositedoc. xml or www.aspfree.com/.

You can find more information on ASP at:

▼ **ASP** http://www.aspfree.com

▲ **Microsoft** http://www.microsoft.com

SERVER-SIDE INCLUDES

Server-Side Includes (SSI) are simple comment tags that can be placed in HTML pages to give the appearance of dynamic web pages. Another term that is used for SSI is *Server-Parsed HTML*. The HTML pages that include SSI tags typically have the file extension .shtml. The *s* that comes before html in the extension notifies the server to parse the SSI tags on the page. SSI is commonly used to list the date a file was last modified or the current date. It also can work with CGI programs. Be careful not to overuse SSI, because the file has to be parsed on the server for each browser page request that contains SSI. Parsing consumes valuable server resources and can put an unacceptable load on a server, especially compared to regular HTML pages that do not change (static pages).

SSI tags have this format:

```
<!--#command tag1="value1" tag2="value2" -->
```

Each command can have one or several arguments, with tags that are discussed in the following sections.

#begin and #end

The #begin and #end tags declare a block of commands and link elements.

SSI Commands	Result

`<!--#begin -->This page has been accessed`
`<!--#exec java="com.hostingresolve.com.`
`ssi.CounterElement"`
`time`
`<!--#end -->`
	This page has been accessed 1 time.

#config

The #config tag displays errors, time format, and size format.

SSI Commands	Result

`<!--#config timefmt="%a %b %d %H:%M:`
`%S %Y" -->`
`<!--#echo var="LAST_MODIFIED" -->`
	Sat Feb 17
	18 0:32:0
	2001

`<!--#config sizefmt="abbrev" -->` `<!--#fsize virtual="preferred.html" -->`	34K

Some of the standard formatting options used for #config include

▼   `%W`   Week of year

■   `%a`   Weekday abbrev.

■   `%w`   Weekday as number, Sun=0

■   `%b`   Month abbreviation

■   `%j`   Day of year

■   `%y`   Year as two digits

■   `%x`   Local date

■   `%c`   Local date and time

■   `%H`   Military hour

■   `%M`   Minutes

■   `%p`   A.M. or P.M. indicator

■   `%w`   Week of year, Sunday first

■   `%A`   Weekday full

■   `%m`   Month as number

■   `%B`   Full month

■   `%d`   Day of month

■   `%Y`   Full year

■   `%X`   Local time

■   `%z, %Z`   Time zone name and location

■   `%I`   Hour in 12-hour format

■   `%S`   Seconds

▲   `%%`   Percent sign

#echo

The #echo tag displays include variables.

SSI Commands	Result
`<!--#echo var="DATE_GMT" -->`	July 30, 1999
`<!--#echo var="DOCUMENT_NAME" -->`	syntax.html
`<!--#echo var="LAST_MODIFIED" -->`	July 22, 1999

#exec

The #exec tag displays the result of a command.

SSI Commands	Result
`<!—#exec java="com.hostingresolve.` `com.ssi.CounterElement" «—>`	7

The #exec tag can run a CGI script or shell program if activated. Valid tags for the #exec tag include

▼ **cmd** Runs a given string using /bin/sh. All of the variables defined in the #config section are defined, and can be used in the command.

▼ **cgi** Runs a CGI script, given a virtual path. Its output will also be included within the SSI.

#flastmod

The #flastmod tag displays the last modified date of a file.

SSI Commands	Result
`<!--#config timefmt="%B %d, %Y" -->` `Use a directive for displaying on a page:` `<B>Date Updated: <!--#flastmod` `file="include_index.html"--></B>`	Date Updated: October 18, 2000

#fsize

The #fsize tag displays the size of a file.

SSI Commands	Result
`<!--#config sizefmt="abbrev" -->`	24K
`<!--#fsize virtual="preferred.html" -->`	

#include

The #include tag includes a file.

SSI Commands	Result
`<!--#include file="_update.ssi" -->`	This text comes from included file

Some include variables are the following:

▼ CONTENT_LENGTH

■ DOCUMENT

■ DATE_GMT

■ DATE_LOCAL

■ LAST_MODIFIED

■ SERVER_SOFTWARE

▲ HTTP_REFERER

Enabling SSI in Apache

To add support for SSI in Apache, you must update the configuration file (httpd.conf) because the SSI feature is disabled by default. To enable this support, you must add the Includes keyword to the <Directory> directive as follows:

```
Options Indexes FollowSymLinks Includes
```

Next, add these statements to the httpd.conf file:

```
# specify MIME type for SSI files
AddType text/html .shtml
AddHandler server-parsed .shtml
```

Now restart Apache for it to associate .shtml with SSI instructions. For further details refer to http://www.apacheweek.com/features/ssi.

PHP

PHP (a recursive acronym of PHP Hypertext Preprocessor) is a popular open-source scripting method that is similar to other server-side technologies and consists of specific PHP tags that can be used with HTML pages to generate dynamic content. When first developed by Rasmus Lerdorf in 1995 as a modified Perl application, PHP (originally short for Personal Home Page), quickly grew in sophistication as an open-source licensed language, and now can run on most all web server platforms. The syntax used for PHP is similar to C and Perl coding, and is quite compact when compared to either JSP or ASP because it is not based on a specific language. As stated on the main web site for the PHP Open Source Development Team at http://www.php.net/, "The goal of the language is to allow web developers to write dynamically generated pages quickly."

Examples of optional ways that PHP can be inserted within a basic HTML page include

Adding PHP Within HTML

```
<HTML>
<HEAD></HEAD>
<BODY>
This is a basic page
<?php echo "This is PHP"; ?>
</BODY>
</HTML>
```

Comments

Use the <?php...?> tags when making coding portable for multiple platforms.

Adding PHP Within HTML

```
<HTML>
<HEAD></HEAD>
<BODY>
This is a basic page
<? echo "This is PHP"; ?>
</BODY>
</HTML>
```

Comments

The <?...?> tags are commonly used. Note that if you are using XML instead of HTML, it might cause coding conflicts.

```
<HTML>
<HEAD></HEAD>
<BODY>
This is a basic page
<SCRIPT LANGUAGE="php"> echo
"This is PHP";
</SCRIPT>
</BODY>
</HTML>
```

Using <SCRIPT LANGUAGE= "php">...</SCRIPT> is another alternative.

```
<HTML>
<HEAD></HEAD>
<BODY>
This is a basic page
<% echo "This is PHP"; %>
</BODY>
</HTML>
```

The <%...%> tags are commonly used with ASP pages or with web design packages such as Microsoft FrontPage.

As you can see, a very basic PHP command (echo) has been inserted inside an HTML document that displays This is PHP in the page when it is loaded by a client from a web server that has PHP enabled. You can add PHP coding in these examples after the semicolon. Files that contain PHP coding normally will have an extension of either .phtml, .php3, or .php (if using PHP4); however, you can modify this to be most any other extension from a PHP-enabled web server.

Setting up PHP Support

There are a few alternative ways for a web server to include support for PHP after PHP has been copied to a server. First, you can install PHP as an Apache module. The AddType command is used in Apache configuration files. On a generic basis, ensure that the Apache http.conf file includes the following comments when PHP is installed

```
# Extra Modules
AddModule mod_php.c
AddModule mod_php3.c
AddModule mod_perl.c
# Extra Modules
LoadModule php_module modules/mod_php.so
LoadModule php3_module modules/libphp3.so (for PHP 3)
LoadModule php4_module modules/libphp4.so (for PHP 4)
LoadModule perl_module modules/libperl.so
```

And add

```
AddType application/x-httpd-php3 .php3 (for PHP 3)
AddType application/x-httpd-php .php (for PHP)
```

You will need to add this for the global properties and the properties of each VirtualDomain that needs PHP capability.

For Microsoft IIS, you must add PHP support as a filter from within IIS. From the Microsoft Management Console (from Control Panel, Administrative Tools in Windows 2000, or Internet Services Manager in Windows NT), right-click the web server node (this probably will appear as Default Web Server) and select Properties.

To use the ISAPI module:

1. If you don't want to perform HTTP Authentication using PHP, you can (and should) skip this step. Under ISAPI Filters, add a new ISAPI filter. Use PHP as the filter name, and supply a path to the php4isapi.dll.

2. Under Home Directory, click Configuration. Add a new entry to the Application Mappings. Use the path to the php4isapi.dll as the executable, supply .php as the extension, leave the method exclusions blank, and check the script engine checkbox.

3. Stop IIS completely.

4. Restart IIS.

There also is a CGI implementation of PHP. If you want to use the CGI binary (for Windows NT/2000), do the following:

1. Under Home Directory, Virtual Directory, or Directory, click Configuration and enter the App Mappings tab.

2. Click Add and in the Executable box, enter c:\php\ php.exe %s %s (assuming you have unzipped PHP in c:\ php\). The %s %s must be on the end. PHP will not function properly if this is not done.

3. In the Extension box, type the file name extension you want associated with PHP scripts. Leave Method exclusions blank and check the Script engine checkbox. Repeat Steps 2 and 3 for each extension that will be associated with PHP scripts (.php and .phtml are common).

4. Set up the appropriate security in Internet Service Manager and, if your Windows NT Server uses the NTFS file system, add execute rights for I_USR_ to the directory that contains php.exe.

Always refer to the install file included with the PHP distribution for complete and updated instructions for the current version available.

New Features of PHP

The current implementation, PHP4, contains numerous advancements over previous versions and is a rewrite of PHP3. Sessions can maintain client state (important for e-commerce applications) that track a user's selections before checkout. An external library was required in the previous PHP version. There are numerous libraries that allow optional PHP extensions to be used. Some of these include support for LDAP, IMAP, databases, and various encryption methods.

Among the many new features included with PHP4 are

▼ Native support for HTTP sessions

■ Standardized build process for UNIX source

■ Support for multithreaded web servers through a web server interface

- ■ Extended API module interface

- ■ Improved syntax emphasis

- ■ Reference calculation

- ■ Support for output buffering

- ▲ Greater flexibility in configuring

Variables are commonly used within PHP coding, and can provide immediate value without a declaration being made. Within PHP, a variable is preceded by a $. For example:

```php
<?php
$this = "loves Raymond";
$list = "Everybody $this";
echo $list;
?>
```

In the example, "Everybody loves Raymond" would be displayed. For a complete set of preset variables, add the <?phpinfo()?> tag within a page and initiate it. This will display special and environmental variables and setup information for PHP.

Support also is provided for arrays. Programmers will be familiar with arrays, which store similar alphanumeric items by datatype; for PHP this is stored in hash tables through the built-in Zend engine.

PHP objects are stored in the same way as arrays.

```php
<?php
$account = new Account;
 $account->add_item("4", 1);
?>
```

For this example, the account object is created, which is of the class Account. The function add_item() of the account object is being called to add 1 item of the article number 4 to the account.

Cookies can be used to track individual client sessions. If this is not supported from the client's browser, a session ID can be added to a relative URL. Other options include adding a SID variable to a query link.

PHP4 also includes the Zend engine (http://www.zend.com), which has many enhancements. The company Zend was formed by

PHP Development Team members to encourage commercial and open source PHP coding development. PHP's lack of language consistency and source code displayed within the HTML has incurred criticism. Zend now has a commercial product that will convert PHP code to byte code, thereby hiding it from view.

PHP and Databases

Because PHP is open source, and has a small memory requirement and concise coding, it is a popular server-side technology. Although PHP lacks a standard database API, or development tools, where PHP really shines is with support and options for working with a wide range of databases. PHP now supports persistent database connectivity, which enables clients to maintain a connection to a server database. The connection is reset if not accessed by the client for a set period of time, or if the server is restarted. PHP has support for a wide variety of databases.

A popular database that is used with PHP is MySQL (http://www. mysql.org). The following instructions demonstrate in general how a customer would connect its MySQL database using PHP, assuming the customer's permissions are set correctly.

```
MYSQL_CONNECT('localhost','USERNAME','PASSWORD');
@mysql_select_db("ENTERDATABASENAME");
```

The first line opens a connection; the second line designates the database that the user will connect to. The customer would use its own database name instead of ENTERDATABASENAME.

Some of the key features MySQL provides include the following:

▼ Multiple programming language APIs such as C, C++, Java, Perl, PHP, Python, Tcl, and Eiffel.

■ A very fast thread-based memory allocation system.

■ Runs on multiple server platforms.

■ ODBC (Open-DataBase-Connectivity) support.

■ Query can access multiple databases (as of version 3.22).

■ Provides secure host-based verification security.

▲ 16 indexes per table are allowed. Each index can consist of 1–16 columns or parts of columns. The maximum index length is 256 bytes (this can be changed when compiling MySQL).

Further information on PHP and related technologies can be located at:

▼ **PHP** http://www.php.net

■ **Zend** http://www.zend.com

▲ **MySQL** http://www.mysql.com

SUMMARY

By focusing on these higher-margin plans and offering the range of services that customers are willing to pay for, web hosts with the right tools and quality personnel are thriving. For the server-side technologies discussed in the chapter, technical personnel will need a higher degree of specialization to provide these services. In some cases it will be more feasible to partner or outsource to other specialty firms, which will be discussed in Chapter 14. The next chapter will discuss infrastructure-scaling issues for web hosts to consider when ensuring highly reliable web services.

PART V

Infrastructure and Security Considerations

CHAPTER 10

Issues in Networking Infrastructure

Having a reliable network is of utmost importance to web hosts that specialize in hosting mission-critical e-commerce web sites and applications. To have this reliability along with the highest availability of services, you must ensure that your network and equipment are redundant. In the simplest terms, this means having multiple mechanisms and backups in place to account for all network components, including servers, routers, bandwidth providers, security measures, power sources, and so on in case of failure of a primary component or provider. These and related factors will be discussed in this chapter.

TARGETING FOR GROWTH

It is estimated that Internet traffic doubles every 100 days. The conservative estimate is that by 2003, there will be more than 500 million users, according to Industry Standard magazine. Methods of accessing the Internet other than a standard browser will become prominent, showing up in new, innovative wireless technologies. And what about e-commerce? Despite the difficulties reported by dot-coms in establishing lasting brand presence on the Internet and going public, the underlying e-commerce opportunities presented by the Internet are unprecedented in our history. More than half the Fortune 1000 companies recently polled by Forrester Research are involved in an e-marketplace. *B2B* (*business to business*) transactions are expected to generate more than $4 billion in revenue by the year 2004, with an increasing emphasis placed on electronic payments.

Web hosts are building their infrastructures in myriad ways, through constructing new data centers, consolidations, purchasing additional bandwidth, or aligning with ASPs for load balancing services. This also can include co-locating server farms within large existing data centers, to ensure a fully scalable environment or by purchasing specialty software to manage.

Having a *server farm* can mean just having multiple servers, but it typically means a group of web servers that are networked together, with the load distributed in combination, to use the combined power of the servers together. This normally is accomplished through the use of load balancing software that enables certain services, tasks, and scheduling processes to be given priority over others, based on the requirements of users.

By enabling their web sites with multiple language translation capability, web hosts are looking beyond the U.S. to attract international markets. This also involves enhancing the capacity of existing networks to accommodate customers within these new markets, and retaining personnel who can converse in these languages. Besides these considerations, there also are differences in currency exchanges, and local taxes and customs to factor in. In 2000 Amazon.com launched a Japanese web site (http://www.amazon.co.jp) that is built around Unicode-enabled software infrastructure. *Unicode* is an open opensource character code standard for recognizing characters that are used in multiple languages. Amazon also has launched several other sites that are geared towards specific cultures. By allowing for multiple languages on the Internet, web hosts will be able to attract new business and acquire additional markets in the process.

FOCUSING ON QOS (QUALITY OF SERVICE)

Many web hosts are adding QoS (Quality of Service) plan guarantees of 100 percent within SLAs (Service Level Agreements) to ensure customers of the utmost reliability and availability of their hosting services. QoS is a phrase that has been used in the industry to identify a wide range of services. QoS is not as easy to define as adding a service to a server. On a large scale it can define the quality of services maintained by carriers that the web host utilizes for Internet connectivity. On an abstract scale, it is the quality of service that is specified or anticipated for an application as part of layer 7 of the OSI model.

In general, QoS can be defined as a method to assign precedence to traffic on the network and to use available bandwidth effectively. When used to its maximum potential, every internal device (servers, routers, switches, and so forth) and external backbone provider's equipment is tuned to support the same QoS standard. To reach this plateau requires a high level of communication and agreement on standards among all parties involved.

The most recent Internet standards that have been proposed and approved (as of August 2000) are included in Appendix E. For later updates to this document, visit http://www.rfc-editor.org. The lists of Internet protocols are specified for each stage of standardization: standard, draft standard, proposed standard, experimental, and historic.

QoS standards are supported by various operating systems and web servers. Microsoft Windows 2000 now includes QoS features that enable you to prioritize network traffic to make the most efficient use of bandwidth. You can designate priority for a set amount of bandwidth to be available for particular applications. Several APIs (Application Programming Interfaces) are available which allow companies to develop and add specific QoS standards of their own that apply to individual user sessions.

A QoS standard module is available for Apache and is called mod_ eclipse. You can find more information on this product at http://www. apache.org/. Numerous other packages are available for monitoring and updating server activity. One such product is SNMP Conductor, commercially available as an Apache module from Covalent (http:// www.covalent.net/products/snmp/). Features include the ability to track real-time utilization and to make optimal configuration changes that can be integrated into a QoS model.

AVAILABLE BANDWIDTH

Available bandwidth is defined as the amount of bandwidth available for use by the web host as arranged through Internet carriers, which determines the capacity available for use by the host's clients. The greater the bandwidth, the faster data can theoretically be assigned. Some types of applications, such as streaming movies and audio (which often are given a priority), can put a strain on bandwidth; especially for special events. Careful monitoring is necessary to ensure that web sites that generate a high level of traffic for a special event or on a continual basis are not detrimental to other web sites on the host's network.

For special events such as these, and for those sites that include services such as two-way video conferencing and real-time voice discussions, latency can become a serious problem if the right network infrastructure is not in place to handle them. Latency was loosely defined in Chapter 6 as the speed of the connection between two computers on the Internet. From a networking perspective, a more precise description for latency is a time delay in receiving a response from a request because a network component (a router, server, switch, and so forth) is busy handling other requests. Latency is discussed later in the chapter. *ATM* (*Asynchronous Transfer Mode*) holds promise as a technology that can prevent latency from occurring, using a type of service called *VBR* (*variable bit rate*), in which the throughput is specific, with data sent in a fluctuating stream.

Web servers enable you to track which web sites are using the most server resources. This can indicate where potential problems lie, such as a server-side script that is not configured properly. The percentage of time that the server spends processing these types of scripts can be limited. This limiting is referred to as *process throttling;* on a web server hosting multiple sites, process throttling can prevent one site from using all the capacity of the server. The network administrator can send a custom error message to the customer through browser and e-mail when a specific application has surpassed its acceptable level. For example, Microsoft IIS (version 5) contains several new process accounting and process throttling features that provide more direct control over how individual web sites use server resources and processes, as described here:

▼ **Process accounting**   Includes information about individual web site usage of server resources on the system. This information is useful in determining which sites are using disproportionately high CPU resources or that might have malfunctioning scripts or CGI processes.

▲ **Process throttling**   Enables you to control the percentage of time the server spends processing out-of-process ASP, ISAPI, and CGI applications for individual Web sites. In addition, misbehaving processes can be stopped and restarted. By default, the interval set for a CGI timeout is 5 minutes for IIS (Version 5). If process throttling is enabled, the CGI timeout should be lowered. This way if a CGI script fails it will not continue to use server processes for the full 5 minutes.

Companies such as Williams Communications are providing *frame relay* services, which include an out-of-region frame relay that can enhance a host's existing bandwidth for peak usage needs that special events require. This enables a host to reserve bandwidth for a specific day or time of day to coordinate with a customer's special events. Depending on the customer's requirements, alternatives include using media players that require a download of software or a plug-in to the client browser for running, instead of a continual stream of data; for example, RealNetwork's RealPlayer and Macromedia Flash.

Other methods for getting expanded bandwidth include installing Fast Ethernet within your facilities. Gigabit Ethernet is another option, although this involves an upgrade to the carrier's equipment; not the web host's. Companies such as Telseon (http://www.telseon.com) and Yipes.com (http://www.yipes.com) are enabling customers to dynamically increase bandwidth on demand through a web interface. This provisioning of bandwidth might redefine current business models, especially within large technology centers of the country.

There are several ways a web host can discover how much bandwidth a server is using. For example, for Microsoft IIS, you can do the following:

1. Examine the Current Bandwidth counter and the Bytes Total/sec by going to the Network Interface object in the System Monitor. From here you can gauge the level of incoming and outgoing traffic levels.

2. Compare the values given to the bandwidth capacity of your network connection. An optimal setting will be around 30 to 50 percent of the total available capacity (depending on the type of customers using the server), with the rest available for heavy usage or peak time frames.

By enabling bandwidth throttling, you can set parameters that specify how much bandwidth is available to customers for specific tasks. For example, a web host can specifically limit the processing of CGI scripts on a per-web-site basis to ensure that other services are able to run efficiently on the network.

Microsoft IIS has bandwidth throttling built in; it can be modified through the IIS snap-in:

1. Using the Microsoft IIS snap-in, select the web site and click the Properties button to list the property sheets.

2. Select Enable Bandwidth Throttling.

3. In the Maximum Network Use box, key in the maximum number of kilobytes per second to be used by the site. Click OK.

For Microsoft IIS, bandwidth throttling limits only the bandwidth used by static HTML files. In addition, *socket pooling* is enabled by default with IIS (Version 5). Socket pooling is the method by which multiple web sites that utilize the same port but different IP addresses, can use the same socket. This allows for conservation of server resources and reduced load, as previous versions assigned sockets for individual sites. Although socket pooling is a more efficient method for managing a greater number of web sites on a server, for web sites (especially e-commerce) that require a high degree of security, this setting can be a security risk. In addition, if you are using bandwidth throttling to maintain limits for individual web sites, you must disable socket pooling for each of these sites (which allows each site to have their own sockets). The following metabase entry (MD_DISABLE_SOCKET_POOLING) can be set for each site that needs to disable socket pooling from /LM/W3SVC/X (where X is the site identifier).

Apache has a module available called mod_throttle that allows bandwidth throttling to control policies for how server requests are completed, and can be based on individual web sites, locations, directories, authenticated users, and so on. Every policy is further specified by variables set which apply limits for specific time periods. There are four levels of throttling policies that are available in mod_throttle:

▼ **ThrottleClientIP**   Sets policies by a customer's IP address

■ **ThrottleUser**   Sets policies by user identification

- ■ **ThrottleRemoteUser**   Sets policies by remote user name that is authenticated

- ▲ **ThrottlePolicy**   Sets policies by virtual host, server, directory, and location

Latency Management

As you know, latency is the amount of time it takes for a server response to be received from a client request, as another component (request, process, and so forth) of the server completes. Latency also can involve the overall wait time factor on a network. Other components of a network, such as a switch or router, also can contribute to latency. A switch delay will cause latency as it determines the route where packets are to be forwarded to next.

When a router becomes congested because of high incoming traffic levels, packet loss of data likely will occur. Within an SLA, packet loss can be specified as being one percent or less as an average on a monthly basis. Additional parameters can be specified for high-end user agreements based on QoS standards. For a router, latency is propagation delay, which includes the time frame from when a packet of data is requested to the time it is forwarded to another network. To increase the speed of forwarding packets, especially for ATM networks, MPLS (Multi-Protocol Label Switching) is used. Through MPLS, definitive routes are specified throughout a network. A label is included with each packet forwarded that has a definitive route. For more information, refer to the web site at http://www.mplsrc.com.

Routers most often are the cause of latency. As a router handles more traffic, latency increases. The combined latency effect when all routers are taken into consideration can be substantial. A quality SLA will include latency details, along with how traffic levels are gauged and the level of throughput. For example, latency could be specified as being 70 milliseconds or less as an average per month. Additional parameters could be outlined to accommodate specific high-end customer requirements within their own SLA, such as outlining that throughput be 99.9% or higher for an average per month.

An SLA should have the capability to track network performance, to measure responsiveness, how long servers have been online, and when service interruptions can be expected (for scheduled network upgrades and so on), adhering to QoS standards. Within the QoS standards are queuing techniques that apply to routers and switches that experience high levels of traffic, whereby data packets are held in sequence for subsequent processing. The router then will process the packets, with the data forwarded based on priority. The IETF has defined a framework for QoS-based routing (RFC 2386), available through ftp://ftp.isi.edu/in-notes/rfc2386.txt.

Jitter

As part of the discussion on latency, one term you should know is *jitter*. With real-time two-way audio and video applications, often there is a noticeable delay or quirkiness to the message, referred to as a jitter in the sound and or video. This is caused by the data packets, which can arrive for the session from different locations across the Internet. When these packets are received, some will be delayed (because of latency), and other packets arrive out of order. The result is a jittery sound or video.

A common workaround is to buffer the traffic coming in, which also creates a delay for the client when loading. For situations in which it is monetarily justified, bandwidth can be purchased on demand for special online media events or webcasts. Under normal traffic levels, latency should not be a problem with one-way real-time media presentations, because each packet is received normally because of being delayed the same amount of time. The *IETF* (*Internet Engineering Task Force*) has released a specification that highlights QoS as a proposed Internet Standard, detailed in a Guaranteed Quality of Service, RFC 2212. Other RFCs in which QoS is specified are in RFC 2990, 2676, 2549, and 2386. As this emerging standard goes beyond the scope of this book, here are some resources for further information:

▼ **IETF QoS Routing Working Group**   http://www.ietf.org/html.charters/qosr-charter.html

▲ **Quality of Service Forum**   http://www.qosforum.com/tech_resources.htm

ROUTING

A small web host may use a single default router to handle forwarding of traffic, and manually add information to a routing table on the router and host server as the needs require. This is referred to as the *static routing* method. The routing table determines the best route to take, and a forwarding table will include directions (IP addresses) to point to the next neighboring router located in the same network segment; not the final destination of the packet being sent. The forwarding table refers to the routing table with updates handled by a routing protocol. This differentiates between static and dynamic routing. Fixed tables are used with static routing, whereas dynamic routing will use routing protocols (as listed in Table 10-1) to enable routers to dynamically exchange data with each other. Each packet's destination address is compared to a locally maintained route table. From here, a packet will either be sent to a local destination on the network, forwarded on to another network, or discarded.

To configure a route with a Windows NT or 2000 server, you can use the `route` command from the command line, or the Routing And Remote Access GUI (if you are using Windows 2000). For example, suppose you want to specify that the host using IP address 200.365.199 should use a router with the IP address 200.365.200.2. You would key in

```
route -p add 200.365.199.0 mask 255.255.255.0
200.365.200.2
```

The -p in the command specifies that the command will be permanent.

By having just the basic IP information, a routing table stays small and efficient. A router forwards traffic (IP datagrams) one hop at a time. A *hop* is the path from one router to the next one it is directly connected to. By using routing protocols, routers can sense the components of a network. This also is referred to as *dynamic routing*, and is more useful for environments that require redundancy and have the personnel to manage such a system. For routers to forward information among networks, they must each use the same routing protocols. Most routers use protocols such as RIP (Routing Information Protocol), OSPF (Open Shortest Path First), or BGP (Border Gate

Protocol) to exchange routing tables. Some of the most common are highlighted in Table 10-1.

Security and Filtering

Routers normally are concerned only with a packet's destination address; not with filtering the actual data that is received, unless they specifically are designed to include firewall capability. Security issues within a hosting environment are discussed in further detail starting in Chapter 11. Security also is available with TCP/IP packet-level filtering. This provides limits to traffic that reaches designated servers and applies application filters. However, the main function is the capability to block incoming traffic that does not include the IP address or port data listed on an exceptions list.

Tracking Performance

Vendors such as Cisco provide add-on statistical capability for their routers and switches through the NetFlow package, which enables

Protocol	Description	Key IETF Related RFC
AppleTalk	Used as a routing protocol for combining Macintosh networks with other networks (Windows, Unix). Developed by Apple.	1583
BGP	Abbreviation for Border Gate Protocol. Enables a web host using multiple backbone provider connections from different bandwidth providers to effectively advertise routes to their BGP router, which then is advertised through the Internet. The current implementation of BGP is BGP-4.	1771

Table 10-1.   Common Routing Protocols

Protocol	Description	Key IETF Related RFC
IGMP	Abbreviation for Internet Group Membership Protocol. Enables Internet hosts to participate in multicasting of video and audio in real time. Allows multiple hosts to receive packets that are based from a single packet. Only works on MBONE (multicast portions of the Internet backbone), with Class D IP addresses (with first octet between 224 and 239).	1112
OSPF	Abbreviation for Open Shortest Path First. Dynamic link state routing protocol. Sends only updated information rather than resending complete routing tables.	1583
RIP for IP	Abbreviation for Routing Information Protocol for IP. Dynamic distance vector routing protocol. Uses substantial overhead as routing table is rebroadcast every 60 seconds. OSPF is considered more efficient than RIP.	1058
RIP for IPX	Abbreviation for Routing Information Protocol for IPX. Similar to RIP for IP. OSPF is considered more efficient than RIP. Only IPX routing protocol supported by Windows 2000 Server.	Microsoft implementation
SAP	Abbreviation for Service Advertising Protocol. A resource broadcast method protocol for IPX/SPX clients. Developed by Novell.	1634

Table 10-1. Common Routing Protocols *(continued)*

you to track such parameters as application metering for billing purposes (useful for ASPs), monitoring of inbound and outbound traffic, and for network planning. You can find more information on NetFlow at http://www.cisco.com/warp/public/cc/cisco/mkt/ios/netflow/tech/napps_wp.htm.

Common Routing Protocols

There are several routing protocols that allow communications among different networks. Some of the most common are highlighted in Table 10-1.

The routing protocols from Table 10-1 that warrant comment here are IGMP (Internet Group Membership Protocol), OSPF (Open Shortest Path First), and RIP (Routing Information Protocol). BGP (Border Gate Protocol), as is commonly used by web hosts to enhance availability of services and redundancy, will be discussed in a separate section.

IGMP (Internet Group Membership Protocol)

IGMP often is referred to as *IP multicasting*, and allows a single packet to be sent to multiple hosts. IGMP runs only on the MBONE (the multicast backbone), which is an assigned portion of the Internet set aside for allowing Internet audio and low bandwidth video broadcasts in real time (as specified in RFC 1112). Class D addresses are used for multicast, which are addresses with their first octet between 224 and 239. Routers that are a part of the network using IGMP must be multicast compatible, and subscribers must be connected through the same subnet on the Internet. According to the Internet Architecture Committee, which is a part of the IETF, IGMP likely will emerge as a recommendation for all hosts and gateways to use in the future.

OSPF (Open Shortest Path First)

OSPF is a robust protocol that allows complex router communications with all other routers within an OSPF-enabled network.

OSPF routing designs are sectioned into three ordered levels:

▼ **OSPF Autonomous System**   A collection of networks that share a common Autonomous System (AS) and are subdivided into OSPF areas. An AS is a set of routers that share one routing policy, and will be under one authority.

- ■ **OSPF area**   A collection of routers that connect to bordering network segments, and are all linked by area border routers (ABR) into a backbone area.

- ▲ **OSPF network**   A network that includes individual segments connected through OSPF routers.

OSPF uses dynamic routing, and is used within medium-sized and larger redundant networks and Intranets, or those that contain greater than 50 subnets. OSPF is an Internet standard defined in RFC 1583. It is the most widely implemented routing protocol in Cisco-based intranets.

RIP (Routing Information Protocol)

RIP is a dynamic routing protocol that has widespread support because it provides legacy support for older routers, as the protocol has been in existence since 1982. Known as a *distance-vector* routing protocol, RIP usually communicates directly only with neighboring routers, and is not as reliable or flexible as newer routing protocols. However, version 2 of RIP can send router updates only when required instead of at timed intervals, as in the previous version. Routers that include support for RIP for IP version 2, OSPF, or BGP allow support for variable- length subnetting.

USING BGP TO MANAGE YOUR NETWORK

For customers who require a high degree of availability, such as an e-commerce or corporate web site, redundant connectivity and routers are required to provide a greater availability of bandwidth. This will enable the web site to be responsive and for page loads to be within an acceptable timeframe, as multiple clients access it through the Internet. As a web host expands its network, it will seek to improve its bandwidth capacity by leasing it as needed and regulating what it has available among its many customers through bandwidth throttling (refer to the section in this chapter on QoS).

In a fully redundant environment, a web host needs to account for all network components. Servers and routers should be clustered to ensure availability, with software or hardware mechanisms in place to detect when a server goes down, and multiple backup connections available through different providers. This is called *multi-homing*. A border router located on the outer edge of your network will control what routes go out to the Internet. In case of downtime by one bandwidth provider, the other one can still maintain connectivity. For web hosts, this is commonly accomplished through the Border Gate Protocol.

BGP is an external routing protocol that enables a web host using multiple backbone provider connections from different bandwidth providers to effectively advertise routes to their BGP router, which then is advertised through the Internet. When routing information is exchanged automatically through BGP, it is referred to as *BGP peering*. This ensures that traffic flows in the most efficient manner.

The key parts of a route include the size of the route (netmask or specificity), base IP address, and what the next destination (hop) is in sending the data to the IP specified address. When traffic is routed into a web host, it is because of the route being first announced over the Internet (as when a new web site becomes fully registered, and the domain name points to your DNS servers). Because of this announcement, packets of data come in through your routers. As traffic leaves, it generally will use routes that have been added dynamically within your border routers, based on rules that you set.

Key features of BGP for external routing include

▼ Capability to choose which provider has the least traffic among multiple provider networks used, and the best place to forward traffic. Instead of just having a default route into a provider's networks, routing can dynamically select the most optimal route.

■ Optimal network redundancy, as traffic can be rerouted automatically to another host's provider if the other provider becomes unavailable

▲ Selection criteria for traffic forwarding can be based on the quickest route instead of by the number of hops.

By sharing information with external sources (providers) about what routes your network uses, the provider's network knows dynamically how to access your network. When routes are announced to providers through BGP, the provider then announces those routes through the Internet. This path route will appear in the provider's routing table, which is distributed to other routers. When initially making known routes with BGP, make sure to configure everything statically; BGP will direct data along the foremost path from one Autonomous System to another located on another network.

Before using BGP, you need to obtain an *Autonomous System Number* (*ASN*) from the *American Registry of Internet Numbers* (*ARIN*). You must complete a template before having an AS number assigned. The template can be found at http://www.arin.net/templates/asntemplate. txt. To complete the form you will need information on your border routers, which will contain the AS information. Border routers that have their own AS on other networks will exchange routing data (internal routing, including addresses of network routers) with BGP. You also must list a Network Operations Center contact person. The ASN is a globally unique number (as noted in Table 10-2) that you use on the Internet, or an intranet, associated with the specific network that is registered with the ASN. In addition, backbone providers typically have some type of route registration process to complete.

To locate the owner of an ASN, you can use a WHOIS query. Simply query on "ASN ###", where ### is the ASN you want to look up. When configured properly, BGP and the ASN number can automatically reroute traffic to another host's provider if one

ASN	Company
701	UUNET
1239	Sprintlink
1	BBN (now Genuity)

Table 10-2. Examples of Autonomous System Numbers

provider becomes unavailable. BGP can be used with Cisco and Bay Network routers, and on Windows or Unix-based systems.

NOTE: The current implementation of BGP is BGP-4. BGP is specified within numerous IETF RFCs.

When a route is received from an AS on another network, it is branded with the associated ASN of the router where it was forwarded. As the route continues to travel to each network, it will include what is referred to as an *AS-PATH*. When the path begins, it is represented by ^$. It then is incremented as it travels from each network until it reaches its destination. The AS-PATH can serve as a log file that includes a list of all ASNs for all ASs that follow the history of the route taken and conduct sophisticated route filtering. The following is an example of AS-PATH access list using a Cisco router:

```
ip as-path access-list 20 permit _701_
ip as-path access-list 20 permit _1239_
ip as-path access-list 20 permit _1_
ip as-path access-list 20 deny .*
```

The _###_ notation means whitespace must be on either side of the number.

For this AS-path access list, it will allow, in order, the routes for UUNET, Sprintlink, and then the BBN routes, and deny all other routes. As you might recall from Table 10-2, the ASN number for each is 701, 1239, and 1.

CHOOSING RELIABLE BACKBONE PROVIDERS

Having a fully redundant network requires more than having a single carrier provide multiple leased line or data link connections to allow the bandwidth that services your customers. If that one provider becomes unavailable, you cannot host your customers' web sites. The result of such a failure, as has been experienced by some hosts, is a marketing nightmare. A redundant network requires multiple carriers to ensure the utmost availability. Bandwidth now can be leased in a multitude of standard connection increments, from DSL (for small offices, or a web host with few accounts) to high-speed data links, as noted in Table 10-3.

Deciding on a backbone provider depends on two key concepts: reliability and value. As markets are deregulated, providers are seeing increased competition, and advances in fiber-optic technologies have driven down the cost of bandwidth to the advantage of web hosts. There are increasing options in how and from whom to purchase bandwidth. Providers can be categorized into four general areas of operations:

▼ Large provider (Example: UUNet)

■ Provider (neutral) (Example: Switch & Data)

Type of Bandwidth	Description	Size
T-1	A leased-line (DS1) circuit connection. A small web host may start out with this type of connection, if you are not going through a reseller.	1.54 Mbps
T-3	A leased-line (DS3) circuit connection. Commonly used.	44.736 Mbps
OC-3	High-speed data links. OC-3 and OC-12 have replaced T-3s as the large backbones on the Internet.	155 Mbps
OC-12	High-speed data links.	622 Mbps
OC-48	High-speed data links.	2.488 Gbps
OC-192	Super-capacity data links. Carriers that provide this service include Williams Communications and GTE.	80 Gbps
DWDM	Dense Wavelength Division Multiplexing	460 Gbps

Table 10-3. Common Bandwidths Used By Web Hosts

- ■ Specialized (Example: Epoch Internet)

- ▲ Independent (Example: Exodus)

The demand for bandwidth remains constant as new services and technologies that use the Internet as a medium are introduced. This includes, but is not limited to content distribution, voice over IP, video conferencing, webcasts, Napster, and wireless technologies; with new applications on the horizon. The largest technology advance has been in *Dense Wavelength Division Multiplexing* (*DWDM*), which enables a single optic fiber to be separated into dozens of channels, creating bandwidth that is several times greater than OC-3 (155 Mbps), creating a huge 460 Gbps (Gigabytes per second) of capacity. This has resulted in a compounded annual rate of growth of DWDM technology worldwide approaching 280 percent. Some web hosts arrange to connect their router directly with a provider that uses DWDM to take advantage of this technology.

Williams Communications is an example of a full-service wholesale provider. With end-to-end services, it has lines that cover more than 33,000 route miles, connecting to more than 125 cities. Using ATM as its underlying transmission platform, Williams provides a range of services including frame relay, high-speed private line, switched voice, satellite, and ATM. The company also utilizes OC-192 for transport over DWDM.

Some providers offer *dark fiber,* which is optical fiber that is assigned directly to a customer to manage, instead of the carrier. The customer decides how to use the line, and from whom to get connectivity, many times relying on companies that specialize in installing and managing. Most current applications of dark fiber are in providing Internet services.

The *Cooperative Association for Internet Data Analysis (CAIDA)* provides tools for analysis of the Internet backbone of major carriers. Designed as a collaborative process, with the input of many organizations, CAIDA is a creation of the University of California at San Diego, and located at the San Diego Supercomputing Center. One of the tools, Mapnet, provides a visual representation of the Internet backbone of various carriers that makes its information available.

For more information, refer to http://www.caida.org/tools/ visualization/mapnet/. Bandwidth business exchange portals are available to allow comparison of carrier services and options. Another site, BandwidthFinders (http://www. bandwidthfinders.com), provides comparisons to more than 30 carriers for review.

CAUSES OF DOWNTIME

You must establish procedures for personnel to follow to reduce or eliminate unscheduled server downtime. According to Cahners In-Stat Group, the most common causes of server downtime can be attributed to the following areas:

▼ **Software failure**   20 percent

■ **Hardware failure**   23 percent

■ **Operator or procedural error**   30 percent

▲ **Environmental failures**   27 percent

For some web hosts, with the complexity of supporting server farms in a diverse array of different server platforms, clusters, and redundant storage, operator error is inevitable. Ongoing tasks, such as server configurations, modifications, and maintenance, require set policies to be established to create order out of the process. The next several chapters will highlight different areas that web hosts can utilize to give personnel the management tools and resources to more effectively complete tasks. Environmental failures usually are related to the loss of power with a data center.

Preventive measures must be in place through redundant power sources and diesel generators as backup. Are you or your partnerships maintaining multiple physical data center locations in different regions of the country in case of disaster? This might be necessary as the volume of more sophisticated customer applications and e-commerce services justifies it. Consider the number of web sites and hosting services that are based in the earthquake-prone areas of California. At the time of this writing, these areas are experiencing critical power shortages, as existing utilities have not been able to keep up with regional energy demands.

SUMMARY

By staying attuned to infrastructure needs, a web host can plan effectively for growth. Through designing a flexible architecture for growth and partnering with the most reliable vendors, a web host can ensure the highest availability of service. The next chapter introduces security concepts and strategies that you must enforce to ensure the utmost protection of a network and customer's data.

CHAPTER 11

Securing Your Infrastructure

What is your definition of security? Depending on your perceptions and assumptions, it has different meanings for different situations. Whatever aim your customers have for their web sites, it is likely that security will be near the top on their list of priorities, especially where e-commerce is concerned. As the Internet has evolved into a critical tool for conducting e-commerce transactions, business analysis, and applications online, security (actually the lack thereof) has become a big concern.

Security measures protect both the external and internal workings of your hosting business. All manner of external intrusion attempts can and have occurred. Tactics have included outright attacks to bring a site down through a DoS (Denial of Service) attack. DoS attacks are designed to disrupt web services by flooding methods which prevent other users from connecting to the service because servers are busy trying to complete bogus requests. New types of DoS methods continue to appear. One method of DoS attack, a SYN flood, will send a barrage of SYN packets using an IP address that is spoofed (claiming to be from within the network). The connection table will eventually become full, as the host attempts to respond to the fake IP address sending each request, which causes the host to become unavailable to requests that are legitimate. Methods to prevent this include reducing the allowable processes running on the system, and by reducing the time out values for connection to the server to thirty seconds. Hidden methods that use *Trojans,* or viruses, with names such as NetBus, Subseven, and ILOVEYOU are also commonly used to attempt to make a network unavailable. Through these techniques, a hacker attempts to find a back door into a network to take advantage of a hidden vulnerability in a server or operating system component.

The techniques also are becoming more advanced, which makes tracking difficult. The number of breaches of security that occur escalates each year. Your customers will have a range of security concerns, from preventive security measures to e-commerce. The extent of their concerns also will relate to how sophisticated their web sites are. Do you have preventive security measures in place that are aligned with your customers' concerns? During January through September of 2000, more than 15,167 reported breaches occurred, up from more than 9,859 for 1999 as a whole (as shown in Figure 11-1). External threats can take other forms that can impact your availability of services, including brute force entry and equipment sabotage. Internal risks also exist, whether from a disgruntled employee or in areas where security procedures are not consistently followed with password changes and patches.

The list of companies, organizations, and government agencies that have experienced successful hacker attacks in one form or another is a long one, including Yahoo, Amazon, eBay, Microsoft, E-Trade, the U.S. Department of Defense, and the U.S. Federal Bureau of Investigation. Consider that only 25 percent of dot-coms that experienced breaches of security in 2000 actually reported it (according to the Computer Security Institute). Why? Concern for how it would look in the media and with their customers. In all likelihood your network has been scanned or tracked by a hacker looking for that one weakness that will make your network vulnerable. Some breaches of security take place over the course of months without full knowledge that it is happening, as occurred with Microsoft during 2000. Some customers are more concerned about security than others, depending on the sensitivity of their data and e-commerce aspects. For heightened security, place hosted services on a secure subnet separate from regular accounts, and charge for

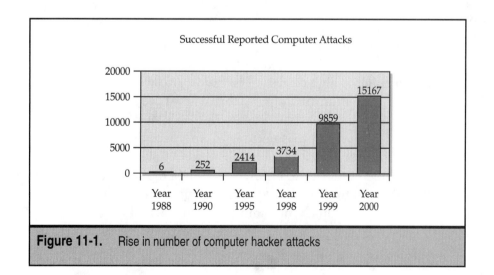

Figure 11-1.   Rise in number of computer hacker attacks

those expanded services detailed in an SLA. With the reports of hacker attacks increasing during 2000, analysts report that businesses are increasing their spending budgets for security by 50 percent or more. If a breach occurs, even the smallest web host that maintains its own network or provides secure services must be prepared to respond effectively, recover, and notify customers that might be affected.

There are no short and guaranteed answers here to securing your network. Security is an ever-changing environment that will require your time, personnel, resources, and money to stay current with the preventive measures, patches, software, and technology measures needed to minimize the risks. Some organizations handle security concerns by assigning the responsibility to existing in-house personnel; others might partner with or outsource to security specialists. When weighing the costs of implementing security measures, consider the cost of not taking preventive actions and the loss of business and reputation because of compromised security. If you are using in-house personnel, make sure their skill sets can handle the wide range of technical knowledge required for security administration.

Depending on the size of your hosting business and the highly specialized dynamics of the security field, there might be ample justification in hiring a full-time security administrator. The person or people who are ultimately responsible for security issues—applying changes where needed and tracking the full extent of security developments—must have an adequate budget and authority to implement a security plan, with full management support.

You also should encourage continuing training, as security issues demand a high degree of technical knowledge and your security staff must be informed of new threats that are introduced daily on the Internet. Otherwise, a plan likely will not be enforced or will be ineffective. There is nothing more frustrating to a security person than to be in charge of an operation but lack the necessary resources or the authority to enforce measures that are needed. This person also might be involved with, or even manage, other network support people who maintain firewalls and routers.

SECURITY PLAN

A security plan should identify all known and likely risk factors of your network, identify acceptable and unacceptable behavior, and be clearly understood and supported by management and employees. A security plan should have the input of management, the IS department, and the customer service department—especially in the early stages—and have members of these departments and management as a part of a security team, which will put the initial security plan into writing.

When preparing for a security plan, question and analyze how you are presently handling security. Here are some initial questions to ask:

▼ Have there been any incidents in which security has been breached, whether it was a system that was compromised or a virus? How was it discovered? Was it a proactive or a reactive approach to the problem? What caused the problem?

■ How are the components of your network tracked now?

■ Are system and log files monitored on a routine basis for any suspicious level of activity?

■ How are existing security patches, updates, router access rules, and patches applied currently managed?

▲ Are user accounts for temporary personnel and contractors deleted when they leave the company?

Examine your infrastructure by conducting an assessment of your risks. Analyze and perform tests on the server farm, connectivity points to other networks, internal systems, operating systems, and firewalls. Take a look at your current level of physical security, especially if you are providing co-location, dedicated, or data center services. A security plan should include a basic overview of what the objectives are, how security policies are to be enforced, and the range of company operations it will have an impact on. It also will include tracking procedures and might include action plans (from a public relations, technical, or legal standpoint) to take based on different scenarios, including security breaches and recovery efforts. A security plan will need to include procedures that are used in how servers are backed up, restored, and that server backups are in a secure off-site location for retrieval as needed. It also might include what actions to take in case of a natural disaster.

Some companies will initially focus a security plan on areas of their network that are discovered through a risk assessment to be vulnerable to possible intrusion or compromise. This will determine the initial level of protection that is required, some likely scenarios if the worst happens, and a cost estimate of a security intrusion. The other key components of the plan include identifying specific security requirements and how each will be accomplished. Specialty firms provide security consulting, including attempting to find openings and vulnerabilities in a network for a negotiated fee.

At the implementation level, a security policy defines guidelines to implement a requirements-level policy, using specific technology in a predefined way to only allow access to resources where absolutely necessary. For example, the implementation-level policy could require access lists to be configured so that only traffic from human resources host computers can access the server containing personnel records. Because networks are constantly open to security breaches, once a security plan is implemented, you must make sure it is updated to actively reflect appropriate defense mechanisms against perceived and real threats. Although a company's size and organization will determine the extent of security necessary, at a minimum, a security plan needs to be reviewed on a quarterly basis by designated security personnel. The major components of a security policy might include, but are not limited to, those highlighted in Figure 11-2. An example security policy is provided later in the chapter to illustrate some components that can be identified by a security plan. A security policy also might reference a separate firewall plan (a sample is included later in the chapter), which will provide specific defensive measures and rules designed for only authorized network personnel and management to view and maintain.

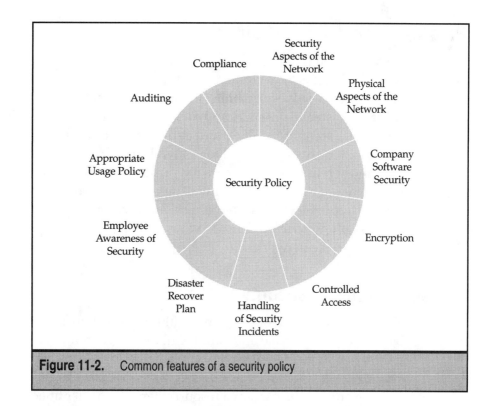

Figure 11-2.   Common features of a security policy

Security Aspects of the Network

Protective measures must be identified for applications, servers, firewalls, routers, and other network components. This also should include details for what types of external and internal access are permitted, what levels of access are authorized for employees and customers to have direct access to, firewalls, routers, and components. Specify all known points of entry in your network, including employees who carry notebooks to and from work, which can be stolen and might contain sensitive information. A separate firewall policy probably also should be referenced to identify specific security measures that need to be enforced. A sample firewall policy also is highlighted later in the chapter. No two organizations are the same, and the same goes for security and firewall policies. Utilize the examples provided to custom fit your operations.

Physical Aspects of the Network

Depending on the types of services provided, you should include controlled access to equipment and servers that are maintained by authorized employee personnel only. Practical measures include securing systems within locked facilities and careful inventory tracking to account for all equipment. This might include data center facilities, which are designed for a high level of security of customer's data and servers. This type of facility usually includes 24/7 security, with guarded entry, keyless entry, fingerprint or retinal scanning, closed circuit televisions, alarms, and an emergency backup system. All possible areas should be identified for ensuring the physical integrity of the network.

Company Software Security

The software section of the plan should describe how software will be used on the internal and external network. With the compliance efforts that many organizations implemented when preparing for the year 2000, an inventory tracking system or database might already be in place and can be used as a resource here. Also identified here will include specifying the accepted procedures for virus scanning of software, files downloaded through the Internet, accepted from customers, vendors, business partners, installed by employees.

Encryption

Encryption can ensure that data transferred through the Internet is protected. Encryption typically is used for highly sensitive material, such as credit transactions or personal records. For example, when using public encryption, keys are used to confirm that each party is identified in the communication process. A *VPN* (*virtual private network*) also often is encrypted or might be bundled within the features of a firewall.

Different vendors use different methods of encryption; there is no single standard. You must take this into consideration when working with customers, vendors, and business partners. Windows 2000 now is capable of generating encrypted keys for a network, eliminating

the need to purchased encryption software from third parties, and
better security measures that are more closely matched to the Unix
environment. This is not to say that Unix is the epitome of security.
Both environments require attention to security measures. You also
must make sure that current operating system patches and service
packs are applied to keep your security measures up to date.

NOTE: It is best to wait until a patch or service pack has been available for
several weeks before applying it so that any hidden drawbacks have been
found and worked out.

Controlled Access

This section of the plan should identify who has the authorization
rights to which level of network resources. This should specify the
users and groups of users that have access to different network
resources, including files, directories, and individual servers. These
permissions lists are known as *Access Control Lists* (*ACLs*). This
method might be more costly and cumbersome for company
personnel, but will provide better preventive measures to discourage
an intruder. Determining an access policy also will determine how
effective a firewall will be, because it enforces rules that are set as to
control the type of access.

Authentication

Authentication usually includes some form of login through an
alphanumeric password, or multiple forms of password, before
gaining entry to a server or the network. Authentication also might
be in combination with a secret word or phrase, or include a more
advanced form of authentication. You must decide where password
data records are kept, how passwords can be modified, and how
access to this location is provided through the network. Third-party
software sometimes is used to keep this organized, or you can use a
secured database.

Handling of Security Incidents

A hacker exploits a weakness in a CGI script, and gains entry to bring down a server. Before doing so, the hacker gains access to sensitive credit information of a customer. In this type of circumstance, a web host has to act quickly and decisively to prevent any further damage, and promptly notify appropriate law enforcement officials and the customer. A security policy should include specific steps to respond as quickly as possible from a preventive, legal, and company standpoint. If the attacker is found and later brought to trial, a court case will need to have sufficient evidence and documentation to prove the guilt of the intruder. This also could include action against an employee who intentionally seeks to compromise the security of data or equipment, such as firing or legal action.

You will need to make a close analysis of all associated system and network log files for the affected systems. What can be learned from the incident? How can this be prevented in the future? Also, by tracking what happens to other organizations where security is compromised, steps can be taken to prevent a similar occurrence from taking place within your network. Incorporate this into your security plan. A security plan should be a constantly evolving document.

Disaster Recovery Plan

Although natural disasters are not a direct security threat, a plan needs to include measures for what to do in case of a disaster. Disaster recovery is a natural addition to ensuring a complete security policy plan, because it can outline steps to take in case of such an emergency, and can be available as a central reference guide. In case an earthquake, flood, tornado, or other natural disaster occurs, the security policy needs to must include an emergency plan listing local and federal emergency official contacts, and identifying employees who will coordinate with officials and handle media and customer inquiries. This team also will report to management on the integrity of systems and data, and the extent of damages. If a web host with data center operations is located in an area that is at risk, ample consideration should be given in planning for a redundant location in another region of the country, or negotiating with a data center provider to provide such a location.

Appropriate Usage Policy

This section of the policy might specify the level of Internet or computer use for personal reasons. An employee doesn't need to be day trading or spending his or her time playing online games on company time. Some companies go further to specify access to network resources only during business hours (with no remote access allowed), although this is no longer widely followed.

Auditing

Servers, systems, personnel, and traffic monitoring should be audited on a routine basis to ensure that a security policy is being complied with. Depending on the critical nature of the data being hosted, this might be monthly or on a quarterly basis. Audits can identify where domains are misconfigured or whether servers need correcting, and other network areas in which enhancements can be identified to increase performance and security. An audit also can identify areas where security is lax and can provide tracking, which hopefully can offer proof of an attempted intrusion before any damage occurs.

Compliance

How will the security policy "have teeth," and be enforced? The compliance section should describe what steps will be taken for external or internal security breaches, and should detail legal remedies and investigations. A security plan should not be so inflexible that personnel must bypass it to do their jobs effectively. If a plan is to be realistic, personnel needs to fully understand it and the benefits of the plan must be fully explained. After review and written approval by management and legal counsel, a security policy can be put into a binder format and given to all employees, and placed on the company intranet.

Employee Awareness of Security

Employees need to understand the range and extent of potential security risks, especially if policies are not followed. Each employee, contract person, or temporary staff member needs to be aware of all security policies, and why they are in place. Conduct a training class to heighten awareness of the importance of enhanced security to the economic viability of the company. As new employees are hired, personnel and managers must instruct them about the importance of the security policy and why its usage is required. This also should include the understanding that passwords need to be updated occasionally, with alphanumeric characters used. For highly secure areas, encrypted passwords must always be used. With a clear understanding of a security plan at the outset by employees, its benefits to them and the company will be fully recognized.

Sample Security Policy Outline

When creating a security policy, define your requirements before defining the security implementations. In that way, you don't end up merely justifying particular technical solutions that might not actually be required for your situation or customers. The following is an example of a generic security policy, which provides a listing of other areas that can be further identified by a web host when preparing a security policy:

1. Introduction

> Overview of the Security Policy
> Objectives

> A. Responsible Organizational Structure

>> 1. Corporate information services

>> 2. Business unit information services

>> 3. International organizations

>> 4. Tenants

B. Security Standards

    1. Confidentiality
    2. Integrity
    3. Authorization
    4. Access
    5. Appropriate use
    6. Employee privacy

2. Domain Services

A. Authentication
B. Password standards
C. Resident personnel departure

    1. Friendly terms
    2. Unfriendly terms

3. E-mail Systems

A. Authentication
B. Intrusion protection
C. Physical access
D. Backups
E. Retention policy
F. Auditing

4. Web Servers

A. Internal
B. External

5. Data Center

A. Authentication
B. Intrusion protection
C. Physical access
D. Backups
E. Retention policy
F. Auditing
G. Disaster recovery

6. LAN/WAN

    A. Authentication
    B. Intrusion protection
    C. Physical access

        1. Modems
        2. Dial-in access
        3. Dial-out

    D. Backups
    E. Retention policy
    F. Content filtering
    G. Auditing
    H. Disaster recovery

        1. Network operations center
        2. Physical network layer

7. Desktop Systems

    A. Authentication
    B. Intrusion protection
    C. Physical access
    D. Backups
    E. Auditing
    F. Disaster recovery

8. Telecommunication Systems

    A. Authentication
    B. Intrusion protection
    C. Physical access
    D. Auditing
    E. Backups
    F. Retention policy
    G. Disaster recovery

9. Strategic Servers

   A. Authentication
   B. Intrusion protection
   C. Physical access
   D. Backups
   E. Retention policy
   F. Auditing
   G. Disaster recovery

10. Legacy Systems

   A. Authentication

      1. Password standards

   B. Intrusion protection
   C. Physical access
   D. Backups
   E. Retention policy
   F. Auditing
   G. Disaster recovery

11. Security Services and Procedures

   A. Auditing
   B. Monitoring

12. Security Incident Handling

   A. Preparing and planning for incident handling
   B. Notification and points of contact
   C. Identifying an incident
   D. Handling an incident
   E. Aftermath of an incident
   F. Forensics and legal implications
   G. Public relations contacts
   H. Key Steps

      A. Containment
      B. Eradication

C. Recovery

D. Follow-up

E. Aftermath / Lessons learned

I. Responsibilities

13. Ongoing Activities

A. Incident warnings

1. Virus warnings
2. Intrusion vulnerabilities
3. Security patches

14. Contacts, Mailing Lists, and Other Resources

15. References

Source: SANS Institute, http://www.sans.org

To be effective, a security plan must be specific to the company. It should be used as a resource and contain strategies for protecting sensitive data, and to ensure network availability from a company standpoint (and to be reiterated to customers if Service Level Agreements are used). This also should identify what minimum levels of security are necessary to accomplish different functions, and what actions to take to recover in case of a security breach or disaster. For further assistance, with writing a security policy, refer to RFC 2196, which is a site security handbook that provides guidelines for further developing network security policies and procedures for web sites. It is available at http://faqs.org/rfcs/rfc2196.html.

FIREWALLS

In its truest sense, a firewall is a web host's defensive strategy, designed to protect the company's network and data (and customers, depending on type of hosting plan) from untrusted or potentially hostile Internet traffic. A firewall can be a firewall box, a *DMZ* (*Demilitarized Zone*), routers, servers, network appliances, or software. Firewalls can serve a variety of different network services, including caching, VPN, proxies, and DNS servers. If a firewall is used for DNS, users on the Internet only see the external firewall connection; not internal server addresses.

To use a firewall for DNS resolution, it must be configured so that no internal network information that provides network web services would be advertised for access by other services on the Internet; these web services should be available only through the firewall. Firewalls can provide an established process for confirming the identity of someone trying to access a system. Some types of authentication include a user login and password, once-only session passwords, and digital certificates. Digital certificates use public key encryption to generate secure certificates. The firewall must be host based to provide this type of feature (router-based firewalls don't provide it). Overall, firewalls provide several types of basic protection:

▼ Firewalls block unwanted traffic. (That is not to say that hackers cannot enter your system through a firewall to a web server.)

■ Firewalls can centrally log traffic coming in and going out from your private network. (For truer detection of hackers, also use some type of detection software, which can monitor for questionable activity that is coming in from the Internet.)

■ Firewalls can direct incoming traffic to more trustworthy internal systems.

▲ Firewalls have more strident authentication than other access methods.

Firewall Architectures

Firewalls can be configured in a number of different architectures. The choice of configuration will depend on the level of security required and existing network utilized.. Some architectures to consider include

▼ Multi-homed

■ Screened

▲ Screened subnet

Multi-homed

The *multi-homed* architecture (also called *dual-homed*) includes a firewall that is configured with more than one *NIC* (network interface card), with each card connecting to a separate network. This separation is both physical and logical. Typically, one network interface is connected to the internal network; the other is connected to the external network (the Internet). Routing is disabled so traffic is not exchanged between the two interfaces.

Screened

The *screened* firewall architecture uses a host (referred to as a *bastion host*) that all external traffic connects to through a router, instead of connecting directly to the internal network. A *bastion host* (sometimes called a *gateway host*) generally is the operating system platform on which the firewall software actually runs. A filtering router directs all traffic intended for the internal network to the bastion host before being sent to the protected network.

Screened Subnet

The *screened* subnet architecture is similar to a screened firewall architecture, with an added security layer that protects the internal network from the external network in case the bastion host is targeted for attack by hackers. The bastion host is within its own perimeter subnet, which prevents an attacker from doing any further damage to the network.

A filtering router is connected between the perimeter and the internal network; it contains rules for access that will either allow or deny traffic, based on permissions set by the firewall administrator. In the context of firewalls, this perimeter area is neither part of the internal network nor directly part of the Internet, and typically is called a Demilitarized Zone, as mentioned earlier in this chapter. The access router contains access control lists for routing of traffic to web services (for incoming connections to HTTP web servers, SMTP e-mail servers, FTP, DNS and so on), which should be located within a DMZ.

There are different kinds of firewalls, including

▼   Packet filtering

■   Application gateway

▲   Combination (complex or hybrid gateway)

Packet Filtering

As the name implies, packet filtering firewalls block traffic based on the source and destination of each data packet, or port, and use routers with packet filtering rules to either grant or deny access. There are tools available to help simplify filtering, maintaining rules, and intelligent logging. *IP spoofing* is when a hacker attempts to connect using an IP address for a known or legitimate host to gain access to a network; DNS can be spoofed in a similar fashion. Packet filtering gateway firewalls do not prevent spoofing. By basing authentication on source address and combining with other security methods, an organization can protect against spoofing attacks. *Source routing* is an uncommon method that involves a packet that includes route information being sent. The only purpose for using source routing should be internal network troubleshooting, or to handle rare situations of high traffic sent through distinct routes. On a firewall, source routing should be disabled, because a hacker could attempt to create reverse traffic by using the IP address of a system that is part of the network. Packet filtering also has been prone to hackers who use IP spoofing and sniffer methods that allow harmful packets through a router onto a network. Other common methods are *ICMP tunneling,* and *buffer overruns. Internet Control Message Protocol* (ICMP) tunneling refers to methods hackers use to add their data onto an ICMP packet. When it accesses the internal network, an external process could be launched.

Depending on the firewall vendor you use, you can set rules to track and block ICMP and to prevent hackers from sending false ICMP redirect packet messages, which may attempt to exploit the firewall's routing tables or to use as a Denial of Service attack. Buffer overruns can occur when buffer data file sizes are more than the amount that was allocated. The following is an example of an access list for a Cisco packet filtering router; some general comments are provided. Rules are applied in order and stop when a first match is found.

```
no ip source-route        //This will deny any source routing.
!
interface ethernet 0
ip address 192.34.32.8
no ip directed-broadcast  //Deny directed broadcasts.
    This is used by Smurf
                          //attacks, where mass packets are
    directed to
                          //specific IP addresses from
    different Internet
                          //destinations in order to make
    the IP addresses
                          //unavailable.
!
interface serial 0
no ip directed-broadcast
ip access-group 101 in    //If a data packet incoming
    claims to be from the
                          //local net, loopback network, or
    private network,
                          //deny. This will prevent a hacker
    from attempting to
                          //spoof as a legitimate host
    coming from within your
                          //network.!
access-list 101 permit tcp any 20 any gt 1024
//Connections incoming from port 20 into high port numbers
//are supposed to be FTP data connections.
```

Application Gateway

Application gateway firewalls typically are used for proxy servers, with no traffic allowed directly between the private network and the Internet. These firewalls can analyze packet contents, with sophisticated logging, robust user authentication, and auditing features, and are designed to hide servers and data from would-be hackers. The proxy analyzes a request and forwards it to an internal host that can satisfy the request. From the outside, the proxy is the only host address that is visible, with all the internal network connections going through the proxy.

Different services (FTP, SMTP, HTTP) use a different application gateway proxy server. They are not used in combination, but as separate services. The advantage of this is to prevent direct access to services on the internal network, which provides protection against insecure or misconfigured servers. However, you should consider the type of service, as the service might require a lot of processing and slow the performance of the firewall as a result.

Application gateway firewalls also can block ICMP packets, and allow the internal network that is behind the firewall to not be seen externally by ICMP packets over the Internet. Given these advantages, application gateway firewalls are considered among the most secure, and generally have a higher price tag (up to $100,000).

Hybrid Gateway

A hybrid gateway provides a combination of the enhanced features of application gateways and packet filtering firewalls that have already been discussed. When utilized in a series as a firewall solution, the connections are highly secure. Brimstone (http://www.soscorp.com) is an example of a hybrid gateway.

Firewall Administration

The firewall administrator should carefully document all firewall rules and procedures; this documentation should be kept in a secure place. The documentation should include a firewall plan, a full record of changes, additions to the firewalls, packet filtering rules, access lists, records of backups, application of patches, and updates. It also should include network diagrams (including IP addresses, subnets, routers, connectivity with Internet carriers), industry notes, and configuration details. Additionally, it should include details on installation, intrusion detection software, and backup diskettes of configuration files.

As shown in Figure 11-3, several firewall products include helpful built-in utilities such as a policy editor to provide a visual representation of policies and rules set for specific hosts and services on a network.

The actual logs for the firewall should be recorded on a daily, weekly, and monthly basis for tracking for possible attacks. This also should include logging of TCP network connect attempts, logins/logouts, system administrator access, inbound and outbound traffic (such as e-mail), connect times, and so on. If an attack occurs, the administrator should be contacted immediately by e-mail, pager, or other method to respond to the security alarm that is a feature with most firewalls. A backup firewall should be preconfigured and placed in secured storage in case it is needed as a replacement. The firewall also should be in a secured area, with limited direct access, and with changes made by encrypted passwords.

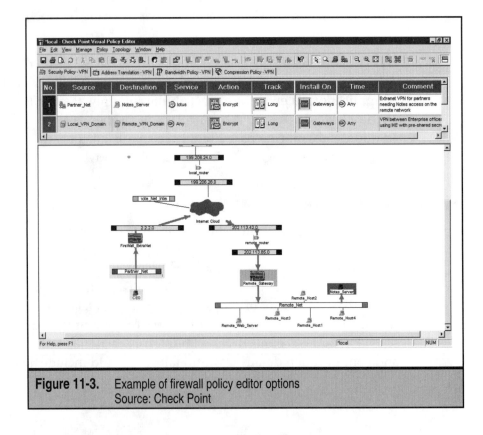

Figure 11-3. Example of firewall policy editor options
Source: Check Point

A firewall administrator must be fully aware of which ports to block for which web servers that provide different web services (SMTP, HTTP, FTP) to ensure that a hacker has no opportunity to come in. For basic web service only (just HTTP), the administrator should limit traffic to only port 80 for that particular web server. This will prevent most DoS-type attacks, although hostile data—say a virus written in Visual Basic—could still get through. A firewall administrator also typically will need to deny all TCP-based connections coming in, including ICMP, in order to further prevent hackers from attempting an intrusion or to scan your network. A firewall and security administrator must be fully educated on all the latest patches and news by subscribing to key security mailing lists and services on an ongoing basis. Some of these are highlighted at the end of this chapter.

Within TCP/IP, ports serve either to listen on reserved ports (from 0 to 1023) for connection requests, or dynamically to open ports for sending data between hosts. The range of ports available for different services is rehe presented as numbers from 0 from 65535. Trange from 0 from 1023 is reserved and the range from 1024 to 65535 is dynamic. As an example, take a look at the ports used by Windows NT Server 4.0 in Table 11-1.

If this system would be used as a server, specific ports would need to be blocked from a security standpoint, depending on the purpose of the web services. To do this from the Windows NT web server, an administrator can go to the Control Panel ¦ Network ¦ Protocols ¦ TCP/IP ¦ Advanced ¦ Enable Security ¦ Configure window. Normally, all TCP ports should be disabled except for port 80 (which is for HTTP), port 6 (IP), and port 17 (UDP). In some cases, IP and UDP (if DNS is not used) also will be disabled.

If part of a DMZ, the filtering router also will need to be configured to block specific ports that can reach the server. As discussed in Chapter 12, there are numerous TCP/IP utilities that allow administrators to verify and track which ports are being used on different systems (because there are no absolutes when it comes to security).

A more sophisticated DMZ security strategy is to have several areas (sometimes referred to as *security zones*) that provide separate

NT 4.0 Service	Static Port Used
WINS replication	TCP: 42
DNS resolution	UDP: 53
DNS administration	TCP: 139
DHCP lease	UDP: 67, 68
WINS manager	TCP: 135
DHCP manager	TCP: 135
Browsing	UDP: 137, 138
Logon sequence	UDP: 137, 138; TCP: 139
Pass through validation	UDP: 137, 138; TCP: 139
WINS registration	TCP: 137
Trusts	UDP: 137, 138; TCP: 139
Printing	UDP: 137, 138 TCP: 139
WinNT secure channel	UDP: 137, 138; TCP: 139
Directory replication	UDP: 138; TCP:139
NetLogon	UDP: 138
Event viewer	TCP: 139
File sharing	TCP: 139
Performance monitor	TCP: 139
Registry Editor	TCP: 139
Server Manager	TCP: 139
User Manager	TCP: 139
WinNT diagnostics	TCP: 139
PPTP	TCP: 1723; IP Protocol: 47

Table 11-1.   List of Ports Used by Windows NT 4.0 Services
Source: Microsoft Knowledgebase Article Q150543

web services within a DMZ. Each zone would have services assigned to it with have similar levels of security requirements. Each zone also will be separated by subnet or on a completely different network, and can be configured to be unaware of the other. Although costly, this can further limit the impact of an intruder going any further than the front door of a particular zone.

Packet Filtering Tools

There are several packet filtering tools available that allow analysis of firewall traffic. These tools provide a greater control in traffic filtering, with elaborate logging available in most cases. These include the following:

▼ **Drawbridge**   ftp://net.tamu.edu/pub/security/TAMU/

■ **KarlBridge**   ftp://coast.cs.purdue.edu/pub/tools/dos/kbridge.zip

▲ **screend**   ftp://ftp.vix.com/pub/vixie/ or ftp://coast.cs.purdue.edu/pub/tools/unix/screend

Firewall Policies

As with a security plan, a firewall policy must be followed for it to be an effective preventive tool. Depending on the range of services which a web host provides, a firewall policy will vary by the same degree. Here are some general guidelines to address in formulating an initial outline:

▼ A firewall needs to be located in between a private network and the Internet to protect a network.

■ A DMZ should be deployed to further prevent unauthorized network intrusion, in combination with intrusion detection software.

■ All traffic must pass through the firewall.

■ Source routing will be disabled on all firewalls and any external routers.

■ A firewall will be configured to deny all but minimum services, with the log tracked and monitored.

■ A firewall will be configured to deny any incoming traffic that appears to be coming from internal network addresses (possible IP spoofing).

■ The host used for the firewall (whether it is a system, network appliance, or other device) will be dedicated to firewall services only.

▲ Detailed logging of traffic will be done at all times, with backups made on a daily basis, and stored securely offsite. In case of intrusion, a firewall administrator and backup administrator will be notified immediately by e-mail, pager, or other method.

By providing guidelines for enhancing the security of a web host, a firewall policy provides a structured framework, which should enhance a security plan and enable network management and security personnel to handle issues before they arise.

Sample Firewall Policy

A firewall policy should identify and enforce the configurations that are established on the firewall. A sample firewall policy is outlined here which lists some specific subject areas to focus on. When designing a workable firewall policy, refer to this sample as a guide.

1. Background and objectives
2. Authentication process
3. Routing compared to forwarding

    A. Source routing
    B. IP spoofing

4. Types of Firewalls

    A. Packet filtering gateways
    B. Application gateways
    C. Hybrid or complex gateways
    D. Rating

5. Firewall Architectures

   A. Multi-homed host
   B. Screened host
   C. Screened subnet

6. Intranet
7. Firewall Administration

   A. Qualifications of the firewall/security administrator
   B. Remote administration of firewall
   C. Managing user accounts
   D. Firewall backups
   E. Network trust relationships
   F. Virtual private networks (VPN)
   G. DNS resolution
   H. E-mail resolution
   I. Integrity of System
   J. Documentation
   K. Physical security of firewall
   L. Handling security incidents
   M. Restoring services
   N. Applying patches and upgrades
   O. Revision/update of firewall policy
   P. Firewall logs and audit trails
   Q. Policy examples
   R. Service-specific policy examples
   S. Manager
   T. Technical
   U. Continuing education of personnel (training, security tracking, industry seminars)

Security Resources

A firewall and security administrator must be fully educated on all the latest patches and industry news by subscribing to key security mailing lists and services on an ongoing basis. Some online resources include

- ▼ **SANS Institute (System Administration, Networking and Security)** http://www.sans.org/topten.htm
- ■ **SecurityFocus** http://www.securityfocus.com/
- ■ **Info Security magazine** http://www.infosecuritymag.com/
- ■ **The Virus Lists** LISTSERV@lehigh.edu (use "subscribe The Virus List" in the body of the message.)
- ■ **Bugtraq Full Disclosure Mailing List** listserv@netspace.org (use :"subscribe" Bugtraq" in the body of the message.)
- ■ **NT Security Issues Mailing List** majordomo@iss.net (use "subscribe NT Security Issues" in the body of the message.)
- ▲ **Linux Security Mailing List** linux-security-request@Redhat.com (use "subscribe Linux Security" in the body of the message.)

Firewall Software

There are numerous firewall packages that are available that can provide enhanced security for your network. Some of these include the following:

- ▼ **Interware** http://www.consensys.com/
- ■ **Microsoft Internet Security and Acceleration (ISA) 2000 Server** http://www.microsoft.com/proxy/ default.asp
- ■ **Firewall-1** http://www.checkpoint.com/
- ▲ **Brimstone** http://www.soscorp.com/

Intrusion Detection Software

There are several intrusion detection packages that can examine log files for suspicious activity, including the following:

▼ **Tripwire** http://www.tripwiresecurity.com/

■ **Nuke Nabber** http://www.dynamsol.com/puppet/nukenabber.html

■ **Snort** http://www.snort.org/

▲ **Nmap** http://www.nmap.org/

Incident Response Centers

The following organizations can be used to report an attack or to find out more about specific vulnerabilities:

▼ **CERT (Computer Emergency Response Team)**
http://www.cert.org/

■ **CIAC (Computer Incident Advisory Capability)**
http://ciac.llnl.gov/ciac/

■ **FIRST (Forum of Incident Response and Security Teams)**
http://first.org/

▲ **FBI (Federal Bureau of Investigation)**
http://www.fbi.gov/

ANTI-VIRUS AND TROJAN PROTECTION

You should install network anti-virus software to protect against viruses on the network sent either by e-mail, FTP, or a variety of different methods. Some vendors include these:

▼ **McAfee Total Virus Defense** http://www.mcafee.com/

■ **Dr. Solomon's Anti-Virus Toolkit**
http://www.drsolomon.com

■ **InterScan VirusWall** http://www.trendmicro.com/

▲ **InoculateIT** http://www.cheyenne.com/

Many anti-virus packages do not account for Trojans. Trojans are designed to do all types of harm to systems, including deletion of data and file corruption. There are a few packages that focus especially on detection of Trojans. One product of note is TDS-3 from DiamondCS, an Australian software company (http://www.diamondcs.com.au/). It also includes a global messaging service that can contact you if a Trojan is encountered.

Some of the more common Trojans that have caused damage to systems include the following:

▼ **NETBUS**   This Trojan, which goes by many names, usually will probe on TCP port 12345. Monitoring of TCP port 12345, 12346, and 20034 is advised.

■ **SUBSEVEN**   Monitoring of TCP port 1243 is advised.

■ **BACK ORIFICE 1.x**   Monitoring of UDP port 31337 is advised.

■ **BACK ORIFICE 2000**   Can use any port, highly advanced.

▲ **IRC THREATS**   Monitoring of TCP port 12345, 1243, and UDP port 31337.

SUMMARY

This chapter stresses the importance of developing and implementing a security plan based on infrastructure requirements, and supported by preventive security measures. As has been proven numerous times, a firewall is not enough to prevent unauthorized access into your network. Web hosts need to consider a wide range of security issues when protecting the external and internal components of their business. A security plan will help you focus on the areas that are most at risk within your network and to plan accordingly. The major components of a security policy were discussed, with an example policy provided. As noted, a security plan must be specific to the company in order to be the most effective. The architectures and types of firewalls were also highlighted. Continuing education is a necessity of security support personnel, as the landscape constantly changes. A web host will never be fully secure, but through an ongoing program of monitoring, analysis, and detection, the reliability and security of a network will be greatly enhanced.

CHAPTER 12

Using Network Monitoring Tools

As was noted in the previous chapter, numerous TCP/IP utilities can assist administrators in verifying and tracking connectivity. These utilities also can provide troubleshooting for connectivity problems, whether locally, remotely, or through a router. As an Internet standard, the TCP/IP protocol is defined by the IETF (Internet Engineering Task Force) in published *RFCs* (Request for Comments), which detail the network services, protocols, implementations, and utilities that comprise the Internet.

Depending on TCP/IP implementation used, it provides other basic network services such as DNS (Domain Name Server) and DHCP (Dynamic Host Configuration Protocol). This chapter presents an introduction to the main TCP/IP utilities available within many Windows and Unix environments. Keep in mind that the commands used with these utilities will vary depending on the operating environment used. Many of the utilities listed here apply only to a Windows environment. Both Windows and Unix platforms have utilities that are unique to their respective environments; some of these also will be noted. We will review third-party software solutions in Chapter 15.

TCP/IP UTILITIES

Each TCP/IP utility provides a clue to where connection problems might be occurring when resolving an IP address to a physical address and packet routing to an intended location. Has a connection problem appeared suddenly? This might indicate that either a router or system change has occurred. This is especially true if systems were connecting properly before the error occurred.

As outlined in Chapter 10, the most common reason for unscheduled server downtime is operator or procedural error. Procedures need to be well established before changes are made to a server or router, as the change might have an effect on a remote host. Are internal network changes recorded? As part of these procedures, you should keep technical notes to record all internal changes to systems on your network. This can provide appropriate tracking to help troubleshoot a connectivity problem. These records also can serve as a technical reference and a training tool for new employees.

Documentation should include basic network information on routers, hubs, default gateways, and subnet masks, and should be shared within a technical departmental database. Another advantage to documentation is ensuring that IP addresses assigned are unique and that none are using the same address (one method to assist with tracking is with the arp [address resolution protocol] command). As will be discussed here in much greater detail later in this chapter, *arp* is a TCP/IP utility for listing of network card addresses, which correspond with IP addresses that are sensed on a network

External problems also can arise, such as an Internet carrier becoming unavailable because of a line cut. In this case, hopefully a web host provides its customers with true redundancy through more than one Internet carrier. If there are connectivity problems that prevent connection to a remote system, the TCP/IP utilities will list errors or will not connect at all.

The following table lists the most common TCP/IP utilities for running diagnostics from the command line (the DOS prompt in Windows). The Unix versions of the commands are very similar.

TCP/IP Diagnostic Utilities	Purpose
arp	Each network card has a unique MAC (Media Access Control) address, which arp identifies on a network after advertising the IP address. This utility will display the arp entries for a system when used with a command line option (such as arp -a, which displays existing arp entries in the cache including the Internet address, physical address type, and dynamic or static address entries).
ipconfig (ifconfig in Unix)	Displays the existing TCP/IP configuration for a system.
hostname	Specifies the host name of a system.

TCP/IP Diagnostic Utilities	Purpose
nbtstat (dig in Unix)	Displays TCP/IP protocol statistics, which include existing network connections through NetBIOS.
netstat	Displays TCP/IP protocol statistics, including addresses, listening ports, Ethernet connections, the routing table, and current network connections.
ping	Confirms connections and sends packets through ICMP (Internet Control Message Protocol) echo requests.
tracert (traceroute in Unix)	Displays detail of hops to confirm route to a remote host. Often used in conjunction with ping.

Each of these executable utilities is described in further detail in this chapter, along with examples showing the most commonly used syntax options. Depending on the host, the operating system used, and the version, TCP/IP command options used might vary. The main TCP/IP utilities available for both Windows and Unix platforms will be discussed next.

Arp

From the command line, the arp utility can display address resolution table entries with associated MAC (Media Access Control) network card addresses, which in turn correspond to the current IP addresses on a network. Sometimes these entries are referred to as the arp cache table. Arp gets this information by broadcasting a request for the MAC address that corresponds with an IP address; this mapping then resides in a cache. When an arp broadcast is made, the results (called an arp reply) are listed in a table, which includes the MAC address of the node communicating on a network, with an associated IP address. This table is cached in memory for a certain time period. If an entry that has been added dynamically is not used within two minutes, it is deleted from the cache. If the destination is remote, the IP address will be resolved through a router into a MAC address.

The syntax for the arp command is as follows:

arp -a [*inet_addr*] [-N [*if_addr*]]
arp -d *inet_addr* [*if_addr*]
arp -s *inet_addr ether_addr* [*if_addr*]

The options for the arp command are listed in the following table:

arp Option	Description
-a arp -a arp -a [inet_addr] [-N if_addr]	Shows existing arp entries in the cache, which include the Internet address and physical address type, and lists each entry as dynamic (unless a static entry has been entered for an address). If inet_addr is specified, the IP address and the corresponding MAC addresses for only the target computer are listed. When more than one NIC card is used, arp tables are listed for each.
-g	Same as -a.
inet_addr	Specifies an Internet address.
-N if_addr arp -N <IP address> arp -N 170.23.1.62	Lists the arp table for the address specified by if_addr.
-s arp -s <MAC address> arp -s 90.0.0.2 00-00-8f-48-24-87	Adds a new static cache entry for an eth_addr. A MAC address is represented in hexadecimal format (as bytes divided by hyphens) and linked to the Internet address (inet_addr).
-d arp -d <IP address> arp -d 170.23.1.62	Deletes the host denoted by inet_addr.

arp Option	Description
if_addr	When present, this denotes the inet_addr of the interface address whose arp table should be modified. If it does not exist, the first applicable interface is used.
eth_addr	Specifies a physical address.

As packets are received, replies might be incorrect, which can cause packets to be sent to incorrect destinations or nowhere at all. When the same IP address is used on more than one host machine, this can cause mysterious problems to occur, again causing packets to be sent to the wrong system or not at all; arp can help to track for this. Some organizations address this potential problem by tracking and recording all static IP addresses with their corresponding MAC addresses, which are part of their network. This then can be referenced when problems occur. The first three bytes of a MAC address indicate the type of NIC card manufacturer, as assigned by the IEEE. Static IP addresses normally should be assigned only to servers and routers; not peripheral devices such as workstations (which should have their IP address assigned dynamically through DHCP).

When multiple machines have the same IP address on a Microsoft Windows NT or 2000 host, an error such as the following will be listed in the System Event Log:

```
Event ID   : 4198 or 4199
   Source    : TCP/IP
   Description: The system detected an address conflict for IP address
      xxx.xxx.xxx.xxx with the system having hardware address
      (the MAC address)
      xx:xx:xx:xx:xx:xx the local interface is being disabled.
```

Besides using other TCP/IP utilities with arp, other methods for troubleshooting include capturing traffic statistics (through log files and through monitoring tools such as Network Monitor or the Event Viewer with Microsoft Windows NT and 2000), or using third-party monitoring products, which will be discussed in the "Microsoft Windows NT and 2000 Utilities" section here in the chapter.

Ipconfig

Ipconfig (Internet Protocol Configuration) for Windows can be used in conjunction with arp to help identify the MAC address for a system. Unix provides a similar utility, ifconfig. Both utilities allow detection of incorrect address settings and display how the interface is configured. This utility is commonly used when there are suspected configuration problems with a host or hosts. Winipcfg, a Windows utility, provides similar ipconfig information in a graphical format on Windows 95, 98, and ME systems. Ipconfig provides information about the existing TCP/IP configuration for a host, which might include details such as the following:

▼ Host name

■ Primary DNS suffix

■ Node type (usually broadcast)

■ NetBIOS scope ID

■ IP routing enabled (yes or no)

■ WINS proxy enabled (yes or no)

■ DNS suffix search list

▲ NetBIOS resolution uses DNS (yes or no)

Ipconfig also provides details for other connected Ethernet adapters within a LAN, including

▼ Connection-specific DNS suffix

■ Description of adapter

■ Physical address

■ DHCP enabled (yes or no)

■ IP address

■ Subnet mask

■ Default IP gateway

■ DHCP server IP address

- DNS server IP addresses

- Primary WINS server IP address

- Secondary WINS server IP address

- Time lease obtained (such as Monday, May 08, 2001 4:53:32 PM)

▲ Time lease expires (such as Wednesday, May 10, 2001 4:53:32 PM)

The following is the syntax for the ipconfig utility:

ipconfig [/all | /renew [adapter] | /release [adapter]]

The following table lists the available options for this utility.

ipconfig Option	Description
/all	Displays detailed IP configuration info
/Batch [file]	Writes to a file; for example, ipconfig /All /Batch c:/temp/ipconfig.txt
/renew N	Renews the host adapter setting
/renew_all	Renews all adapter settings
/release N	Releases the host adapter setting
/release_all	Releases all adapter setting

Microsoft Windows 2000 also includes additional options for ipconfig, which are listed in the following table.

ipconfig Option	Description
/registerdns	Refreshs leases for DHCP; reregisters DNS names
/displaydns	Displays the cache listing for DNS
/flushdns	Removes all entries from DNS name cache
/showclassid <adapter>	Displays all the DHCP class IDs that are allowed for the specified adapter
/setclassid <adapter> <classID to set>	Modifies the DHCP class ID for the specified adapter
/?	Displays the list of options available

The ifconfig utility for Unix has the following syntax:

ifconfig [-a | [*interface* [[alias | -alias] *address*] [up | down]
[netmask *mask*] [broadcast *address*][mtusize *size*] [mediatype { tp |
tp-fd | 100tx | 100tx-fd | 1000fx | auto }] [flowcontrol { none |
receive | send | full }] [trusted | untrusted][wins | -wins]
[[partner { *address* | *interface* }] | [-*partner*]]]]

The options for ifconfig are listed in the following table.

ifconfig Option	Description
-a	Shows all the configuration information, including IP address, netmask, and broadcast address for each interface on the host
alias	Allows creation of an alias name
-alias	Removes any aliases
arp	Enables arp mapping
-arp	Disables arp mapping
debug	Enables detailed error messages
up	Denotes interface as being up
down	Denotes interface as being down
netmask	Specifies the subnet mask
-p	Establishes a link via interface to TCP/IP

hostname

The hostname utility simply specifies the host name of a system on which it is running; no options are available with the utility. If the hostname is not known, you can also display it from a Windows host machine by running ipconfig at a command prompt (or winipcfg.exe if Windows 9x).

nbtstat

Nbtstat (short for NetBIOS test status) lists details about existing TCP/IP connections through NetBIOS and associated IP addresses on Windows-based systems (Unix does not have an equivalent utility). It also can update the NetBIOS name cache, and resolve scope ID and registered names. Scope ID enables NetBIOS systems to communicate with each other using a character string that is added on to the end of the NetBIOS name.

Nbtstat will provide information about existing NetBIOS connections through TCP/IP for a host, which might include details such as the following:

▼ Bytes received (Represented as In).

■ Bytes sent (Represented as Out).

■ Connection type (Inbound or Outbound).

■ Time to live of name table cache entry.

■ NetBIOS Name (local and remote).

■ IP Address (remote).

▲ Unique NetBIOS End Identifiers (For example, <24> denotes a Microsoft Exchange Directory.)

NOTE: Refer to http://support.microsoft.com/support/kb/articles/ Q163/4/09.ASP for a full listing of the 34 different suffixes that can be used as unique hexadecimal end identifiers for a NetBIOS connection.

The connection's State also is identified. State describes the existing nature of a connection. An IP address and a corresponding TCP port number identify each connection endpoint within in a finite timeframe. The following are options used to describe State:

▼ **Connected**   The session is active.

■ **Associated**   The connection endpoint has been created and now is associated with an IP address.

■ **Listening**   The endpoint is available for an inbound connection.

■ **Idle**   The connection endpoint is open but is not enabled to receive connections.

- **Connecting**   The name-to-IP address is being resolved in the connection stage.

- **Accepting**   An inbound connection session is in the process of being accepted and will be connected shortly.

- **Reconnecting**   A connection session is attempting to reconnect after failing the first time.

- **Outbound**   A TCP connection is being created for a session.

- **Inbound**   A session that is inbound is currently connecting.

- **Disconnecting**   A connection session is in the process of disconnecting.

- ▲ **Disconnected**   The local host has issued a disconnect state and is waiting for the remote host to confirm.

The following is the syntax for the nbtstat utility:

nbtstat [-a *remotename*] [-A *IPaddress*] [-c] [-n] [-R] [-r] [-S] [-s] [*interval*]

The following table lists the options available with this utility.

nbtstat Option	Description
-a nbtstat [-a RemoteName]	Shows a remote computer's name table when given its host name
-A nbtstat [-A IP address]	Show a remote computer's name table when given its IP address
-c	List the remote name cache, which includes the IP addresses
-n	Lists local NetBIOS names
-r	Provides names that are resolved by broadcast and through WINS
-R	Purges and reloads the remote cache name table
-S	Provides a list of the sessions table with the destination IP addresses
-s	Lists sessions table, converting to host names from the IP address via a hosts file

The following is an example of using nbtstat -n. This will display NetBIOS connected systems:

```
NetBIOS Local Name Table
Name Type Status
----------------------
Registered Registered Registered Registered
CAESAR01 <00> UNIQUE
ROMEO <00> GROUP
CAESAR01 <03> UNIQUE
PLATO <03> UNIQUE
```

netstat

Nnetstat (short for Network Statistics) is another method to list information on existing TCP/IP connections over a network, including protocol statistics, addresses, listening ports, Ethernet connections, and the routing table. It also can help troubleshoot problems with route tables, Ethernet connectivity, or a particular system. For example, the following command displays Ethernet statistics for a host:

```
C:\WINDOWS>netstat -e
Interface Statistics

                      Received            Sent
Bytes                 17718860         7656081
Unicast packets          44605           41571
Non-unicast packets       1058            1146
Discards                     0               0
Errors                       0               0
Unknown protocols         7611
```

If there are a large number of send and receive packet errors, you might have a network problem. Run a ping (described in the next section) on the system; then run netstat -e again. Try the command on different systems, and compare the send and receive packet errors. If errors are displayed on other systems on the network, this indicates a network problem, and not just a problem with one system.

Another useful option is the netstat -r option, which lists the routing table. This will display routes with various statistics. For active IP routes, the following data is listed:

▼ Network address

■ Netmask

■ Gateway address

■ Interface

▲ Metric

For active connections, the following data is listed:

▼ Proto (listed as TCP or UDP)

■ Local address (by host address and port #)

■ Foreign address (open connections address and port #)

▲ State (established or time-wait)

The syntax for the netstat command is as follows:

netstat [-a] [-e][-n][-s] [-p *protocol*] [-r] [*interval*]

The options for netstat are listed in the following table.

netstat Option	Description
-a	Show all connections and ports that are listening.
-e	Lists Ethernet statistics. Can be used with the -s option.
-n	Lists addresses and port numbers in numerical format.
-p proto	Displays connections for the specified protocol, either TCP or UDP. When used with the -s option, the protocol can be TCP, UDP, or IP.
-r	Lists the route table.
-s	Shows protocol information by TCP, UDP, and IP. When used with the -p option, it may be used to specify the default subset.

ping

The ping (packet Internet groper) utility is useful for verifying host connectivity, both local and remote. If the network is operating correctly, a ping that is sent to a remote host will receive a return echo packet that lists basic response data. For troubleshooting, ping can indicate whether a particular host is down, the pings are lost, or there is a large amount of traffic that is preventing normal responsiveness in connectivity.

For example, you would perform a ping on Yahoo! by typing the following at a command prompt:

```
ping www.yahoo.com
```

If you already know the IP address you are trying to reach, you can ping the address directly. In the case of yahoo.com, that would be ping 216.115.105.2. The following results will be displayed on a Windows system, depending on the speed of your connection:

```
C:\WINDOWS>ping www.yahoo.com
Pinging www.yahoo.akadns.net [216.115.105.2] with 32 bytes of data:
Reply from 216.115.105.2: bytes=32 time=88ms TTL=242
Reply from 216.115.105.2: bytes=32 time=76ms TTL=242
Reply from 216.115.105.2: bytes=32 time=93ms TTL=242
Reply from 216.115.105.2: bytes=32 time=89ms TTL=242
```

For a Solaris system, the response will be similar to www.yahoo.com is alive.

If the local host is not connected, the following message will appear on a Windows-based system (and many Unix systems):

```
Unknown host www.yahoo.com or Request timed out
```

Of course, this might indicate that there is some type of problem with TCP/IP connectivity or settings on the local host. To check for this, the first step is to do a ping on the local host using the standard IP loopback address (which will not access the network card) from a command prompt:

```
ping 127.0.0.1
```

If the local host is working properly, the following message will appear on a Windows-based system:

```
C:\WINDOWS>ping 127.0.0.1
Pinging 127.0.0.0 with 32 bytes of data:
Reply from 127.0.0.1: bytes=32 time<10ms TTL=128
Reply from 127.0.0.1: bytes=32 time<10ms TTL=128
Reply from 127.0.0.1: bytes=32 time<10ms TTL=128
Reply from 127.0.0.1: bytes=32 time<10ms TTL=128
Ping statistics for 127.0.0.1:
    Packets: Sent = 4, Received = 4, Lost = 0 (0% loss),
Approximate round trip times in milli-seconds:
    Minimum = 0ms, Maximum =  0ms, Average =  0ms
```

After pinging the loopback address, ping the IP address of the local host. If the local host responds to the ping, ping another host on the same subnet of the network. If that host responds to the ping, ping the default gateway. Once this is confirmed, ping a remote host on another subnet and then one on the Internet. Also keep in mind that a remote router or firewall might have ping disabled for security reasons and you will need to use other utilities to determine what is wrong.

You can change the size and number of packets ping sends to get more specific data from your tests. You also can compare responses from other hosts on the local network to find out how long it takes in milliseconds to reach another device on the network or the Internet.

The syntax for the ping command is as follows:

ping [-t] [-a] [-n *count*] [-l *length*] [-f] [-i *ttl*] [-v *tos*] [-r *count*]
[-s *count*] [[-j *host-list*] | [-k *host-list*]] [-w *timeout*] *destination-list*

The following table lists the options available with ping on Windows systems. Many other options are available for the Unix version of ping.

ping Option	Description
-a	Resolves addresses to host names
-f	Designates the Don't Fragment flag within packet
-i TTL	Designates time-to-live

ping Option	Description
-j host-list	Uses a loose source route along host-list
-k host-list	Uses a strict source route along host-list
-l size	Sends the buffer size
-n count	Specifies the number of echo requests to send
-r count	Records the route for count hops
-s count	Records the time stamp for count hops
-t	Pings a specific host until interrupted
-v TOS	Designates the type of service
w timeout	Specifies the time-out wait in milliseconds for each reply

tracert

The Windows tracert utility (the equivalent utility in Unix is traceroute) is used to verify that a particular destination route is reachable, and to display the route from the local host to the remote host. The utility also can ascertain the connection speed of individual routes, and displays the amount of time that each hop (route) takes. Depending on the TCP/IP implementation used, an ICMP (Internet Control Message Protocol) packet will be sent with a default time limit to the first router that will tell the tracert utility to increase each time. The utility sends the next packet to the next router, with a higher time limit. This process is repeated until the route reaches the requested destination.

The results show how long each hop took to reach the remote host. In some cases, with particular firewalls, the utility will not provide a full listing. Tracert, along with ping, often is one of the first utilities to use to trace where a connection problem is occurring.

The syntax for tracert is as follows:

tracert [-d] [-h maximum_hops] [-j host-list] [-w timeout] target_name

The options available for use with tracert are shown in the following table.

tracert Option	Description
-d	Specifies not to resolve addresses to host names
-h *maximum_hops*	Specifies the greatest number of hops to search for a target host
-j *host-list*	Designates the loose source route along host-list
-w *timeout*	Designates the timeout period, in milliseconds, for each reply

The tracert utility verifies the route used from the local host to a remote host. For the following example, the trace will display the route taken from the origin through routers to the destination (11.110.10.0).

```
C:\Windows>tracert 11.110.10.0
   Tracing route to 11.110.10.0 over a maximum of 30 hops


1      2 ms      3 ms      2 ms   159.16.32.7
2     75 ms     83 ms     88 ms   11.110.10.43
3     73 ms     79 ms     93 ms   11.110.10.0


Trace complete.
```

If a particular destination can't be reached, the following message is displayed:

```
Destination host unreachable (if there are problems with the TCP/IP
connection)
```

or

```
* * * Request timed out
```

This can indicate problems with a particular router, or indicate a high degree of traffic congestion (especially if packet loss is high).

The Unix traceroute utility is similar to ping because both can determine the time it takes a packet to travel from one destination to another, and check into the round-trip time in milliseconds for each hop made along the route. The syntax for traceroute is as follows:

traceroute [*ip address, hostname*]

The options for traceroute are listed in the following table.

traceroute Option	Description
-m *max_ttl*	Specifies the maximum number of hops for packets, with the default being 30.
-n	Displays hop addresses numerically instead of symbolically and numerically.
-p *port*	Assigns the base port number to be used for probes. This UDP number typically is 33434.
-q *nqueries*	Specifies the number of probes per time to live, with the default being 3.
-r	Specifies a local host instead of remote host.
-s *src_addr*	Requires that the source address in outgoing packet probes must be the IP address.
-t *tos*	Specifies the type of service that will be used for probe packets, with the default being 0.
-v	Lists detail statistics.
-w *timeout*	Designates the timeout period, in milliseconds, for each reply.

nslookup

Nslookup is a TCP/IP command line utility that enables you to make detailed queries to DNS servers to verify records, host aliases, services, or operating system information.

NOTE: For Unix, nslookup is available with BIND (Berkeley Internet Name Domain), which provides elaborate DNS security features. More information is available from http://www.isc.org/.

nslookup also is available for the Windows environments. A simple nslookup query of Yahoo.com would look like this:

```
Name: yahoo.com
Addresses: 216.115.108.245, 216.115.108.243
```

The results of nslookup queries can help to correct confirmation of zone resource records for a domain, or for resolving domain names. You can use nslookup either from the command line or in interactive mode. Interactive mode makes an ongoing query to designated servers, and displays the results. Use fully qualified domain names with nslookup (for example, doing an nslookup on www.yahoo.com would display 216.115.105.2 as the result).

The syntax for nslookup is as follows:

nslookup [-*option U*] [*hostname* | - [*server*]]

The options for nslookup are listed in Table 12-1.

nslookup Option	Description
-exit	Exits the utility.
-finger	Provides connection with the finger server on the existing host.
-help or -?	Provides a listing of nslookup commands.
-ls [*Option*] *DOMAIN*	Displays information on a given DNS domain, with IP addresses and host names.
-lserver *NAME*	Sets the default server to another DNS domain name, using the initial server.
-root	Updates the current default server to the root server.
-server *NAME*	Updates the current default server to the specified DNS domain.
-set	Updates settings, which changes the behavior of the nslookup commands.
-set all	Prints current server, host, and option values.
-set class=	Modifies a class query.
-set [no]d2 or -set [no]debug	Prints extensive debugging information, or just minimal information.

Table 12-1. nslookup Command Options

nslookup Option	Description
-set [no]*defname*	Each query will have the domain name appended to it.
-set domain=*NAME*	Changes the default DNS domain to a name that is specified.
-set querytype=	Updates the query type to A, ANY, CNAME, MX, NS, PTR, or SOA.
-set [no]recurse	Instructs the DNS name server to query other servers for data.
-set retry=*X*	Specifies the number of retries.
-set root=*NAME*	Changes the name of the root server to a name specified.
-set [no]search	Uses the DNS domain search list.
-set srchlist=N1 [/N2/.../N6]	Changes the default DNS domain name to N1, and the search list.
-set timeout=*X*	Sets the timeout period to a specified number of seconds before reply.
-set type=*X*	Synonym for querytype.
-set [no]vc	Specifies to use a virtual circuit.
-U	Used to specify one or more commands.
-view	Sorts an ls file for viewing.

Table 12-1.   nslookup Command Options *(continued)*

When nslookup cannot complete a lookup request, one of the following errors is displayed:

▼ *No Response from Server*   The requested name server is not running on the server.

■ *No Records*   The server does not have the query resource records for the host, even if the host name is valid.

■ *Non-Existent Domain*   The domain name or host does not exist.

- *Connection Refused*   The connection to the name or finger server could not be completed when the request was made.

- *Timed Out*   The server did not respond to the request made, even after a number of attempts.

- *Network Is Unreachable*   The connection to the name or finger server could not be reached when the request was made.

- *Refused*   The name server refused to handle the request.

- *Format Error*   The name server refused a request packet because it was not in the proper format.

- *Server Failure*   The name server experienced an internal error and could not respond to a request.

NOTE: There also is a utility named dig (domain internet grouper), which is included with many Unix implementations. Dig provides functions similar to nslookup, but is more detailed in its results.

Additional Utilities

Many other utilities are available for both the Unix and Windows environments that provide more detailed network connectivity information. The Unix environment provides additional utilities, which will vary, depending on the Unix implementation.

Two Unix utilities of note that are especially useful, include the following:

- **snoop**   This utility is an analyzer that allows each packet header and information sent from local to remote hosts to be tracked. A similar tool is tcpdump, available from http://www.tcpdump.org/.

- **ripquery**   This utility, which runs on RIP (Routing Information Protocol)-enabled hosts, tracks packets that are sent or received.

Windows 2000 includes additional TCP/IP tools for monitoring and connectivity:

▼ **netdiag**   This utility is quite useful because it verifies network connectivity through a series of tests that diagnose where a connectivity problem is occurring. It can be installed from the Windows 2000 CD.

■ **pathping**   This utility tracks packet losses from each remote router that is along a connection path from the local to remote host.

▲ **route**   This utility enables you to list, modify, or delete the local routing table, which contains IP information on the default route, host, subnet, and network.

MICROSOFT WINDOWS NT AND 2000 UTILITIES

Windows NT and 2000 include several server-based utilities that are useful for managing and diagnosing where potential problems may be occurring. For network administrators, these utilities (which include the Event Log, Performance Monitor, Network Monitor, and System Monitor) allow for monitoring of a server and network traffic. When used in combination with the TCP/IP utilities already discussed in this chapter, the source of server and network traffic problems can be more clearly identified. These server-based utilities include the following:

▼ **Event Log (located in Event Viewer)**   Used to track events and errors occurring relative to the system

■ **Performance Monitor**   Used to detect where bottlenecks or network congestion may be occurring, and to gauge network performance

■ **Network Monitor**   Allows TCP/IP monitoring of incoming and outgoing traffic for review

▲ **System Monitor (Windows 2000 only)**   Analysis of TCP/IP network performance and traffic

Event Log

The Event Log can be used to track events and errors. All critical messages related to the system are stored in the System Event Log. Event messages can indicate where problems lie before they become performance issues. Three types of log files can be viewed from within Event Viewer: System, Security, and Application. If a host is not performing optimally, view the System Event Log. Security Log can track audited events, which are categorized by success or failure. The Application Log tracks native Windows applications.

If there is a duplicate IP address, it should show up in the Event Log. This will be described in the Event Detail section with an error such as this:

```
The system detected an address conflict for IP address 192.168.101.12
with the system having network hardware address 00:D0:2H:E2:CC:DG:3H.
Network operations on this system may be disrupted as a result."
```

If this occurs, run the ipconfig command utility; then go to Network in the Control Panel and select TCP/IP properties to verify the IP address. Go back and run ipconfig again to verify the IP address that is listed.

Performance Monitor

Performance Monitor counters also can be used to measure statistics for TCP/IP and other protocols, running over a selected period of time. You must install *SNMP* (Simple Network Management Protocol) on hosts you want to monitor this way. SNMP is a management protocol that enables tracking and troubleshooting of a network in detail. SNMP provides tools that enable you to capture MIB (Management Information Base) information from devices that support SNMP agents. It also initiates an alert when default parameters are exceeded. Extensions called *RMON* (*Remote MONitoring*) are available to extend SNMP. RMON is more interactive in providing network monitoring, with tracking that can be gauged for applications and particular types of errors.

An administrator will need to establish what the baseline will be to compare against for monitoring performance. You then can set

Performance Monitor to generate alerts when conditions go above or below certain levels.

Network Monitor

Network Monitor is used to track network traffic that a host either generates or receives. The utility uses display and capture filters, which can trigger certain preset actions to take place automatically (such as security or antivirus measures, or sending an e-mail to notify an administrator). Network Monitor places a network card on a capturing host into *promiscuous mode,* which enables every frame on the network to pass through the monitoring tool. Filtering parameters can be based on different patterns, including source address, destination network relative to the source, and destination protocol addresses.

The SMS (Systems Management Server) provides additional functions to Network Monitor, which allows for packets, protocols, and ports to be closely tracked, either on a local host or on remote hosts. It is a management tool for configuring networks with many workstations. You can make modifications to packets, and individual users can be gauged. Some of the functions that can be monitored include the following:

▼ Objects

■ Processor

■ PhysicalDisk

■ Process

■ System

▲ Thread

System Monitor

System Monitor, available only in Windows 2000, allows for the viewing of detailed log and data files in real-time. Accessed from the Performance Console of Windows 2000, System Monitor provides detailed analysis of how a network is performing, along with Internet Information Server, to gauge how bandwidth is being used, and to manage the load on individual hosts in order to ensure the best performance. Services such as Active Directory™ and DNS can be tracked for a specified period of time, which can be used to gauge how a server is responding. Keep in mind, though, that running System Monitor on a connected system can take up a significant portion of a system's resources, so use sparingly for testing purposes.

TROUBLESHOOTING TIPS

Although the utilities mentioned in this chapter can provide a lot of data to help you track down a network problem, they shouldn't be your only troubleshooting tools. Don't overlook other possibilities, such as potential physical problems including:

▼ **Faulty cabling or loose wiring** Check the back of the host, and the cables that lead to a router or other devices (depending on infrastructure).

■ **Faulty hardware (port, network card, operating system, or system failure)** Many network cards have indicator link lights on the back of the board to display whether or not there is a valid connection (indicated by green, yellow, or red). If the card is not responding, the host might require rebooting or you might need to reinstall the interface card.

■ **The host has become flooded with traffic and cannot handle requests** This can be due to a hacker, who is forwarding traffic to your server in bulk in an attempt to make your host unavailable. Refer to Chapter 11 for more information on security.

■ **Remote host misconfiguration of router, firewall, server, or other device.** This problem prevents packets from being forwarded correctly.

■ **A carrier providing Internet backbone connectivity is having problems or becomes unavailable.** This is especially critical if a web host does not have true redundancy in place.

▲ **Has there been any construction in the immediate area where your building is?** A connectivity line might have been cut, depending on the type of infrastructure used.

SUMMARY

This chapter introduces key TCP/IP utilities, which can be used in conjunction with other monitoring tools to perform diagnostics, gauge performance, and troubleshoot connectivity issues. From an enterprise perspective, in the next several chapters we will discuss third-party monitoring tools that optimize performance. The next chapter will discuss scalability and methods of enhancing network performance.

Numerous resources are available to provide in-depth details on TCP/IP utilities and advanced options that can be used to help in administering a network. These include the following reference books:

▼ *TCP/IP Illustrated, Volume 1,* Richard Stevens, Addison-Wesley (describes the TCP/IP protocols)

■ *TCP/IP Illustrated, Volume 2,* Richard Stevens, Addison-Wesley (describes the TCP/IP stack from the source code level)

■ *TCP/IP Illustrated, Volume 3,* Richard Stevens, Addison-Wesley (describes HTTP, NNTP, etc.)

■ *TCP/IP: Architecture, Protocols, and Implementation with IPv6 and IP Security,* Dr. Sidnie Feit, McGraw-Hill

▲ *TCP/IP Network Administration,* Craig Hunt, Gigi Estabrook, O'Reilly & Associates

Other TCP/IP references online include the following:

▼ **RFC 1739, A Primer On Internet and TCP/IP Tools**
http://www.ietf.org/rfc/rfc1739.txt

■ **TCP/IP For Internet Administrators**
http://techref.ezine.com/tc/

■ **IP Overview, by Cisco**
http://www.cisco.com/univercd/cc/td/doc/cisintwk/ito_doc/ip.htm

▲ **TCP/IP Newsgroup**   comp.protocols.tcp-ip

CHAPTER 13

Enhancing Network Performance

To manage a system effectively, you might focus on the interactions of the parts rather than their behavior taken separately.

- Russell L. Ackoff

As your web hosting business encounters increased traffic demands from customers, you will need to address performance issues and consider various optimization methods to ensure the best availability and redundancy of services. First you must ensure that an abundant supply of bandwidth is available from multiple providers to meet the requirements of your customers and their web sites. If the heart of the problem is a lack of available bandwidth, the performance enhancements discussed in this chapter will not have a positive impact. See Chapter 10 for more information about ensuring sufficient bandwidth.

This chapter discusses technologies that provide hardware and software solutions designed to improve server responsiveness on different platforms. When considering how your network is performing, questions will need to keep in mind include these:

▼ Where are the current bottlenecks in the network?

■ Do current customers complain of slow loading pages for their web sites?

■ Are connections being dropped or are slow server responses being noted?

■ How many simultaneous connections are being made to key systems?

■ Which applications are generating the most traffic at specific intervals?

▲ Have systems been optimized with additional memory, fast processors, and sufficient storage resources to address the problem?

Before committing to any performance solution, consider the following questions:

▼ Is the solution scalable?

■ Are security features available?

- Is specialized hardware required?
- Is there a single point of failure?
- Is it open source or proprietary?
- What protocols are supported?
- ▲ Do you have the personnel resources to devote to managing the solution? If not, a partnership might be necessary to acquire the expertise that you need.

The solutions discussed in this chapter enhance network availability and performance, including clustering, load balancing, and caching solutions.

CLUSTERING

In general, a *cluster* can be defined simply as a group of computers that together provide web services as needed. Clustering provides failover protection for back-end databases and web servers, and is the method commonly used with load balancing. The general rule in server administration is that if a specific server cannot be down for more than 5–10 minutes, a clustering solution is necessary.

In clustering servers that are synchronized; if a primary server goes down, another server in the cluster is automatically contacted to process requests. When using clustering technology, confirm that servers and applications are enabled to fail over automatically. Technologies that use clustering include several alternative methods for ensuring that data is always available to multiple participating servers, including

- ▼ **Disk mirroring**   This method synchronizes data from one server with another. It is commonly used to mirror data to an offsite server location in case a primary server becomes unavailable.

- **Disk sharing**   In this scenario, each member server can access another participating server's disk. This method generally requires specific applications, and is limited in scalability.

- ▲ **No sharing**   Also termed as a "shared nothing" approach, each member server manages its own data. If a member server fails, the cluster can assign the management of a disk to another member server, and does not require special applications. Applications also can be spread among more than one member server, providing enhanced availability. This method provides the most administration manageability and scalability, with the addition of resources as needed, and appears as one resource to users.

Cluster services are available for most web servers, and are supported by many popular messaging and workgroup applications to ensure greater reliability of server farms. Applications that support clustering can automatically transfer to an active server in a cluster if one of the servers fails. *Failure* is when the server stops sending a heartbeat message to other servers in a cluster. If a failure occurs during an application session, the user will see that the session disconnects and will be able to restart with the application now running in the background on another node. For noncluster applications, this step requires a manual restart to make the transfer. Within a clustering environment, multiple network cards are installed in each server, with one card configured for a network segment, while the other is used for clustering communications with the other cluster members. Routers also can be clustered to ensure the utmost availability.

Linux Clustering Solutions

As part of a project with NASA's Goddard Space Flight Center in 1994, Donald Becker initiated the Beowulf Project, one of the first clustering developments. During this time, clustering to support 16 nodes was developed. It now is an open source standard for Linux clustering, and is used by universities and research facilities. More information can be found at http://www.beowulf.org and http://www.scyld.com. As a result of these early efforts, many other clustering product implementations are available for the Unix server environment.

From VA Linux, ClusterCity provides advanced clustering for Linux-based servers as a rack-mounted solution, and is based on Beowulf. Through the included VACM (VA Cluster Management) software, remote management can be accomplished for all clustering functions, including the capability to run diagnostics, manage configuration settings, and control RAID components. Up to 48 nodes (servers) can be used together and combined in parallel with other clusters to enable massive clustered environments. Further information on ClusterCity is available at http://www.valinux.com/systems/clustercity.html.

Another product, LifeKeeper, available from SteelEye Technology, includes tools for recovery of applications for several Linux-compatible products within a clustered environment, including Apache Web Server, Sendmail, Oracle, and Informix databases. More information is available at http://www.steeleye.com.

Windows Clustering Solutions

For Microsoft Windows servers, there are several products that cater to environments of different sizes. Microsoft has two products, which also can be used together: MSCS (Microsoft Cluster Server) and NLB (Network Load Balancing, which is available with Microsoft Windows 2000 Advanced Server). MSCS supports two-node clustering (with servers on site) for failover protection, with parameters that can be set for responding to failures.

MSCS (originally code named "Wolfpack" with Microsoft NT Advanced Server Enterprise Edition) can be used in combination with the Microsoft ClusterSentinel, for close monitoring of applications. Microsoft ClusterSentinel is available with the Windows 2000 Resource Kit. Microsoft ClusterSentinel monitors at the application level, and can work with Microsoft's NLB clustering technology. ClusterSentinel monitors the health of servers and uses the testing results to determine if the server is available.

The Windows 2000 Datacenter Server provides support for 4 nodes (servers). Through NLB, available as a feature within Windows 2000, Datacenter Server can support up to 32 nodes for high-end clustering scalability. When NLB is installed it is given a virtual IP address, which is the central address that all other cluster nodes respond to. Content often will be load balanced equally among clustered servers for enhanced delivery of content to the browser, although priority levels and port rules for unique requirements can be set for each node. In addition, failover protection is a built-in feature, which prevents one system from having a detrimental effect on performance.

When designing clusters for high-traffic situations that come with services such as streaming media, web servers should be pretested to ensure they can handle the load. For Windows server environments,

Microsoft Windows Media Load Simulator tests the stability of a system under high traffic loads and can simulate Microsoft Windows Media Player connections. The Microsoft Web Application Stress Tool provides testing of server performance while running various applications. You can perform tests to determine optimal settings.

LOAD BALANCING

The basic function of a load balancing solution (sometimes referred to as *traffic management*) is to send incoming traffic to targeted servers. The targeting is based on defined parameters, and accounts for the responsiveness and traffic volume of servers. As with other solutions, there are many hardware and software combinations that provide varying degrees of load balancing scalability and functionality. The flexibility in available solutions allows you to use different platforms and hardware combinations.

Many load balancing solutions today are sophisticated offerings, with functions to accommodate different load variations on servers. Optional settings can send requests to the most optimal server connection and the server that is most responsive. You also can use the DNS *round-robin* approach, which handles requests in a prearranged server sequence, using alternative algorithms to provide an elaborate weighted scale for determining how requests are assigned. Traffic can be distributed based on a user's session or by the type of content.

From a disaster planning perspective, a load balancing solution also can be used to dynamically divert traffic to another physical hosting server location in case primary servers become unavailable due to earthquake, tornado, fire, extended power outage, or other unforeseen emergency. With the energy crisis in California during 2001, many web hosts are adjusting their strategies to include load balancing scenarios and developing partnerships to seamlessly divert web traffic to other offsite U.S. locations in case central servers became unavailable. For some data centers that have experienced disaster, load balancing has provided continuation of critical business services that otherwise could have forced them out of business.

Some types of load balancing products, which can be used singularly or in combination, include the following:

▼ Software-based load balancing

■ Hardware-based load balancing

▲ Load balancing appliances

Software-based Load Balancing

Software-based load balancing solutions operate as an application stored on a server; often they are an affordable option. A simplified method of load balancing is through enabling round-robin DNS. This configuration involves assigning two or more IP addresses for a given domain, using A (address) records located in a DNS server configuration file. As requests are made for the domain, the DNS server will consecutively access the IP addresses, requesting the same web site from different servers. This is designed to simplify the load on a network, because each time DNS resolves the requested domain name, the request is forwarded to a different IP address that is specified in the DNS record for the domain name. Here is a sample DNS record for four servers that are part of a cluster:

```
www   300   IN   A   172.17.0.0
      300   IN   A   172.17.0.1
      300   IN   A   172.17.0.2
      300   IN   A   172.17.0.3
```

One limitation of this method is that if a server in the round-robin list goes down, connections made to that particular server fail. As one server receives the bulk of requests, other servers remain underutilized. Other methods or approaches to load balancing involve a *weighted percentage distribution,* in which the traffic is divided among servers or *least connects,* in which the server with the smallest level of traffic receives incoming traffic.

Through optional modules, the Apache web server can support load balancing functionality to allow utmost data availability among servers; these optional modules are discussed in the following.

mod_rewrite

The mod_rewrite module is described as a rule-based rewriting engine that uses parsing to rewrite requested URLs dynamically. It also has been eloquently termed the "Swiss Army knife of URL manipulation."

The module was invented by Ralf S. Engelschall in 1996, and then provided as open source to the Apache Group. A limitless number of rules and conditions are available to provide URL control and definition. The basis for the rules can include environment variables, server variables, HTTP headers, query to external data sources, and so on.

Control of the URL also can be fine-tuned to be based on a specific server within a cluster or a designated directory. A sophisticated DNS-based method for load balancing that can be used with mod_rewrite to provide increased functionality is a program called lbnamed, written in Perl, which is located at http://www.stanford.edu/~schemers/docs/lbnamed/lbnamed.html.

Further information on mod_rewrite can be located at

▼   http://www.apache.org/docs/mod/mod_rewrite.html

▲   http://www.apache.org/docs/misc/rewriteguide.html

mod_backhand

The mod_backhand module is capable of redirecting browser requests from one web server to another that is part of a cluster, depending on what system resources are available to handle a request. Initially developed in 1999 as a network replication project at the Johns Hopkins University, Department of Computer Science, now it is available as an open source add-on module for Apache. With the mod_backhand module you can pinpoint specific servers that have plenty of capacity to handle HTTP requests.

mod_backhand operates on a per-request basis and has a wide range of available configurations. This is a more efficient approach than some load balancing solutions that deal with only network connections coming in to a server, and run as a process separate from the web server. As part of a clustering environment, each node is provided with information on how resources are being used.

Based on this information, you also can determine proper allocation of resources, as each node communicates with the other. Functions are executed in the order in which they appear in the configuration file. These functions, called *candidacy functions,* include several built-in functions that provide a great deal of flexibility in managing traffic loads. A few of the many candidacy functions that are available with mod_backhand include these:

▼   **byAge [time in seconds]**   Traffic is not forwarded to servers that do not respond to queries within a designated time span.

■   **byLoad [bias]**   Only the servers with the lowest load are used.

■   **byCost**   Using this framework, a cost is associated with a request for every machine that is part of a cluster. The least costly machine is used by default. This framework is further defined in a paper entitled, "A Cost Benefit Framework for Online Management of a Metacomputing System," available at http://www.backhand.org/mod_backhand/.

■   **HTTPRedirectToIP**   Requests are forwarded over IP instead of the standard proxy method; for example, the http://192.168.255.250/request/uri format is used.

■   **bySession [identifier]**   With this function, user sessions can be enabled to provide a specific user access to a designated machine that is part of the cluster.

▲   **off**   This function disables mod_backhand for a particular directory.

Besides the included candidacy functions, you can create others, because the module is open source. As an add-in module, mod_backhand can operate by itself or in conjunction with other load balancing products in providing sophisticated load balancing functionality and server-based monitoring for Apache web server environments. The mod_backhand module and source code are available at http://www.backhand.org/mod_backhand/.

mod_redundancy

The mod_redundancy module provides load balancing functionality by combining mod_proxy and mod_rewrite. The standard configuration involves configuring two servers for handling dynamic pages, with a third server configured to handle static pages. Through reverse proxying that operates from the web server, random requests are sent. At the time of this writing, mod_redundancy has announced its intent to become open source, and was available for Linux and Solaris.

LinuxDirector

LinuxDirector is a connection director with support for load balancing among several web servers in a cluster. Three IP load balancing techniques, VS/NAT, VS/TUN, and VS/DR are used, through extending the TCP/IP stack of the Linux kernel. Written by Jacob Rief, LinxDirector is a standalone daemon designed to monitor the services of web servers. Nodes that are a part of a cluster can be transparently added or removed to allow for scalability. To encourage high availability, daemon failures are monitored, and backups are made, to provide failover protection for the load balancing functions. Further information can be located at http://www.linuxvirtualserver.org.

Hardware-based Load Balancing

Hardware-based load balancing (sometimes referred to as *switches*) forwards IP-based packets to enhance the availability and reliability of data. The optimal placement of a load balancer within a server farm is between routers and servers. They often serve as a proxy, which functions for servers that are part of a cluster, or in conjunction with multiple firewalls to avoid bottlenecks and to provide failover protection. Traffic also can be distributed to different physical server farm locations to enhance services, reduce slowdowns, and provide for additional insurance against a site becoming unavailable.

An additional advantage of hardware-based load balancing is intelligent load balancing, which provides the ability of parsing a URL among web servers and forwarding traffic that is based on HTTP header information. This provides for optimal use of server resources because traffic can be forwarded to a specific server in a group (or referred to as a pool) of servers, depending on rules that are set. These rules can be determined by several factors, including

- ▼ According to requesting address
- ▲ By HTTP header content

One vendor of note, F5 Networks (http://www.f5.com) offers a range of load balancing solutions in its product line, including BIG/IP. Through parsing the URL via an HTTP request, BIG-IP can establish a session on the server that is best able to handle the request. The source IP address also can determine the destination server to receive the request. An added benefit is the capability to assign priority service to your best hosting customers; for example, by looking at the HTTP Cookie Header. According to F5, its products are based on Layers 2–7 of the OSI model, which accounts for both the connection and the application.

Companies such as Dell have integrated F5's BIG-IP software with their PowerApp appliance servers to provide their customers with turnkey access to sophisticated traffic and content management. Dell PowerApp.BIG-IP and Dell PowerApp.cache have been engineered with fault tolerance in mind:

▼ Dual power supplies are standard on PowerApp.cache 200 and PowerApp.BIG-IP.

■ The multiple disk configurations of PowerApp.cache use mirrored partitions so that the OS and associated software are automatically backed up and restored if they are corrupted.

▲ PowerApp.BIG-IP employs a watchdog timer that automatically restarts the appliance if it becomes unresponsive.

A load balancing solution can provide automatic switching of incoming traffic by forwarding to caching servers for accelerated delivery of content to the end user's browser. "A load balancer can be a single point of failure unless additional precautions are taken," according to Dr. Craig Lowery, Senior Engineer for Internet Server Products with Dell's Enterprise Systems Group. Dell PowerApp.BIG-IP can be deployed in a high-availability redundant pair. One loadss balancer is designated as the active member of the pair; the other member is designated as passive.

According to Dr. Lowery, in this scenario the active member routes requests to caches in the array and the passive member simply monitors the health of the active member. If the active member fails, the passive member assumes its functions and becomes active. This arrangement is known as an *active/passive redundant pair*. Employing the Dell PowerApp load balanced cache array, high-availability redundancy yields a scalable and cost-effective caching solution, as shown in Figure 13-1.

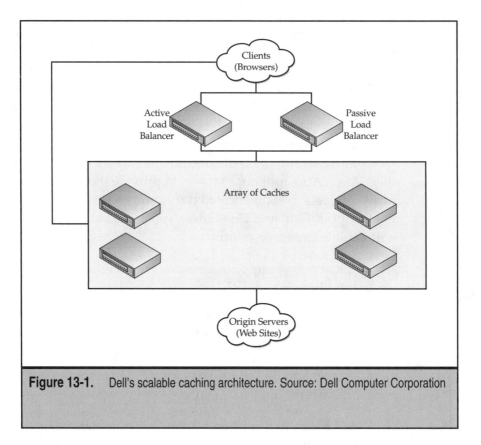

Figure 13-1.   Dell's scalable caching architecture. Source: Dell Computer Corporation

For more information about Dell products, see http://www.dell.com/us/en/gen/default.htm.

Load Balancing Appliances

Cisco LocalDirector, IOS Server (bundled into its Cisco Catalyst 6500 switches), and Distributed Director (for multiple locations) are part of a full suite of hardware and software bundled products. The Cisco LocalDirector is a high-end load balancing appliance that is rack mountable, and includes 92 Mbps throughput. It also can support scaling for up to 1 million TCP/IP connections simultaneously.

By dynamically managing traffic based on IP, the LocalDirector serves as a single-path bridge for traffic and distributes requests for up to 64,000 real or virtual servers. Dynamic-feedback command options can be configured to gauge each server's IP address and port number. Incoming TCP/IP requests can be forwarded to different web servers based on the number of connections, speed, or service criteria. Individual tracking options include setting dynamic feedback update, timeout, and connection retries, which are collectively defined by Cisco as *DFP* (*Dynamic Feedback Protocol*).

Other configuration options allow for maximizing the number of TCP/IP connections a server farm is able to maintain. Several security features are included with the LocalDirector, which can restrict access to particular IP addresses and ports. You can translate Web server IP addresses to virtual addresses using the LocalDirector. The LocalDirector comes with optional hot-standby failover functionality to ensure additional redundancy for a network. For more information about Cisco LocalDirector, see http://www.cisco.com/warp/public/cc/pd/cxsr/400/index.shtml.

CACHING SOLUTIONS

Web hosts are using caching solutions to help diminish the effect of sudden surges in traffic, enhance content delivery, and make technologies such as streaming media feasible. The bandwidth that is saved by having frequently accessed images, streaming media, and content pages stored in a cache can range at 25 percent or more of the site's total bandwidth. The web host enjoys the added benefit of being able to make available as an advanced hosting service add-on for customers, especially beneficial for sites with a need for enhanced content distribution.

According to Dr. Craig Lowery, Senior Engineer for Internet Server Products with Dell's Enterprise Systems Group, "Internet caching provides a way to improve the performance of a user's Internet session by storing frequently accessed objects such as web pages, graphics, streaming media, and general-purpose data files, in a high-speed caching server. Instead of requesting content directly from an origin server, web browsers make requests from a caching server, which exists on the network somewhere between the browser and the origin server."

Other companies such as CacheFlow and Cisco provide products that use caching software in combination with hardware and their own proprietary operating systems. These appliances often are rack-mounted devices that fit well in a server farm. Caching appliances are easy to use and maintain. For small web hosts that do not have large server farm resources, caching solutions can greatly enhance content delivery for customers. The most common use of caching is to store popular site pages and images without accessing the actual web site that contains the original data each time. As wireless technology is being used more for content delivery, caching servers can be used in innovative ways to modify original web server content to be readable on wireless devices.

Some types of caching solutions include

▼ Proxy caching

■ Reverse proxy caching

■ Data center caching

■ Caching appliances

■ Transparent caching

▲ Multimedia (streaming media) caching

CacheFlow provides a range of caching management products in its cIQ line, which uses patent-pending algorithms and protocols that allow content to be generated based on the type of request, as noted in Figure 13-2. These include the cIQ Streaming Services product, which is designed to enhance the delivery of streaming media content, and cIQ Edge Accelerators, which are focused on improving content delivery within WANs. This type of solution would benefit a slow WAN connection by being placed at the ends of the connection, resolving requests.

Another product, the cIQ Server Accelerator, is asserted by CacheFlow to be the only appliance that is designated to offload web servers from having to handle routine content delivery and security tasks, which results in optimized site performance and scalability by up to 10 times, and a reduction of 60 percent in upstream bandwidth usage for web hosts. It also includes protection against *DoS* (*Denial of Service*) attacks, which includes the ability to distinguish between valid and malicious connections, and servicing users while resisting

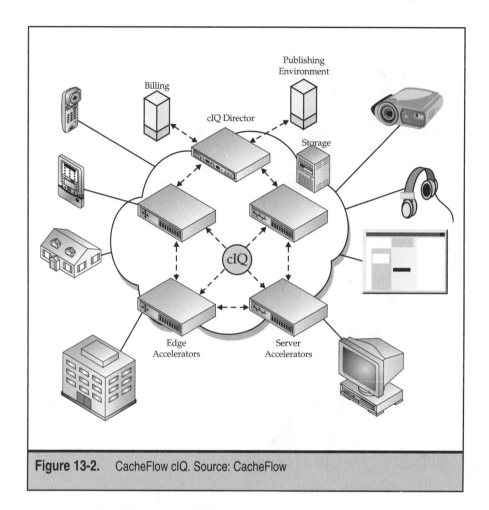

Figure 13-2. CacheFlow cIQ. Source: CacheFlow

the attack, according to CacheFlow. Its features also include an integrated SSL cryptographic processor that is able to handle 200 secure key negotiations per second, which is an average of 10 times greater than many standard web servers.

CacheFlow customers include GlobalOne, Excite, Sprint, and MCI Worldcom. "Our web site is an essential information channel, so service and availability cannot be compromised," explained Sidsel Nordhagen, head of IT operations and technical services at the Oslo Stock Exchange. "CacheFlow's cIQ Server Accelerator equips us to meet any and all situations and ensures that unexpected peaks in traffic won't cause problems in the future.

CacheFlow also provides a tool that can be used to gauge how responsive a cache is for a site under different load criteria. The CacheFlow Cache Performance Testing Tool (available from http://www.cacheflow.com/technology/tools/index.cfm), is available for several server platforms.

Cisco also provides caching appliances, which are a combination of hardware and software. The Cache Engine 500 series includes router switching capability that uses Cisco's IOS software and *WCCP* (*Web Cache Communications Protocol*) to cache content requests. Inktomi's caching solution, Traffic Server, provides high-end caching that includes the capability of dynamically refreshing the contents of one or more cache servers, which ensures the most current content is available to the user.

Other vendors that offer a range of products that include caching functionality include

▼ **Network Appliance**   (http://www.netapp.com)

■ **Cobalt**   (http://www.cobalt.com)

■ **InfoLibria**   (http://www.infolibria.com)

▲ **Microsoft Proxy Server**   (http://www.microsoft.com/proxy)

CONTENT DELIVERY SERVICES

For web hosts who do not want to be concerned with the cost of maintaining in-house content delivery services, leading companies such as Akamai, SolidSpeed, and Digital Island have a wide array of distribution services for enhanced delivery of content-matched customer needs. Content hosting often is used to power the enhanced content delivery for high-volume web sites that have downloadable files, streaming media, or large graphics files. The content delivery service often will host the actual content that needs the enhanced speed, with other portions of the customer web site remaining on the original server. This form of outsourcing is discussed in further detail in Chapter 14.

OTHER METHODS OF ENHANCING AVAILABILITY

Another form of hardware redundancy is *RAID* (*Redundant Arrays of Independent Disks*) technology, which provides different levels of redundancy. By ensuring that dual drives are maintained, a copy of data can be made available if a primary drive stops functioning. Backup data also can be available through *hot swapping,* which is intelligent controller technology that enables drives to be swapped without restarting a server. RAID can be either software of hardware based. RAID-5 has been a common choice for many environments that require a high level of redundancy; hardware arrays being the most fault tolerant. Newer RAID technology, which provides even more redundancy, is increasingly available. You can find an in-depth article on RAID technology at http://www.dell.com/us/en/gen/topics/power_ps3q99-raid.htm.

In ensuring that servers are responsive, a device available for Windows-based servers, Heart Beat Rebooter, can reboot a system automatically (default is 30 seconds), if it stops responding and a locked condition is detected. This is especially beneficial to a network administrator if a system becomes unavailable in the middle of the night.

Two models are available, Heart Beat ReBooter and an AC version, which both connect through a dedicated serial port on the PC. When the PC platform reboots, the software reinitializes the system, with an error file generated for logging when a reset occurs. Software is included that sends a heartbeat signal to the serial port during normal operation. The Rebooter version physically connects to the motherboard through the reset jumper pins and receives its power through the serial port. If needed, a reset takes place through this connection when a signal is not received. The AC version can connect through an optional intelligent AC power strip for rebooting.

The company also is testing to allow software to monitor and have direct control over the rebooting process in the event an application may hang a system. A DLL also can be used, making it an almost foolproof method for automatic rebooting. For more information, refer to http://www.cpscom.com/gprod/hb.htm.

PERFORMANCE TESTING

Performance testing software provides measurements to gauge how a particular web server platform operates under stress. Depending on the package used, measures can include scoring for requests per second and for throughput in bytes per second for static and dynamic page loads. These tests can help track how a web server is operating within a set timeframe. Available free from ZD Labs, WebBench (http://www.zdnet.com/etestinglabs/stories/benchmarks/0,8829,2326243,00.html), provides comparative analysis results to gauge how well your web server performs compared to other server platforms, using different scenarios. SPECweb99 Benchmark also is available at http://open.specbench.org/osg/web99/. WebStone, available from Mindcraft, also provides a benchmark analysis package and is free to download from http://www.mindcraft.com/webstone/.

An independent development and consulting company, the Measurement Factory, provides an annual competition in which participating web server vendors compete on defined areas of performance. Some of the benchmarked areas include web components used to enhance the speed of web content to the browser. The results of the competition can be viewed at http://www.measurement-factory.com/.

For Windows environments Microsoft provides a free testing tool, Web Capacity Analysis Tool, which analyzes Windows 2000 and NT with Internet Information Server, operating under various loads to gauge the capacity of servers in responding to requests. Tests include gauging HTTP, ASP pages, SSL, PCT (Private Communications Technology) encryption, and the use of cookies. It is available for download: Simply reference http://msdn.microsoft.com and do a search from the web site. Another tool, Httpmon for Windows 2000, monitors information on a web site through an Httpmon.ini configuration file. The purpose of the tool is to allow real-time monitoring and testing of a Windows 2000 web server.

In seeking performance enhancements for web services, do not overlook improvements that can be made from routinely defragmenting hard drives. According to an Execsoft report, which quoted NSTL (National Software Testing Laboratories), the most common configurations (by survey) make improvements of as much as 81 percent for Windows NT and as much as 219 percent for Windows 2000. Tools such as Diskeeper from Execsoft provide enhanced disk defragmentation products. For more information on the report, refer to http://www.execsoft.com/whats-new/whitepaper.asp. Statistics were not available on improvements that can be realized for Unix-based systems, because fragmentation is not as much of an issue.

When disk partitions are nearing 100 percent capacity, defragmentation might be needed. For Unix systems, a common method to use is through the use of backup utilities such as tar, cpio, and tar. More information can be found at ftp://sunsite.unc.edu/pub/Linux/docs/HOWTO/mini/Partition.

SUMMARY

This chapter introduces methods that can enhance network performance and reliability, reduce bottlenecks, and enable faster content delivery. The next chapter will discuss the benefits of outsourcing for various technology needs, which allows a web host to offer highly specialized Web services to customers without having to fully maintain support for those services through in-house staff.

CHAPTER 14

Developing Partnerships and Outsourcing Services

Partnerships are the rule of the day in complementing the range of services you can offer, because a web host has only so many internal resources available to deploy. Several examples of niche markets and services are introduced here that allow web hosts to enhance their revenue streams while fulfilling customer needs as a one-source web host. Besides the potential additional revenues from partnerships, substantial cost savings can also be realized through automating internal processes and outsourcing where justified.

In choosing among the wide range of opportunities available via partnerships, be sure to review some preliminary questions such as the following:

▼ Have customers expressed an interest in having access to specific products or services (through online interaction, customer surveys, and so on) that you do not currently provide in-house?

■ Do the products or services being considered complement your range of offerings?

■ Can products or services be customized? Can they be privately labeled, to be resold using your company name?

■ What about licensing? Is open source available to allow custom development?

■ How long has the product or service been offered? What other types of customers does the company service, which are in the Internet or web hosting market?

■ Are there win-win opportunities available to market to the prospective partner's customers as well?

■ Are there setup costs involved? What about monthly costs?

■ What revenue sharing options are available? What is it based on?

■ Is there an annual fee involved in addition to setup costs or monthly fees? What about any hidden costs? Does the partnership include different discount pricing levels?

■ Does the solution involve a long-term commitment? Is it justified?

■ Is there a low-cost option of entry, or a test run for offering the product or service prior to a full commitment?

■ What is the business impact, or penalty, if any, if a campaign is unsuccessful or the partner's business fails? Are other partners available that provide a similar quality program for customers?

■ Does the company provide responsive backup customer support for their product or service?

▲ Will the partnership provide incentives for certification of employees on the product or service?

The landscape is constantly changing, as mergers and consolidations occur within the industry. Partnering is also available within the hosting market for web hosts to partner with each other, utilizing specialty services provided by ASPs, MSPs, and other high-end types of hosting providers, in order to become a one-source host for customers. In referring to this trend, Lew Moorman, chief marketing officer of Rackspace Managed Hosting states, "Companies now want to focus on the core competency of their business rather than maintaining a server, which colocation requires. For example, magazine publishers outsource printing so they can concentrate on the content of the publication, not the intricacies of the printing press. In particular, we believe that small- to medium-sized companies see the most value in managed services and software combined with a zero-dollar hardware investment."

For web services who offer partnering plans, further information will generally be located in a partner or reseller section of a web site, with pricing requirements ranging from nothing to quite expensive. Many of the solutions that have been discussed in previous chapters provide some type of partnership program. Within the customer service and technical support areas, numerous software packages have been identified, which can provide substantial improvements in the servicing of customer accounts through partnering (refer back to Chapters 6 and 7). For resellers, as part of a web hosting plan, as discussed in Chapter 8, a Control Panel may be bundled within a plan, which allows access to various in-house and third party services.

Some of the various revenue models for a product or service include

▼ **Revenue Sharing**   Sales are shared with the web host.

■ **Resell**   Provided at a discount to web host, which resells at a markup.

■ **Licensing Per Item**   Pricing based per sale.

■ **Commissions**   Pricing plans include a set percentage based on sales volume.

▲ **Affiliate Program**   The web host is paid an agreed-upon basic rate.

These revenue models may also often include co-marketing, such as mutual advertising via emails, tradeshows, direct mail, or other media. Other benefits are usually provided as well, such as training materials, technical support, and co-branding. Web hosts can extend the range of competitive services they offer by outsourcing in certain areas and developing win-win alliances. These alliances may be with a reseller, VAR (value added reseller), affiliate, partnership, alliance, or even a referral arrangement. The following individual areas are presented to provide an overview of some of the best partnering opportunities that allow web hosts to expand upon their range of services available.

WEB SITE MONITORING

Tracking a customer's web site activity through log files and third-party monitoring software, such as Urchin and WebTrends, can provide useful information. A customer can view data in a graphical format to help gauge how well their site is reaching their target audience. Monitoring can also pinpoint problem areas with pages or images that are not loading properly.

Some of the individual customer data that can be measured through log file analysis and monitoring programs, that are especially of interest to the web host, include the following:

▼ Amount of bandwidth used per day

■ How the site is performing with search engines based on keywords or phrases

■ Domain names and IP addresses of visitors

▲ Pages that are not loading properly

There are numerous site monitoring packages are available that can retrieve web server log files, and present the data in graphical format for visual interpretation of customer web site activity. The trend is to provide basic monitoring functions to customers bundled within their hosting account plan. It can also be the basis for billing that is based on the amount of bandwidth used, and to provide justification to customers when a hosting plan upgrade is necessary for their account. Other possibilities for the web host include using the data to provide additional consulting services, such as offering to optimize the customer's web site pages for search engines or to redesign site pages for faster loading. Additional services could also include providing customers with advanced web site information including detailed graphical reporting on the types of web site visitors and site performance tracking.

Some of the standard log formats that are supported by site monitoring packages include Apache Common, Apache Extended, Apache Multiple Log File Format, IIS, NCSA Common, NCSA Combined, CERN Common, CERN Combined, Standard Common Log File Format, Standard Combined Log File Format, and IIS.

Logging with Apache

The default log file format that works best with Apache to generate the most useful information is the Combined log file format. Apache allows you to designate this log file format in the httpd.conf configuration file, located in the /Apache/conf/ directory. You would change the Apache configuration file to this log file format by adding the following to the http.conf file:

```
# This defines a "nickname" for specified log file format.
# The nickname is "combined".
```

```
LogFormat "%h %l %u %t \"%r\" %>s %b \"%{Referer}i\"
\"%{User-Agent}i\""
combined
# Specify that we want to store combined log file in location
# "logs/combined.log".
CustomLog logs/combined.log
combined
```

Logging with IIS

The standard log format that works best with IIS is the W3C Extended Log File Format, which is specified from within IIS. In order to do this, modify the following:

1. From within IIS, select either a Web or FTP site, and click Properties.

2. Select the Enable Logging check box.

3. Choose the W3C Extended Log File Format as the Active log format.

4. Click on Properties again.

5. Click Extended Properties (or Advanced Properties for some versions of IIS).

6. Select the following fields: Date, Time, Client IP Address, Method, URI Stem, HTTP Status, Bytes Received, Bytes Sent, User Agent, Referrer.

7. Now click Apply, and click OK to close all the dialog box windows.

Urchin

Urchin, available from Quantified Systems, is a visitor web site reporting system for gauging key information on a web site, with advanced traffic reporting. As reported by the company, Urchin has the capability of processing a 1-gigabyte log file in an estimated 10 minutes. As stated by Ed Douglas, director of marketing with

EarthLink, "We looked for over two years to find a web stats system that could work with our large and fast-growing hosting network, and we are excited to have found Quantified's Urchin."

With Urchin 3, two types of site tracking reports can be run via a web browser, to display the following:

▼ **Site Report**   Displays daily and historical traffic report for each site on a web server.

▲ **Server Report**   Displays daily and historical network traffic reporting from the server level.

A range of views are available to display a summary of site visitors, page views, and hits for a given period, as displayed in Figure 14-1. With the separate e-commerce module available, actual dollars spent on a site can also be tracked.

Also available, Urchin Enterprise 3, especially for large hosting environments, the package has the functionality to provide centralized reporting for web sites that are hosted via a shared hosting account under a single IP address. Some of Urchin's

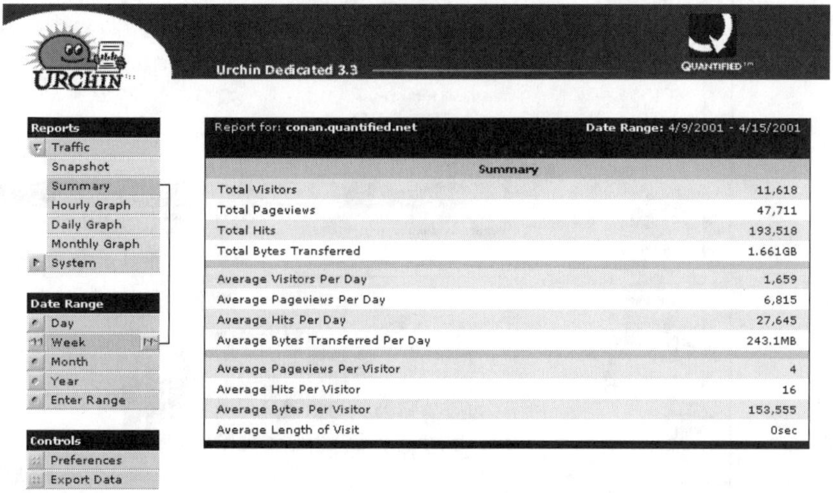

Figure 14-1.   Urchin Reporting
Source: Quantified Systems

customers include web hosts and data centers, including Cable & Wireless, EarthLink, Winstar, Worldport, Fastnet, HostMe, Interliant, and KeyBridge. More information on Urchin is available at http://www.urchin.com.

WebTrends

WebTrends provides a range of site analysis and intelligence reporting solutions. As shown in Figure 14-2, overall site information can be made available for customers to access within a web browser, allowing a record of site activity to be displayed for during different time periods and criteria. Shown here are the overall number of visitors during a one-day period.

As quoted by Clifton Robin, senior product manager with Interliant, "Having WebTrends has cut down on technical support time. WebTrends gives us the performance, scalability and features to meet all our customers' needs." Web hosts often use the WebTrends

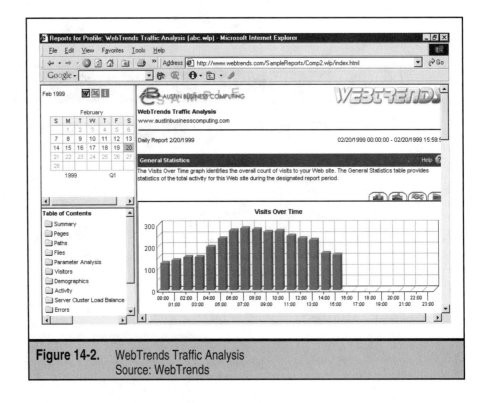

Figure 14-2. WebTrends Traffic Analysis
Source: WebTrends

Enterprise solution, which allows multiple users to access traffic analysis, reporting, and monitoring information, via a web browser. Reports can be generated that focus on Security Analysis, Streaming Media Usage, or Bandwidth Utilization for a web site. Additional solutions are available for generating of reports and analysis for large clustering environments.

Customers that have partnered with WebTrends, include Interliant, XO Communications, Digex, and GTE. More information on WebTrends is available at http://www.webtrends.com.

ORDER PROCESSING SERVICES

A common value-added service for web hosts is to offer add-on e-commerce storefront capabilities for customers. Two of the top three web services that respondents plan to purchase within the next twelve months were online credit card processing (26%) and order management systems (24%). An order processing solution should always include secure online ordering capability, either directly or through a secure third-party payment service such as VeriSign or Cardservice Gateway. Security is typically accomplished through 768-bit RSA encryption for transactions, which is considered more secure than SSL (Secure Socket Layer). Real-time transactions can take place online, acting as a bridge that connects a web site securely to a participating bank. An order processing solution will typically also allow inventory items to be organized in a catalog format, with search enabled functionality, with connection to a back-end database containing product inventory details. In May 2000, B2SB Technologies Corp (formerly SmartAge.com) commissioned Millward Brown IntelliQuest to conduct a poll among small businesses that currently have a web presence or are in the process of developing one. Vendors that provide e-commerce storefront capabilities include Intershop (http://www.intershop.com), Interworld (http://www.interworld.com), and Miva (http://www.miva.com), which is discussed here.

Miva

Miva Corporation (http://www.miva.com) provides a set of premier e-commerce software and services for web hosts to resell. Miva states that the number of small merchants on the Internet will increase 40%

by the year 2004, to nearly 3 million merchants online. Two primary products within the Miva line include Miva Merchant and Miva Order.

Miva Merchant is described by the company as "a dynamic browser based storefront development and management system that allows merchants to create multiple online stores." Many stores can be maintained by an administrator. Through the interface, numerous options are available to manage catalog information, modify customer interaction screens, and promotion campaigns, and to handle order fulfillment. Reports can be generated that provide details of the best selling items, and tracking of individual web site pages.

According to George DeVack, CEO of OLM.net, "The Miva e-commerce platform provides our customers with a complete solution that meets the needs of almost every business. The modular architecture, combined with Miva Script, makes it possible to customize the application to fit most any business requirement. Add on modules can be purchased from third-party developers or made from scratch." Reports can be generated which provide details of the best-selling items, and tracking of individual web site pages. For the customer, Miva Merchant wizards are included to ease the process of creating a web store, with handling of credit card processing via the Miva Order product, as well as having access to online partners which provide third-party merchant services as well. Miva Order is a customizable browser-based order form and order processing system. It can be personalized with specific color, graphics, product descriptions and other layout options. Businesses simply incorporate a link from the web page where their products are sold, permitting customers to seamlessly access the order form and make purchases.

Users are able to create and manage custom product order forms with provisions that simplify the process of calculating sales tax, shipping costs and currency formatting. More information on Miva is available at http://www.miva.com. Other secure third-party payment services which can be used with Miva Order and business merchant accounts, includes Signio Payflow Pro, Cardservice Gateway, CyberCash, CyberSource, Anacom, and Authorize.Net.

PayPal

Another order processing service available, PayPal, was originally designed for personal accounts in sending and receiving money to checking or credit card accounts. PayPal now includes a business account feature, which can handle an unlimited number of transactions. A shopping cart feature is being developed. PayPal does not offer the range of services that are available with vendors such as Miva, but does feature low fees for receiving payments. More information is available at http://www.paypal.com.

BILLING SOLUTIONS

As with any solution, pricing varies widely on billing solutions available. A billing solution for web hosts requires unique billing features not found with traditional billing packages, such as billing for bandwidth usage or for a large number of customers as a web host expands.

Some areas to ask questions prior to partnering for a billing solution include

▼ How many customers can be supported by the product?

■ Is the product expandable?

▲ Can it be customized to fit any unique billing requirements for mycustomers?

Ensure that a billing solution is expandable with your business as the base of your customers grow. Some billing packages of note for web hosts that are discussed in this section are Portal Software and Rodopi.

Portal Software

Portal Software provides billing and customer management solutions for web hosts to manage billing for a wide range of hosting plans, which includes tracking for bandwidth usage. The cornerstone of the services provided to its over 400 customers is via the billing and customer management software called Infranet. Introduced in 1996, the software is now commonly used with ISPs and in web hosting data centers. The Infranet package is object-oriented, and includes the capability to track usage based on the type of data and storage that is used, which eases the billing process, and simplifies the introduction of new services. An added benefit is support for multiple currencies and languages, which customers such as BT Ignite use in its worldwide web hosting data centers. The Application provider, iNNERHOST, also utilizes the Infranet package in supporting its services. "To maintain our leadership position and respond to changes in today's rapidly evolving managed hosting and application services market, we need a business platform that gives us the flexibility to quickly launch new business models and price plans, and scale to any size customer base," said Luis Navarro, chairman and CEO of iNNERHOST. "We chose Infranet because it meets these needs, and also because Portal's Infranet integrates with other industry-leading technologies, which allows us to reduce our costs by automating key tasks."

Another component available, the Infranet Manager for Cisco NetFlow allows web hosts to easily measure bandwidth actually used, as well as use of network resources for billing purposes. By combining the capabilities of Cisco NetFlow and Portal's Infranet software, web hosts can charge based on actual bandwidth usage, bandwidth on demand, for content delivery services, and expanded services, such as VPNs (Virtual Private Networks). This may also be specified as value-added services which is based on customer IP address, or upper tier of services as outlined via QoS (Quality of Service) guarantees, and agreed via SLA (Service Level Agreements).

Rodopi

Rodopi provides a suite of online billing, provisioning, and customer care software, which is designed to improve the process of billing and supporting customers. When a subscription is made, Rodopi automatically creates a web site account. For shared servers, billing can be individually assigned. A customer care section includes data on a customer, including tracking that can be associated with service ticketing. Through the Bandwidth Manager, web hosts can allow customers access to modify their bandwidth increments online, with charges automatically recorded for bandwidth that customers utilize, via logging or in combination with the NetFlow functions that are included within many Cisco routers. Secure online credit card processing is also available, through Rodopi's Payment Gateway.

Rodopi Software is being used by over 700 Internet providers for automation of provisioning, billing, and customer care. "Rodopi offerings are a market leader, not only because the software is well suited to some of the applications that we are addressing, but also because I have looked at the software quite thoroughly and I think it is excellent," according to Errol Pollnow, with Brooktech.com. More information on Rodopi is available at http://www.rodopi.com.

CONTENT DELIVERY SERVICES

In the previous chapter, several infrastructure technologies were highlighted that are designed to enhance the speed of web services to the user. As was discussed, for content to reach its intended destination (the end-user's browser), it must go through several varying routes over the Internet. Content delivery is one of the new services highlighted in this section, which provides an attractive, behind-the-scenes solution to overcoming bandwidth limits, and is designed for hosts that do not want to manage caching infrastructure issues, but have customers which require caching. The customer may need to enhance delivery for page content, including streaming media, images, or other embedded objects.

Through the adoption of caching technologies, the delivery of content to the browser can be speeded up. Another benefit is to conserve bandwidth, because some technologies such as streaming media can fluctuate greatly depending on how often they are accessed. Hosts also use caching for special events or unique promotions that draws a lot of traffic. By 2003, Forrester Research estimates that content delivery services and edge caching to grow to reach 2.52 billion.

Content delivery services provide an array of distribution services, through partnerships, to speed the delivery of content to the customer's browser. Hosts often need these services when powering the enhanced content delivery for high-volume web sites, which have downloadable files, streaming audio and video, or large graphics files, including banner ads or brand logos. This will many times include hosting a portion of a customer's content, placed in caching devices that are located closest to the user within a content delivery service's global network, with the remaining content (which is updated often) still residing on the customer's original server.

Some web hosts use these content delivery services in addition to their internal caching devices in order to enhance the speed of delivery even further for their best customers. Content delivery services are "going to be one of the biggest growth markets on the 'Net for the next three years," predicts Al Lill, vice president and research director for Gartner Group. Another likely area that can benefit from this technology is with Extranets, which enhance the delivery of services to key business partners. "It's a virtual no-brainer. [For customers,] the risks associated with these services are so low," states the *Network World Fusion News*.

Factors to consider when looking at content delivery services as partners are what type of content is handled (some services do not work with static page files, only graphics technologies), and making certain that pages appear seamlessly to the customer. Another consideration is having access to the most current log files for how much traffic the content is generating, which can be tracked via a web browser. Real-time monitoring of the caching content is generally available to track traffic data and other details related to the content. Cisco has formed a content delivery alliance to encourage the adoption of overall standards for content delivery networks. Find out more about this initiative by visiting http://www.content-bridge.com.

For your customer web sites with high traffic, or those that schedule special events that attract many to their sites, you can enhance your solutions provided by partnering with a content delivery service. This will also further enhance your web services in relation to your competition, as being a one-source solution for your customers. Large companies such as AOL are able to speed the delivery of their content to members through Digital Island's content services. By using services across AOL's network, content can be served directly from within AOL. Akamai (http://www.akamai.com), Digital Island (http://www.digitalisland.com) and SolidSpeed (http://www.solidspeed.com) are three of the top content delivery service companies in the industry. Because Akamai is the leader in the content delivery technology market, it will be discussed further in this section.

Akamai

Akamai has by far the leadership role in content delivery services, with over 11,600 servers within its globally distributed network. Akamai offers a service known as EdgeSuite for handling dynamic Web traffic needs. The proprietary technology uses algorithms developed by M.I.T. researchers, and cache servers to handle efficient content distribution within Akamai's network. According to Akamai, its content delivery services can deliver content to browsers from two to ten times faster than traditional load-balancing technologies. Akamai's flagship, the EdgeSuite service, is designed to reduce Internet infrastructure costs by extending the scalability, reliability, and performance benefits of content delivery across an entire web site. Akamai EdgeSuite enables the generation and delivery of dynamic content by building web pages from component pieces that can be targeted and delivered from locations optimized for each end user. Akamai's EdgeSuite pricing is based on a platform, services, and usage model. Akamai offers extensive traffic monitoring, activity logs, and service guarantees, as well as specializes in working with large-sized web sites. According to Akamai, it is also the largest CDN (content delivery network) in existence.

In Japan, for example, where Akamai and SOFTBANK have entered into a venture to create a jointly owned company in Japan to be known as Akamai Technologies Japan KK, there is heightened demand for enhancing streaming media services. Japan ranks second only to the U.S. in total Internet usage. According to the Electronic Commerce Promotion Council of Japan as noted by Akamai, business-to-consumer e-commerce is expected to grow to 6.7 trillion yen by 2004, a 762% increase from 2000 purchases.

During the 2000 presidential election, the CNN web site was able to deliver more than 100 million page impressions and 6.3 million unique visitors by using Akamai's service. According to Mike

Kilpatrick, technical content manager for Microsoft's Event Marketing Group, and user of Akamai's enterprise streaming services, "Through Akamai, we achieved a compelling return on investment by reaching out to new audiences that can further benefit from the technical content of our premium events via the Web." More information on Akamai is available at http://www.akamai.com.

SUMMARY

This chapter has introduced some examples of niche areas that web hosts can incorporate via partnerships in order to enhance their level of services provided. When considering the wide selection of web services to partner with, keep in mind the initial questions provided at the beginning of the chapter. Also, take into account how well each solution will complement your core business and actually benefit your customers. Find out what your customer's current and future needs are through surveys, questionnaires, and other interaction. The next chapter will focus on providing services for the enterprise, including offering data center and application services, either directly or via partnerships, with the goal of providing one-source solutions for customer needs.

PART VI

Advanced
Hosting Markets

CHAPTER 15

Growing Your Web Hosting Business

The loftier the building, the deeper must the foundation be laid.
—Thomas Kempis

As has been discussed in previous chapters, through partnerships with other ASPs, MSPs, and specialized web services, a web host can provide many value-added services that otherwise would not be available. As web applications become more sophisticated, it will be especially important for new entrants into this market to form partnership alliances in order to meet the array of customer requirements for e-commerce transactions and high server availability. In this chapter we will discuss several topics you will need to consider as your web hosting business expands. These subjects will include partnering with data centers, developing redundancy, ASPs, application servers, and utilizing network analysis tools. Case studies of web hosts will be highlighted that are successfully meeting customer needs within the market.

DEVELOPING PARTNERSHIPS WITH DATA CENTERS

Building a fully scalable data center requires a high-infrastructure investment, time, and a high degree of technical specialization in designing secure and protected operational facilities. Cisco offers a Hosting Business Modeling Tool that can help you forecast data center costs of construction, operations, sales, capital costs, backbone, and Internet connectivity costs. It also offers options for estimating the costs of purchasing from existing providers. More information is available at http://www.cisco.com.

As a web host's server farm expands, unless it has deep pockets, building a fully scalable data center from scratch is not a practical entry point for many in today's economy; especially if you are targeting customers who require highly scalable and secure solutions. Besides the cost of servers, routers, equipment, bandwidth, and security, personnel is a sizable percentage of expenses, especially if 24/7 support is provided.

By partnering with existing data centers or larger web hosts that provides co-location, dedicated, managed, and highly secure web services, it becomes more economically feasible. By co-locating servers within a partner's server facilities, the web host has the advantage of having access to the infrastructure, enhanced security, greater bandwidth, and 24/7 support services. The web host can also be able to resell these services and provide a greater range of hosting options to customers, especially on the high end. Pricing for co-location placement can range from $800 to $1,500 per month, depending on facilities. As part of an end-to-end solution, a data center may also market or resell bandwidth to partners. Some providers do not maintain ownership of their own network, but instead mark up the price of bandwidth to customers, while others do not sell bandwidth at all.

As with web hosts, there is no across-the-board standard to which all data centers adhere to. When reviewing providers to consider which have these data center capabilities, here is a checklist of some primary questions to keep in mind:

▼   How is the network managed? Is it actively manned by support personnel on a 24/7 basis?

■   What types of peering agreements are in place with other Tier 1 providers? Are methods such as BGP (Border Gateway Protocol) routing used among providers to reduce latency on the network, with the proper ASN (Autonomous System Number) registered? Where does this peering actually take place? Are public and private peering used?

■   What types of fiber optic connections does the provider have with the major exchange points on the Internet?

■   Are SLAs (Service Level Agreements) utilized that address conformance to individual customer requirements?

■   Are measures in place to regulate and maintain the internal environment of the facility (raised flooring, industrial-rated air conditioning system, fire retardant, backup power)?

■   What types of servers, network topologies, and routers are utilized and supported? How many servers are actively maintained?

■   How are the actual data backups maintained? Are backup media archived in a secure, ventilated, off-sight location?

- Is a high level of security maintained for the network and the facility? Are company security policies available for reviewing? What types of security policies are in place to prevent unauthorized data access through the Internet or the actual facilities, and to ensure network security and availability of services in case of emergencies, natural disasters, or hostile attack?

- Does the provider have staff assigned to keep up to date with the latest security concerns, and to ensure that the latest security measures and patches are applied, as well as to enforce the utmost internal and external network and firewall security?

- What levels of security are in place for limited clearance access to a data center (24 hour guarded security, digital cameras, PIN codes, photo badges, scanned palm readers, locked cages and racks, bulletproof glass)?

- Are security patches applied to all system builds, and operating systems installed that cover all known security holes?

- Are external security audits routinely made of data center operations?

- Is equipment kept up to date with technology advancements (which incorporate load balancing and caching), with systems routinely optimized for the best performance?

- How are rollouts coordinated through the provider, the customer, and your company?

- What is the standard rollout time for putting a customer's server and required applications in place? Is access to the root directory available on servers that need this type of access?

- How are customer support issues coordinated? Does the customer deal with your company exclusively?

- Does the provider have staff members that are certified in the technology represented? What types of relationships does the provider have in place with technology vendors?

■   Are spare servers, routers, and other equipment available in case of hardware failure?

■   What is the reputation, growth rate, and track record of the company? Are customer referrals available? How long has the provider been offering data center services?

■   Can monitoring of the availability and performance of the network be accomplished on a real-time basis through a standard web browser?

■   Are multiple data center locations maintained in different regions of the country or the world to address load balancing and network scalability, and ensure full backup and disaster recovery of the network?

▲   What levels of redundancy are enforced throughout the network and the infrastructure of the provider?

Be sure to research the data center facilities completely. Know the infrastructure and meet with support personnel. Depending on the range of services selected, once a server farm is fully in place, extensive network monitoring, security, product testing support, and 24/7 manned technical support should be available. Optional plans should allow for load balancing and scalable expansion as your needs require.

TOWARD FULL REDUNDANCY

When evaluating data center facilities, the criteria should especially focus on the level of redundancy of the operations available throughout, and should account for the types of requirements your customers have and what you can afford. Redundancy should be the central component throughout the decision process, which encompasses the smallest to the largest components in the data center. This includes not only the clustering of servers, daily backups, multiple firewalls, and security policies in place; it also should include redundancy of server power supplies, spare equipment, excess capacity, and cooling and electrical systems in case of extended power outages.

NOTE: One example of the importance of cooling and electrical systems has been the 2001 energy crisis and rolling blackouts in California; more than 500 of the top Internet companies are headquartered in the state. Web hosts that co-locate within California (or any other state that has experienced similar energy shortages) should contact their data center providers to plan for the local power company's schedule for blackouts. Alternate power sources such as high-performance diesel generators should be a required feature in a data center provider.

Redundancy encompasses multiple bandwidth providers, which includes peering agreements (as a Tier One provider) with other providers to enhance the routing of traffic, and to avoid delays because of latency. Investigate the types of connections the data center has with the more than 70 major exchange points on the Internet. This also will include multiple data center locations to globally distribute services in case another location becomes unavailable because of a regional disaster or hostile physical attack.

For high-end performance in the data center environment, solutions such as Sun Solaris and Compaq Tru64 have long provided scalable systems based on Unix. For example, Sun Solaris supports 64 processors, with advanced partitioning features. Microsoft has introduced a new operating system for the data center market, Datacenter, which will support as many as 32 processors (compared to 8 with other versions of Windows), including partitioning, clustering, and load balancing. The operating system is marketed only through hardware vendors that have been certified by Microsoft, with only certified vendors to provide the installation and after sales support for. Some of the vendors that have been certified include Dell, IBM, Unisys, and Compaq, which will market and provide support directly for Datacenter.

Products such as NSI's Double-Take provides real-time replication of data from primary to secondary servers either locally or through the Internet, providing disaster recovery protection for server farms and enhancing existing backup methods. If a primary server fails, the secondary server provides failover protection, containing backup copies of key data files, with the secondary server capable of handling user requests. Double-Take is available from NSI Software; more information can be found at http://www.nsisoftware.com.

In 1999, as Hurricane Floyd approached Florida, Dnet Internet, a web hosting company, knew that web services would need to be quickly transferred to another location. "We're a hosting and Internet consulting company and we wanted to make absolutely sure that if there were any power outages in Florida, our clients wouldn't be affected. It's great to have a company (Rackspace) follow through and do what it says it will do," asserts Mark Footer, CEO of Dnet Internet. Based in San Antonio, Texas, Rackspace provides managed web services through its data centers which allow rapid deployment for made-to-order servers, and dedicated services on the Unix and Microsoft platforms. Rackspace provides a range of monitoring services, including RackWatch. RackWatch provides the capability of monitoring and testing specific server ports that run web services such as DNS, HTTP, and FTP. These ports can be tested routinely on servers that are hosted by Rackspace, with alerts sent to the customer. More information on Rackspace is available at http://www.rackspace.com.

Internet attacking methods, which attempt to maliciously penetrate servers through the Internet, are ever evolving and include port scanning, Trojan worms or viruses (through e-mail or other methods), multiple logon attempts to protected areas, network mapping attempts, flooding attempts to send bursts of large packets, spoofing, and other cracking efforts. Data centers must have a sophisticated intrusion detection system in place, in addition to virus and Trojan prevention software, and firewalls. Redundant routing capability, security tracking, server logging, and event monitoring within a data center are critical. Inquire about the availability of spare routers that are already preconfigured (within fully secured areas), to diminish the potential for downtime because of a router. Through a comprehensive and evolving security policy, a data center can anticipate the unexpected. With a fully redundant environment and a fully knowledgeable and continually trained staff, a single point of failure will be alleviated.

APPLICATION SERVICE PROVIDERS

As with the leaders in the web hosting space, ASPs will continue to form consolidations and mergers as the market emerges, and companies continue to redefine their ranges of services beyond basic online rental of office applications. The market is expected to reach $2 billion by 2003 according to some industry estimates. For ASPs providing the hosting of many applications, the short- and long-term savings in IT costs have proven substantial for customers. Regardless of whether the ASP manages its own infrastructure, or partners with a web host or data center for co-location or other services, there are parameters to keep in mind when representing solutions:

▼   Partner with infrastructure providers (data centers, bandwidth providers, carriers) that can be coordinated with for extensive application beta testing before going live, which provide performance enhanced technologies (caching, load balancing, clustering), enhanced security, and monitoring.

■   Explain with clarity (no vague industry terms here), the range of application services provided, using the customer's viewpoint.

■   Explain any components of the service provided that is the responsibility of the customer, such as off-site training. Delineate between what is and is not covered within the customer's unique contractual and service level agreements. Specify an uptime guarantee in coordination with back-end providers of Internet services, identified through SLAs.

■   Clearly identify within the contractual agreement, installation costs, monthly recurring costs, hidden costs, and a range of pricing for custom services at the outset of the relationship.

■   Provide customers with access to monitoring, if the application is made available through the customer's web site.

■   Identify the amount of time for the initial and ongoing training you will provide, and what subjects are covered within training programs. Provide a detailed manual or online help screens, and instant online customer assistance for the web application interface.

■   Specify your customer, web presence, privacy, security, and support policies within your contracts and SLAs.

- ■ At the beginning of the relationship, assign a customer and support person as first-level contact for the customer, with a clear chain of contact for resolving questions or concerns.

- ■ Provide case studies and quotations of positive customer experiences.

- ▲ Refer to previous chapters to review tips on customer relations and effective marketing strategies.

The Application Usage Tracking Service, shown in Figure 15-1, is a package freely available from Microsoft that tracks customer hosted services specifically for ASPs and data centers. Another function of the package that can also be utilized by web hosts is to provide SLA (Service Level Agreement) tracking for specific hosting functions, and to make these detailed reports available to individual customers.

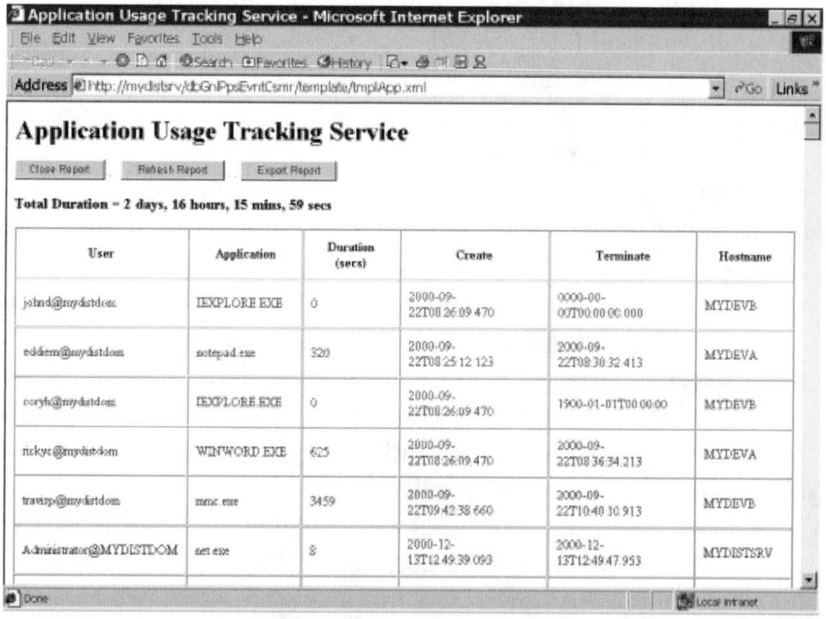

Figure 15-1.   Application Usage Tracking Service reporting example
Source: Microsoft Corporation

An ASP or data center also could use report data to determine customer pricing. For data centers, individual operational tasks completed by company personnel can be tracked for each customer, which also can target where tasks might need to be automated. You can individually track applications and processes, and generate reports to gauge when and how each is run. The Application Usage Tracking Service package can also be used as a tool for troubleshooting where potential problems may be occurring. Available as a free download with source code, you can find tracking service software at ftp://ftp.microsoft.com/services/isn/svcPvdrs/ops/monitoring/.

APPLICATION SERVERS

Application servers allow highly sophisticated web solutions to be developed, incorporating business concepts with advanced programming logic. An extensive array of application servers is available in the market in which web hosts can specialize. By 2002 the market for application servers is expected to reach $2.1 billion. Many application servers are built around J2EE (Java 2 Enterprise Edition), which uses Enterprise JavaBeans technology, including BEA WebLogic, IBM WebSphere, and iPlanet Application Server, to provide high scalability and functionality using the robust features provided by the Java platform-independent architecture (refer to Appendix B for a full listing).

Ensure that an EJB server solution that is considered is certified by JavaSoft fully supports the EJB 1.1 specification. Most vendors that have Enterprise JavaBeans solutions also provide a version of the JSP (Java Server Pages) engine. Many application server solutions include built-in load balancing and fault tolerance functionality. Individual vendor pricing varies widely.

Other application servers available include Allaire Cold Fusion and Microsoft Application Center 2000 Server. Some web hosts such as Digex are starting to support Microsoft Application Center. "Application Center 2000 will give us a true component/business logic tier with the ability to load balance and provide automatic failover, as well as the ability to rapidly expand or rebuild clusters with minimal human intervention based on the cluster controller replication functionality," according to Shawn Bice, Director of Engineering for Digex. Microsoft's Application Center now includes CDLB (Component Dynamic Load Balancing) which allows COM+ to do component processing within a clustering environment, which has long been supported by EJBs. When deciding on what architecture to use, consider the range of platforms and devices you need to support, whether the server needs to be open source or proprietary, licensing issues, the requirements of the customer, performance issues, scalability, and where developers' experienced lies.

Online resources available for Application Servers can be located in Appendix B, and the following:

▼ **Sun Microsystems Java 2 Enterprise Edition**
   http:// java.sun.com/j2ee/

▲ **Microsoft Application Center 2000**
   http://www. microsoft.com/applicationcenter

ENHANCING SQL SERVER PERFORMANCE

A common database server that is supported within many data center environment is Microsoft's SQL Server. In addressing the need for enhanced performance, Microsoft has initiated an architecture standard known as the VI (Virtual Interface) architecture, shown in Figure 15-2, made standard within SQL Server 2000 Enterprise Edition. For SQL database applications, the VI standard can allow for less system overhead, lower latency, clustering functionality, and is supported by many computer vendors such as Giganet, Intel, and Microsoft.

As identified within a Dell Power Solutions article (March 2000, by Jamie Gruener, with Giganet), VI adds the following performance enhancements for Microsoft SQL–based database applications:

▼ Higher throughput for faster application to application communications

■ Reduced system overhead for greater scalability

▲ Lower message latency (delays) for greater application responsiveness

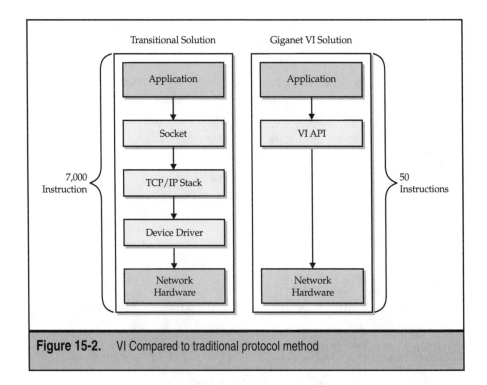

Figure 15-2. VI Compared to traditional protocol method

All servers can communicate with each other across a data center VI-enabled network (such as Giganet cLAN), with data accessed seamlessly by users across a server farm. This distributed approach can result in increased speed of access to data and redundancy, for less cost than the purchasing of large traditional systems. More information can be located at http://www.giganet.com.

OTHER SECURITY CONSIDERATIONS

In addition to the use of firewalls and preventative measures, which were discussed in Chapter 11, enhanced security services are being offered by web hosts to ensure privacy of data. Many web hosts provide VPN (Virtual Private Networks) services through firewalls and encryption to allow customers to access a private network via the Internet. IPSec is an IETF standard that provides enhanced security at the network layer, has been available for some time with Unix platforms and now is supported with Windows 2000.

IPSec can support applications through IP, providing the utmost integrity of confidential data. By using IPSec with Network Load Balancing (NLB) in Windows 2000 as part of a clustering solution, incoming Internet traffic can be distributed among servers. For enhanced security and encryption, two VPN methods are supported: IPSec (IP Security Protocol), shown in Figure 15-3 and MPPE (Microsoft Point-to-Point Encryption). IPSec is the most commonly used, because it is an open protocol.

For real-time security, packages such as Network ICE are available which seamlessly provide advanced intrusion detection for VPNs. More information can found at http://www.networkice.com/sans. Enhanced encryption and security at times comes at the price of speed. For secure e-commerce transactions, other resources are provided by web hosts to enhance the speed of processing, such as with Radware

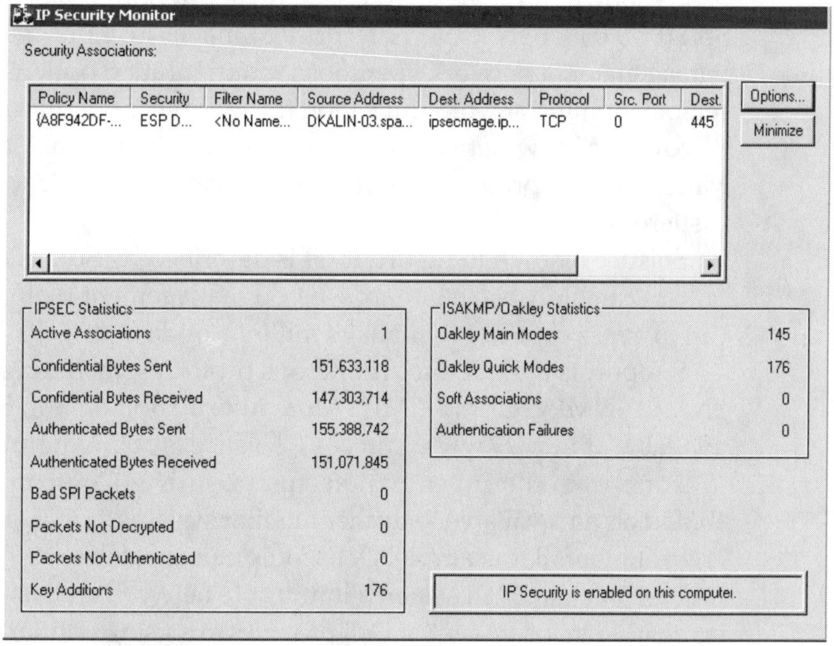

Source: Microsoft Corporation

Figure 15-3. IP Security Protocol

(http://www.radware.com). As CEO of Ordermarket Mike Belson says, "Secure transactions are slow and tedious and often consume a large portion of network resources. Our experience with handling hundreds of simultaneous secure transactions has led us to the conclusion that Radware's SSL acceleration product is a critical solution for alleviating much of the associated overhead."

NETWORK ANALYSIS TOOLS

There are numerous network analysis tools that provide sophisticated monitoring of servers, with the real-time ability to page, call, or e-mail support personnel if a server becomes unavailable. Some of the these (which are commonly used within data centers and server farm operations) include HP OpenView, Computer Associates Unicenter TNG, Tivoli, Microsoft SMS (Systems Management Server), Sun Solstice, Intel LANDesk, Castle Rock, IBM NetView, and Cabletron Spectrum.

As shown in Figure 15-4, Castle Rock provides scalable packages, SNMPc 5.0 Network and Enterprise Manager Editions, which allows management of network operations. Configuration options can include remote monitoring with utilization tracking, event notifications, instant discovery of new network components, and an optional Java console. More information on Castle Rock is available at http://www. castlerock.com.

Solstice (shown in Figure 15-5) is described by Sun as being an "ultra scalable, open standards–based management platform, which can increase capacity to manage millions of devices."

Support is included for numerous protocols, including RPC, SNMP, SNMPv2C, and CMIP. More information on Sun Solstice is available at http://www.sun.com/solstice/system.mgmt.html.

For certain computer manufacturers, such as Compaq, Dell, and IBM, tools are available to further monitor systems within an operations environment. For example, Dell Computers provides an integration tool for tracking Dell systems if multiple network analysis tools are being used in a data center. Dell provides this using standard protocols including SNMP (Simple Network Management Protocol), DMI

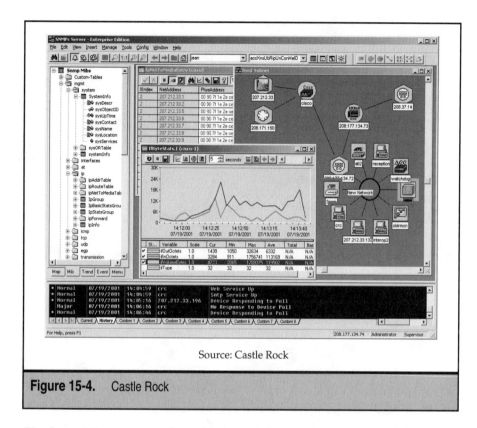

Source: Castle Rock

Figure 15-4. Castle Rock

(Desktop Management Interface), and CIM (Common Information Model). Further online sources on network monitoring and analysis tools are noted in Appendix D.

CASE STUDY: DIGEX

Digex, which began operations in 1991 as a regional ISP, was the first provider of dedicated hosting services. In 1993, the company started providing managed web hosting services. Besides managed services, Digex also provides ASP, VPN, and managed firewall services. Digex has now grown to become the largest provider of web hosting services, with a variety of partnership plans available for IT professionals to resell. Digex utilizes an OC-48 Tier One network backbone with caching services through Inktomi.

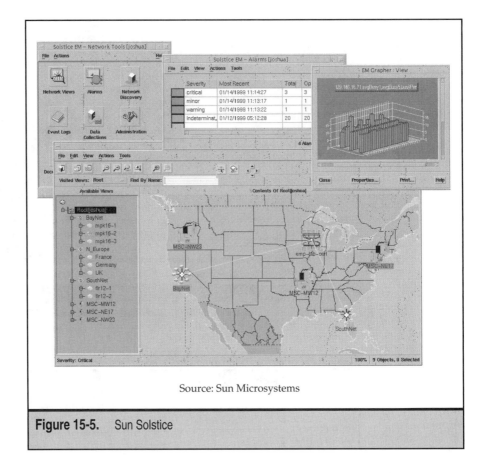

Source: Sun Microsystems

Figure 15-5. Sun Solstice

According to Digex, it maintains over 4,200 servers, with the average customer using 6 servers. For ASPs, Digex provides a partner program called app-Link, which allows ASPs to test their applications prior to launch, and provides a quick turnaround for new installations, partner incentives, and joint marketing opportunities. Using its custom- built Digex Application Platform, which operates through a graphical interface on the Microsoft Windows 2000 platform, network administrators are able to quickly design and install new web servers in a matter of minutes to meet changing customer needs. For customers who utilize the platform, this allows updates to be made quickly instead of modifying the actual coding.

Digex is one of the first web and application hosts to utilize the Microsoft .NET architecture of Enterprise Servers, which includes

Application Center 2000 and Exchange 2000 Server. For advanced server requirements, Digex uses clustering with Microsoft's *CRS* (*Content Replication Server*) to ensure that dedicated servers that are clustered are always synchronized in meeting the parameters of individual customer SLAs.

For customers seeking enhanced security, traffic can be segmented separately on Cisco switches through VLANs (Virtual Local Area Networks), with each server farm independently maintained. Digex also provides solutions that are based on the Sun Solaris for Unix platform, and was among the first hosting providers to receive Sun Microsystem's SunTone certification. Digex operates five data centers, located in California, Maryland, and Great Britain, with customers including Ford Motor Company, PeoplePC, Nike, Spalding, J. P. Morgan, and Forbes. Digex was purchased by Intermedia Communications in 1997 and became a subsidiary of WorldCom following a $3 billion merger with Intermedia Communications in 2001. More information on Digex is available at http://www.digex.com.

CASE STUDY: DIGITAL ISLAND

Digital Island provides a three-tiered approach to allow a range of partnerships, utilizing from their six available data center facilities located around the world. There is a range of managed hosting options that allow partners to provide customers with access to Digital Island's data center facility services. There also are Internet security services that include Denial of Service backoff protection, according to Digital Island. Digital Island also offers specific application-level services to meet network service requirements, including VistaWare (shown in Figure 15-6), a management tool that monitors applications for server utilization and performance statistics, data centers, and the Digital Island network.

The Digital Island network itself encompasses a private fiber optic ATM backbone, which is available within oven more than 30 countries. Using a process defined as *BSD* (*Best Distributor Selection*), content is further enhanced to speed the delivery of packets and avoid Internet congestion points. Further information on Digital Island can be located at http://www.digitalisland.net.

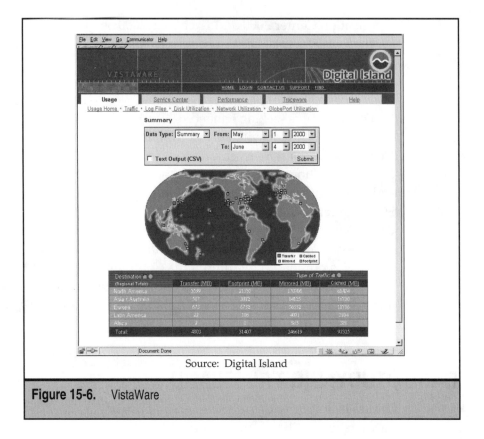

Source: Digital Island

Figure 15-6.   VistaWare

SUMMARY

This chapter has introduced factors for web hosts to consider as their markets expand into managed services, for which more than half of the growth in hosting is predicted by 2004. Web hosts must review these areas as they partner with existing data centers and utilize technologies that will best be able to meet their customers' high-end needs.

CHAPTER 16

Emerging Markets

The widespread acceptance of the Internet has been unprecedented, surpassing television, radio, and the telephone in its rapid rate of adoption as an innovative form of communication. In the mad rush to instant e-commerce riches, which can be compared to the most feverish gold rushes of the past, many dot-coms quickly used up the majority of their venture capital and IPO funding on marketing, believing that market share could be instantly acquired. Others forgot the most basic tenet of sound business practice: having a good business model in the first place.

Businesses realize the importance of the Internet as a very effective overall business and marketing tool; thus they are increasingly utilizing it to be globally competitive. Predictions for the web hosting market overall are an estimated expansion rate of 85–105 percent between 1999 and 2003 (according to Forrester Research and IDC). The web hosts that stand out from the competition will clearly communicate the value of solutions that focus on business processes and go well beyond just basic web hosting. Web hosts will provide enhanced productivity tools including marketing and even call center services to customers. The line between the web host and consultant role will become further blurred, as web hosts offer professional insights and best solutions that can complement the existing core processes in a business and provide enhanced control of IT costs and management through outsourcing. Small businesses and brick-and-mortar companies especially can greatly benefit from this level of enhanced IT services.

A web host also can serve as a frontline consultant, offering professional insights and best solutions that can complement the existing processes in a business and provide enhanced control of IT costs and management. For web hosts to fully accomplish this, they need to become knowledgeable in their customers' businesses; to speak their language and avoid "technospeak" terminology." These small companies are looking for a virtual partner that can give them the tools they need to expand online and, more important, offer the guidance to do it successfully. "It's about building relationships," acknowledged Kneko Burney, Cahners In-Stat Group.

As identified in Chapter 10, look for QoS (Quality of Service) guarantees of 100 percent availability to be fully utilized by web hosts as a value-added service feature in preallocating a designated portion of their available bandwidth for specific customer subscribers, and for speeding up functions such as distributed content on demand. Further routing enhancements are being made with MPLS (Multiprotocol Label Switch) routing, which provides measures for guaranteeing bandwidth; the IETF (Internet Engineering Task Force) is working on standards. For bandwidth providers, rapid enhancements also are being made in the routing and optical switching capabilities of fiber optics for Internet usage, which will continue to open market opportunities. The problem for carriers has been high operational costs that cut into revenues—sometimes as much as 50 percent. These new optical technologies will significantly reduce these recurring operating costs. Providers such as Telseon (http://www.telseon.com) also are introducing services that allow web hosts (and their customers) to control the amount of bandwidth they need in real time through their online web portals.

Businesses seek to partner with hosts that understand their organizations and can implement strategic plans in cost-effective ways that fully complement, and are consistent with their ways of doing business with customers, employees, and suppliers. Even with the dot-com slowdown, online business-to-business sales are expected to reach $1 trillion before 2005, with more than half coming from outside the U.S.

Businesses and web hosts must increasingly cater to global markets to increase their market share, which includes having web sites that can be displayed in multiple languages instead of English only, and that have support representatives capable of interpreting. A web host also needs to be knowledgeable of and prepared for other variables such as Internet taxation, and be able to accommodate customers for this service need as new legislation emerges. The three primary hosting markets that present the most potential revenues are MSPs (Managed Service Providers), ASPs (Applications Service Providers), and One-Source Service Providers that can combine MSP, ASP, and other online services to provide end-to-end Web solutions for customers.

MSPs

Popular aspects of managed web services include customized server management, applications monitoring and hosting, and network integration of enterprise processes. The primary component provided by MSPs is in handling specific IT infrastructure needs of customers. Web services I see as being especially in demand in the near future include these:

▼ **Performance monitoring**   Monitors how servers and applications are performing and the tracking of web site visitors.

■ **Load balancing**   Servers or applications are distributed among several computers within a network to balance the load and better ensure reliability of services.

■ **Distributed content**   Includes special one-time events and variable traffic needs to accommodate capacity upon demand. This niche market is anticipated to approach $1.1 billion during 2001.

■ **E-commerce processing of transactions**   Capability to process customer orders securely online. As noted by Forrester Research, web hosts will obtain an estimated 91 percent of all revenues from web sites that are e-commerce enabled by 2004 (accounting for $18 billion of the estimated $19.8 billion in revenues for web hosts).

■ **Streaming media services**   The process of supporting high quality audio and video content. As technologies improve, imagine in the near future being able to rent movies for viewing online anytime through the Internet.

▲ **Security**   Protection of data is a continual process. Hosts can capture niche markets by marketing specialized security services such as firewalls, virus and Trojan prevention, secure data centers, intrusion detection and notification services, enhanced encryption services, and VPNs. Hosts also can adopt stringent security policies to protect critical network and customer data, which includes ongoing monitoring and awareness of security issues in the industry.

The market growth of web hosts that provide managed services is anticipated to be more extensive than any other type of hosting. As has been noted in previous chapters, analysts predict more than half the growth in web hosting to be in managed services alone by 2004. With the recent energy shortages experienced in California and appearing in other regions of the country, businesses are concerned with their operations and infrastructure availability. Web hosts that can represent their hosting and applications as being highly available and redundant, and can provide reliable solutions to this energy problem will be able to capture substantial market share. This can be especially beneficial to hosts that provide end-to-end solutions for enterprises, with direct ownership of their own managed facilities (distributed regional data centers and bandwidth), or through strategic partnerships. Within the area of server automation, some web hosts might go with turnkey solutions such as those provided by Sphera or Plesk, or develop their own, which will enable companies to manage and scale servers and applications.

ASPs

As identified by Cahners In-Stat Group, by 2004, more than 3 million businesses will use ASPs for their online efforts. As with other types of web hosts, ASPs will need to differentiate their services to gain identification within the emerging market. As markets evolve, look for ASPs to go beyond providing distributed IT-based monitoring and office productivity–type enterprise applications.

ASPs must develop alliances within the industry and focus on research and development to provide competitive services in the future. These highly sophisticated applications will be developed through a combination of technologies such as Java, EJB, XML, XHTML, COM+, and SOAP, providing customized add-on components developed in house for both general and specific niche markets for a wide variety of new Internet connected devices.

For example, you will be able to securely manage your house utility or burglar alarm settings through an Internet cellular phone, PDA, or PC. Some of this will be made possible through developmental partnerships with regional utilities, associations, and industry-associated companies.

As Microsoft evolves as a .NET-centered organization for distributing Microsoft-based applications through the Internet, it will increasingly partner with web hosts. In addition, UML (Uniformed Modeling Language) will be further utilized to encourage rapid application development among teams of programmers. If you are providing developed or customized applications, you will need to ensure thorough beta testing of applications before introducing them. The speed at which the market can further evolve will partially depend on targeted industry partnerships that allow coordinated standards, and research and development to occur.

From an ongoing expense basis, ASPs have to negotiate software licensing arrangements and infrastructure requirements necessary for supporting an application, and provide all the necessary training and management of the application. Some of this is being accomplished through strategic partnerships with market leaders such as with Microsoft, Sun, IBM, Cisco, and Oracle. From an infrastructure standpoint, according to Cahners In-Stat Group, ASPs spent more than $1 billion in the U.S. during 2000.

Many web hosts have established strategic partnerships with consultant firms, systems integrators, accounting firms, telephone companies, and ISPs that might include negotiated arrangements to market their services to partners' customers. "Our partners are HP, Sun, SAP, Oracle, Siebel, KPMG Consulting, and the list goes on," stated John Charters, President and CEO of Qwest Cyber.Solutions; he further stated, "At QCS we believe that developing and maintaining the right industry partnerships is key to successful delivery of value-driven ASP solutions." ASPs such as Qwest Cyber.Solutions maintain their own data center operations, unlike many ASPs, which rely on partnership arrangements for their infrastructure needs.

ASPs such as Cirqit.com specialize in the niche market of business communications, which includes ordering, procurement, and estimating. ASPs also are making inroads within the real estate, insurance, legal, and financial sectors, especially those with key executive experience in those industries; other ASPs seek to acquire overall market share. Applications are being developed which are integrated with advanced Internet search functionality to be able to more effectively find targeted information online quickly. Voice recognition applications will finally evolve to allow practical everyday usage.

The need for web sites to be highly personalized is leading web hosts to fill the niche for *portals* through which customers can enable web site visitors to customize appearance settings with search functionality and targeted content. With the application development time needed to specialize, some web hosts are using packaged solutions for resell. Utilizing a package such as OptimalView from Compuware provides web hosts with a turnkey solution for portals, which includes workflow processes and component-based development

As with other types of web hosting within the market, consolidations and mergers will steadily increase. If you are starting out as a web host, consider forming the type of business that will be beneficial to your continued operations, such as an LLC (Limited Liability Corporation), in case of liability or other action. Consult with an attorney for professional advice on this subject.

Many smaller web hosting firms are partnering with ISPs for beneficial routing peering agreements, in some cases having access to customer accounts for marketing. The ISP also benefits by being able to provide enhanced specialty hosting services beyond dial-up, which is provided through the partner web host. The ISP must be able to expand its bandwidth capability to accommodate for the expanded services offered through these partnerships; some ISPs are expanding their specialties through acquisitions or mergers to directly provide specialized ASP-level services themselves.

HARDWARE INNOVATIONS

There are many new technologies on the horizon that will continue to increase the speed and performance of web servers, network appliances, and routers. One innovative new memory technology from IBM might substantially bolster web hosting services within the next few years: *MRAM* (*Magnetic Random Access Memory*), scheduled to be in production by 2004, is designed to use magnetism instead of electricity to store data in memory. IBM, in conjunction with Infineon Technologies AG, plans to manufacture the memory chips, which have the potential to greatly improve the speed and capabilities of PCs and other devices that access the Internet. Other areas that would benefit from these memory enhancements include voice recognition, streaming multimedia and, complex applications, which will encourage the development of many new portable Internet devices. Look for a multitude of these portable Internet devices which will be geared toward making the Internet more widely available to consumers and employees from any location (always on and available), and will be used as a personal information tool. These developments also will continue to expand opportunities for employees to work from anywhere.

Technologies that take advantage of wireless technology are increasingly in demand as cellular phones, PDAs, handhelds, and other new methods are developed to access the Internet and provide increased functionality, communication, and convenience. Cellular phones currently are used by 50 percent of global users for Internet access; primarily in Japan and Europe. The U.S. has lagged behind in its adoption for this purpose, due primarily to the delayed market availability for Internet-enabled cellular phones, widespread PC usage, and slow adoption of wireless standards. Higher-speed carrier networks are increasingly available overseas for cellular, which will greatly expand the capabilities of delivering HTML/XHTML-style content, and should be widely available by 2003 in the U.S.

By 2003 analysts project that there will be more than 1 billion cellular phones in use, most with fully integrated Internet capability. ASPs such as Aether Systems, Everypath, and AnyDevice.com specialize in applications for wireless devices. Web hosts must learn how to develop for cellular and other wireless devices, create content, and handle security using XHTML, Java, WML, and 3G/OS (a new interface standard for enabling more sophisticated applications) to prepare and account for wireless technologies and be able to market these services to customers. Web hosts also can partner with device manufacturers such as Ericsson, Motorola, Nokia, and Palm in advertising their links, and with telephone carriers such as AT&T, Verizon, and Nextel.

SECURITY ENHANCEMENTS

Security concerns are brought on by potential hackers and crackers causing network breaches of security, Denial of Service attacks, and computer viruses almost daily, all of which have the potential to do significant damage to web hosts and customers' data on their networks. These potentially harmful methods are meant to find hidden vulnerabilities in operating systems and networks. Since first being reported on in 1988 by CERT, the number of computer security incidents has grown from 6 to 58,000. These types of attacks have at one time affected most of the more popular web sites through widely known system vulnerabilities that were not accounted for. Supposedly secure U.S. government web sites also have proven to be vulnerable.

Besides having a security policy, a web host today needs to have a security specialist and staff who are designated to fulfill important functions. These include active security maintenance of the network, further bolstering and hardening systems that might be exposed, updating intrusion detection methods and security policies as needed, and making available enhanced customer services that go beyond simply having a firewall. Keep an updated security and usage policy—and enforce it. It's one thing to allow employees to play Doom; quite another to allow employees free rein to access customer maintained systems without the proper clearance, or to visit porn sites on company time.

As vulnerabilities are discovered and viruses developed, a web host must have staff dedicated to full awareness of these security issues and know how to prevent them. Ensure that new employees and contractors are checked out, agree to security policies, and have appropriate clearance only to systems that they are responsible for. Complete internal audits that gauge how well security is implemented, including the tracking of all software and hardware inventory. A stolen notebook could expose your systems to many hidden vulnerabilities. For customers, media coverage has resulted in a heightened awareness of the need for ongoing preventive security measures, for which web hosts now provide online solutions. Enhancements continue to be made for stronger encryption methods, security tools, procedures, and secure routing protocols.

SUMMARY

In preparing for emerging market opportunities, a web host will need to be in a constant state of evolution to help customers realize the many practical benefits that can be realized. This will include an increasing range of enhanced web services and professional consultation, and a high-availability infrastructure and responsive customer service, either directly or through alliances and partnerships. Review the questions presented throughout this book, which provide the new or existing web host with areas they can address in providing an overall hosting solution. This also will assist a web host with being fully prepared to formulate services that, both match customer needs and also are geared to best take advantage of emerging markets.

APPENDIX A

Web Hosting
Scripting Resources

In Chapters 8 and 9 of this book we discussed web server scripting resources for popular technologies such as CGI, PHP, JSP, and ASP. Refer to these for links to web sites, scripting examples, and coding, which help you learn more about these technologies. Other online resources that provide scripts and coding for web hosts to download and modify for their own usage include

▼ **Apache Software Foundation** http://www.apache.org/

■ **Apache Week** http://www.apacheweek.com/

■ **Apache Today.com** http://www.apachetoday.com/

■ **Microsoft Internet Services Network ISN Code Samples Resource Center** http://www.microsoft.com/ISN/ISP/downloads.asp

■ **ASP Objects** http://www.aspobjects.com/

■ **ASP Code** http://www.aspcode.net/

■ **Servlets** http://staging.servlets.com/isps/servlet/ISPViewAll

■ **PHP Resources** http://www.weberdev.com/

■ **Gamelan** http://www.gamelan.com/javaprogramming/

■ **ScriptSearch** http://scriptsearch.internet.com/

▲ **Website Abstrations** http://www.wsabstract.com/

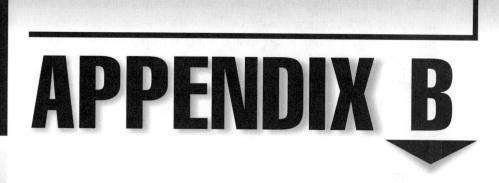

APPENDIX B

Application Server Resources

The Application Server comparison charts on the following pages are provided as a resource for Internet application developers that focus on providing Java-based enterprise hosting solutions. Web hosts and ASPs now provide hosting plans and solutions for some of the vendor enterprise–based products listed. Refer to Flashline at http://www.flashline.com/ for updates. Not listed are Microsoft-specific application server products, which are discussed in Chapter 15 (you can find more information at http://www.microsoft.com/applicationcenter.htm).

Vendor Product	Edition Version	Release	JDK	EJB	JSP	JMS	J2EE Lic.	J2EE Cert.	Platform
Allaire JRun	Developer v3.0	Jun-00	1.2 1.3	1.1	1.1	1.0	X		NT, Solaris, Linux, HP-UX, Mac MRJ 2.0, Tru64, AIX, SGI IRIX
	Professional v3.0	Jun-00	1.2 1.3		1.1		X		
	Advanced v3.0	Feb-01	1.2 1.3		1.1		X		
	Enterprise v3.0	Jun-00	1.2 1.3	1.1	1.1	1.0	X	X	
Apache Tomcat	v3.3	Mar-01	1.8 1.2.2 1.3		1.1				Anything running a JDK 1.1.8 JVM
Apple WebObjects	v4.5	Mar-00	1.1.6						Mac OS X Server, NT 4.0, Win2K, Solaris 2.6 and 2.7, HP-UX 11

Table B-1.   Application Server Comparison Matrix

Vendor Product	Edition Version	Release	JDK	EJB	JSP	JMS	J2EE Lic.	J2EE Cert.	Platform
ATG Dynamo	v5.0	Sep-00	1.2.2	1.1	1.1	1.0.2	X	X	NT, Solaris, AIX, HP-UX
BEA WebLogic	Express v6.0	Dec-00	1.3		1.1		X		NT, Solaris, HP-UX, AIX, Tru64, Win2K, Open VMS, AIX 4.3.3, Sequent Dynix 4.4.4, OS/400 V4R4, Linux, SGI Irix 6.5, SNI Reliant 5.44C, Unisys OS1100, Unisys Burroughs, OS 390 V2R6
	Server v6.0		1.3	1.1 2.0 (Limited)	1.1	1.0.2	X	X	
	Enterprise v5.1	Jun-00	1.2	1.1	1.1	1.0.2	X	X	NT, Solaris, HP-UX, AIX, Compaq Tru64, Win2K, SCO Unixware, OS/390 Unix System Services, CORBA

Table B-1.   Application Server Comparison Matrix *(continued)*

Vendor Product	Edition Version	Release	JDK	EJB	JSP	JMS	J2EE Lic.	J2EE Cert.	Platform
Borland (Formerly Inprise) AppServer	v4.5	Jan-01	1.2.2 1.3	1.1	1.1	1.0.1	X	X	NT, Win2k, Solaris, HP-UX, AIX, Linux
Caucho Resin	Core v1.2	Oct-00	1.1.x 1.2.x 1.3.x		1.1				NT, Win2K, Solaris, Linux (any system running a JDK)
Compaq NonStop Enterprise	v1.0	Jan-00	1.2 1.3	1.1	N/A		X		Compaq NonStop ™ Himalaya ™
Digital Creations ;Zope	Standard v2.3	Feb-01							Solaris, xBSD, Linux, Windows (win32) (Anything that supports Python)
Evidian	v2.2	Feb-01	1.2 1.3	1.1		1.0.2			NT, Linux, Solaris, AIX, HP-UX, Win2K, Netware
JonAS Fujistsu Siemens Bean Transactions	v2.0	Sep-00	1.2	1.1					NT, Solaris, Linux, Reliant Unix, BS2000
Fujitsu Software Corp. Interstage	Web v3.0	Jul-00	1.2 1.3		1.1 1.2		X		Linux, HP UX, Sun Solaris, NT

Table B-1.   Application Server Comparison Matrix *(continued)*

Vendor Product	Edition Version	Release	JDK	EJB	JSP	JMS	J2EE Lic.	J2EE Cert.	Platform
	Standard v3.0	Jul-00	1.2 1.3		1.1 1.2		X		
	Enterprise v3.0	Jul-00	1.2 1.3	1.1	1.1 1.2	1.0.2	X	X	
Gemstone *Gemstone/J*	Web v4.1	Oct-00	1.2		1.1		X		NT, Solaris
	Component v4.1	Oct-00	1.2	1.0	1.1		X		
	Enterprise v4.1	Oct-00	1.2	1.0	1.1		X		
	Commerce Automation v4.1	Oct-00	1.2	1.0	1.1		X		
HP Bluestone Total-e-Server	Server v7.3	Mar-01	1.2.2 1.3	1.1	1.1	1.0.2	X	X	NT, Solaris, Linux, OS/390, AIX, HP-UX, SGI IRIX, Digital Alpha UNIX, Digital Alpha Intel
	Mobile v1.0	Mar-01	1.2.2 1.3	1.1	1.1	1.0.2	X	X	
HHPN XLiRAD	Enterprise v1.5	Feb-01	1.2 1.3	1.1					Any platform running a JVM 1.2.x
	Lite v1.5	Feb-01	1.2 1.3	1.1					
Hitachi Cosminexus	Web v03-05	Apr-01	1.3		1.1				NT 4.0, Win2K Server, Solaris, HP-UX
	Standard v03-05	Apr-01	1.3	1.1	1.1	1.0.2	X	X	

Table B-1. Application Server Comparison Matrix *(continued)*

Vendor Product	Edition Version	Release	JDK	EJB	JSP	JMS	J2EE Lic.	J2EE Cert.	Platform
	Enterprise v03-05	Apr-01	1.3	1.1	1.1	1.0.2	X	X	
IBM WebSphere	Standard v3.5.3	Mar-01	1.2.2		1.1	1.0.2	X		NT, Win2K, Solaris, AIX, AS/400, HP-UX, Netware, Linux
	Advanced v3.5.3	Mar-01	1.2.2	11	1.1	1.0.2	X		
	Enterprise v3.5	Oct-00	1.2.2	1.0	1.0		X		NT, Solaris, AIX
	V4.0	Mar-01	1.2.2	1.1	1.1	1.0.2	X	X	Z/OS, OS/390
In-Q-My Application Server	V4.0.2	Mar-01	1.2.2 1.3	1.1	1.1	1.0.2	X		NT, Solaris, HP-UX, AIX, Linux
IBS Enterprise Application Server	v1.0	Jul-00	1.2	1.1	1.0				NT, Solaris, AIX
IONA IPortal	Standard v1.3	Nov-00	13	1.1	1.2	1.1	X	X	NT 4, Solaris 7, HP-UX 11, AIX 4.3.3, Tru64
	Enterprise v1.3	Nov-00	1.3	1.1	1.2	1.0.2	X	X	NT 4, Solaris 7, HP-UX 11, AIX 4.3.3
IPlanet	Enterprise V6.0	May-00	1.2	1.1	1.1	1.0.2	X	X	NT, Solaris, HP-UX, AIX
	Enterprise Pro v6.0	Mar-01	1.2	1.1	1.1	1.0.2	X	X	NT, Solaris

Table B-1. Application Server Comparison Matrix *(continued)*

Vendor Product	Edition Version	Release	JDK	EJB	JSP	JMS	J2EE Lic.	J2EE Cert.	Platform
Ironflare (formerly Evermind) *Orion*	v1.4	Oct-00	1.2 1.3	1.1	1.1				NT, Solaris, Linux
JBoss.org JBoss	v2.1	Feb-01	1.2.2 1.3	1.1	1.1	1.0.2			NT, OS/390, Solaris, OS/400, Unix, Netware, Linux, HP-UX
Lutris Enhydra	Enhydra v3.1	Dec-00	1.2.2 1.3		1.1				NT, Solaris, Linux
	Lutris Enhydra v3.5	Dec-00	1.2.2 1.3		1.1				
	Enhydra Enterprise v4.0 (early access)	Jun-01	1.3	1.1					
ObjectSpace Voyager	v3.3	May-00	1.2.2	11	1.1				NT, Solaris, Linux, AIX
Open Connect OC:// WebConnect Enterprise Integration Server	v1.5	Jul-00	1.1		1.2. 2				NT, Solaris, HPUX, AIX
Oracle 9i AS	Standard v1.0.2	Oct- 00	1.1.8 1.2.2	1.1	1.1		X		NT, Solaris, HPUX, Linux, AIX, Tru64
Orbware Orcas Enterprise Server	Standard v4.1	Oct- 00	1.2.2 1.3	1.1	1.1		X		NT, Linux, Solaris

Table B-1. Application Server Comparison Matrix *(continued)*

Vendor Product	Edition Version	Release	JDK	EJB	JSP	JMS	J2EE Lic.	J2EE Cert.	Platform
Persistence Power Tier for J2EE	v6.5	Nov-00	1.2 1.3	1.1	1.1		X		NT, Solaris, HPUX, AIX, Linux
Pramati Server	Deployment v2.0	Nov-00	1.2.2 1.3	1.1	1.1				NT, Solaris, Linux, AIX
Secant	Extreme Internet Server v3.5	Jun-00	1.2.2		1.0				NT, Linux, Solaris, HPUX, BSD/OS
	Extreme Enterprise Server v3.5	Jun-00	1.2.2	1.1	1.0				NT, Linux, Solaris and HPUX
SilverStream Application Server	Developer v3.7.1	Feb-01	1.2 1.3	1.1	1.1	1.0.2	X	X	NT, Win2k, Linux
	Enterprise v3.7.1	Feb-01	1.2 1.3	1.1	1.1	1.0.2	X	X	NT, Win2K, Solaris, AIX, HPUX, Linux
Sybase Enterprise Application Server	Small Business v3.6	Oct-00	1.2	1.1	1.1	1.0.2	X	X	NT, Solaris, AIX, HPUX
	Advanced v3.6	Oct-00	1.2	1.1	1.1	1.0.2	X	X	
	Enterprise v3.6	Oct-00	1.2	1.1	1.1	1.0.2	X	X	
Unify eWave Engine	Access v4.0	Feb-01	1.2	1.1	1.1				NT, Unix, Linux
	Enterprise v4.0	Feb-01	1.2	1.1	1.1				

Table B-1.   Application Server Comparison Matrix *(continued)*

Vendor Product	Edition Version	Release	JDK	EJB	JSP	JMS	J2EE Lic.	J2EE Cert.	Platform
X03 OpenJODA	Standard v1.0	Sep-00	1.3	1.1	1.2				Linux, NT, Solaris, Win9x
Xoology Solo	Developer v2.1	Oct-00		1.2 1.3	1.2				NT, Win2K, Solaris, Linux
	Deployment v2.1	Oct-00		1.2 1.3	1.2				

* Source: Flashline.com

Table B-1.   Application Server Comparison Matrix *(continued)*

APPENDIX C

Network Monitoring Resources

The following web site resources are provided where specific network monitoring software solutions are available for review, purchase, and download.

NETWORK MONITORING PLATFORMS (NMPS)

- ▼ **HP OpenView** http://www.hp.com/openview/
- ■ **Sun Solstice** http://www.sun.com/solstice/system.mgmt.html
- ■ **IBM Netview/AIX** http://www.raleigh.ibm.com/nv6/nv6prod.html
- ■ **DEC Polycenter** http://www.digital.com/info/key-polycenter-index.html
- ■ **Cabletron Spectrum** http://www.cabletron.com/spectrum/
- ▲ **Castle Rock** http://www.castlerock.com/

MONITORING TOOLS INTEGRATED WITH NETWORK MONITORING PLATFORMS

- ▼ **Cabletron Remote LAN Manager** http://www.cabletron.com/
- ■ **Ciscoworks** http://www.cisco.com/warp/public/cc/cisco/mkt/enm/cw2000/. (Cisco also provides solutions that are standalone monitoring tools.)
- ■ **DEC-Bridge** http://www.digital.com
- ■ **NetMetrix** http://www.tmo.hp.com/tmo/ntd/products/netmetrix/netmet-main.html
- ▲ **Optimal Networks** http://www.optimal.com/

COMMERCIAL MONITORING TOOLS NOT INTEGRATED WITH A NETWORK MONITORING PLATFORM

- ▼ **Akamai EdgeScape** http://www.akamai.com/html/sv/edse_eshow.html. EdgeScape tracks IP addresses with geographic and network points of origin.

- **Argent** http://www.argent.com/. The Argent Guardian is a real-time monitoring and alerting system for NT/2000 servers as well as SNMP-compliant devices. The Argent Predictor is a trend analysis product for both NT/2000 servers and SNMP devices. The Argent Sentinel is a web monitoring product.

- **Ganymede** http://www.ganymede.com/index.htm. Ganymede addresses performance management of networks and components.

- **GeoBoy** http://www.clevertools.com/products/netboys/. GeoBoy allows for 3-dimensional views of networks.

- **InMon** http://www.inmon.com/. InMon monitors the flow of traffic for high-speed switches.

- **Keynote** http://www.keynote.com/. Provides software and services for measurement of performance of web-based applications.

- **Netflow** http://www.cisco.com/go/netflow. A Cisco product for monitoring traffic.

- **NetOps** http://www.netops.com/. NetOps is a bundled assortment of monitoring tools.

- **NextPoint** http://www.nextpoint.com/S3. NextPoint provides service level monitoring of networks.

- **PacketBoy** http://www.clevertools.com/products/netboys/pb.html. PacketBoy is a packet sniffer analyzer for networks.

- **ResponseNetworks** http://www.responsenetworks.com/. Response-Networks allows for measuring of Web services on a network.

- **SNMP Tools**:

  - **Quallaby Proviso** http://www.quallaby.com/. Proviso is a quality assurance product targeted towards network service providers.

  - **WinTDS** http://www.tdslink.com/download.html. WinTDS is a monitoring network status tool for IP-SNMP devices and networks.

- **Sniffer** http://www.sniffer.com/. Sniffer protocol analyzers.

- ▲ **VisualRoute** http://www.visualroute.com/. VisualRoute provides a graphical view of traceroute for Windows.

PUBLIC DOMAIN OR FREE NETWORK MONITORING TOOLS

■ **Big Brother** http://www.bb4.com. Big Brother tests for network availability.

■ **Bing** http://spengler.econ.duke.edu/~ferizs/bing.txt. Bing is a point-to-point bandwidth measurement tool.

■ **CAIDA Measurement Tool Taxonomy** http://www.caida.org/tools/. CAIDA provides measurement performance TCP/IP tools.

■ **Cricket** http://cricket.sourceforge.net/. Cricket provides for network trends analysis, provided in time-series format.

■ **Dig** http://ciac.llnl.gov/ciac/ToolsUnixGeneral.html. A Unix-specific network diagnostics tool.

■ **Mapnet** http://www.caida.org/Tools/Mapnet/Backbones/. Available from NLANR/CAIDA, Mapnet is a tool for graphically showing the backbone infrastructure of multiple providers.

■ **netman** ftp://ftp.cs.curtin.edu.au/pub/netman/. Netman displays data and the status of connections among networks.

■ **NetNow** http://www.merit.edu/ipma/analysis/. NetNow provides real-time monitoring of NAP & ISP-based backbones.

■ **Nmap** http://www.insecure.org/nmap/. Nmap is a port scanning utility for networks.

■ **RouteViews** http://www.antc.uoregon.edu/route-views/. RouteViews provides real-time traffic data on multiple backbones.

A more comprehensive web site listing is available through the Stanford Linear Accelerator Center, Stanford University Web site. For an updated listing, reference http://www.slac.stanford.edu/xorg/nmtf/nmtf-tools.html.

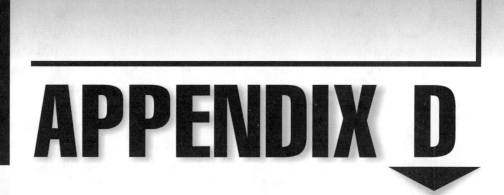

APPENDIX D

Introduction
to Networking

On an abstract scale, the various components that allow a computer to access a network can be defined in *layers,* and are referred to as the OSI (Open Systems Interconnection) Model of Networking. The OSI Model references the process of communication that takes place within seven layers, with each layer having defined functions as shown in Table D-1. The model is used to depict how data flows from the physical connection (Layer 1) to the network and to the end-user application (Layer 7).

Each layer provides functionality to the next layer. The *upper tier* encompasses Layers 4 through 7, and includes the functions for the data passing to and from the user. Layers 1–3 include the functions for data passing through a host. Except for the physical layer (Layer 1), no layer can forward information directly to the same layer on another computer. Data on the sending computer must pass through all the lower layers. Communication that takes place between neighboring layers is referred to as an *interface.* The interface determines which services the lower layer offers to the next highest layer, and how those services will be accessed. The set of standards used in passing information between layers is defined as a *protocol.* On a computer each layer will perform as if passing information to the same layer on another computer.

At the most basic level, TCP/IP (Transmission Control Protocol and Internet Protocol) is the suite of protocols and applications used to enable Internet, local-area network (LAN), and wide-area network (WAN) communications.

Layer Level	Description	Example of Usage
Layer 7	Application	HTTP, FTP, SMTP, etc.
Layer 6	Presentation	Interfaces with Applications and Session Layer
Layer 5	Session	NetBIOS over TCP/IP
Layer 4	Transport	TCP and UDP
Layer 3	Network	IP, IPX, NDIS (Network Driver Interface Specification)
Layer 2	Data Link	FDDI (Fiber Distributed Data Interface), Token Ring, Ethernet
Layer 1	Physical	NIC (Network Interface Card)

Table D-1.   OSI Model

TCP/IP applications provide ways to gauge the responsiveness of individual hosts and track the level of traffic from one host to another, such as ping and tracert. Some of the various TCP/IP protocols available with the suite of applications include TCP, IP, FTP, Telnet, and ARP, which are discussed in further detail in Chapter 12. Each server, workstation, standalone PC, or other device that is connected to the Internet uses TCP/IP, with each using a static or dynamic 32-bit IP address in the format xxx.xxx.xxx.xxx; each xxx represents an integer value (also referred to as an octet) from 0 to 255. An example is 216.25.36.117. This is a public, externally visible IP address assigned by a domain registration service or ISP to be accessible via the Internet, and is based on the IP version 4 addressing scheme (which was introduced in 1981 with RFC 791, see http://www.rfc-editor.org/rfc/rfc791.txt).

At the most basic, Web servers, routers, and externally visible machines will have static (external) IP addresses to match the forward and reverse (if enabled) mapping records contained in DNS (Domain Name System). For a host to be seen, and to communicate outside of a local network segment via the Internet, a default gateway (router) is required. The default gateway also will handle forwarding and receiving of packets, both for the network and for packets that is destined for another network.

DNS enables you to associate each IP address to a Domain name. Over the Internet, BIND (Berkeley Internet Name Domain) software is commonly used for managing DNS within the Unix environment, whereas Windows NT and 2000 uses its own (which is also compatible with BIND). BIND versions 8.2 and higher allows zone data verification and authentication. BIND includes zone configuration file information, with router addresses, domain name servers, IP addresses, ACLs (Access Control Lists), forward mappings (which translate a domain name into an IP address), reverse mappings (which translate an IP address into a domain name), and might include other details on customer accounts.

Each customer needs to have its own individual zone files, with zone transfers located on a secondary DNS. A web hosting company typically will have two DNS servers that store IP addresses, which correspond with name servers hosted and are registered through a domain registration service. One server will be assigned as the primary DNS; the other the secondary DNS server. Typically, each DNS service must run on a separate machine from other server processes, such as shared hosting or SMTP services.

For our discussion here in relation to the Internet, three classes of IP addresses normally are used for TCP/IP: Classes A, B, and C. Each IP address has two components: the network section and a host section. The network section defines the address as being a member of a Class A, B, or C network, as noted in Table D-2.

The following IP address ranges are recognized as private (or internal). These addresses are not viewable over the Internet; they are detailed in Internet RFC (Request for Comments) 1918:

▼ 10.0.0.0 through 10.255.255.255

■ 172.16.0.0 through 172.31.255.255

▲ 192.168.0.0 through 192.168.255.255

If your network uses IP addresses within this range for internal purposes, they will be translated to a public IP address through a proxy or a Network Address Translation (NAT) server; the public address then can be routed over the Internet. Routers have specific rules for where to send data packets, based on what the IP address is, and often will have firewall or proxy capabilities built in to prevent unauthorized access to a network.

A *subnet mask* is a 32-bit numbering method that determines whether a host is local or on a remote network. It distinguishes the network ID from the host ID. The host ID is divided into sections for sharing by other sub-networks that are

Network Class	Address Range	Subnet Mask (by default)	# of Networks Possible	# of Hosts Available per Network
Class A	1.0.0.0 to 127.0.0.0*	255.0.0.0	126	16,777,214
Class B	128.0.0.0 to 191.255.0.0	255.255.0.0	16,384	65,534
Class C	192.0.0.0 to 223.255.255.0	255.255.255.0	2,097,152	254

* 127.0.0.1 is the static loopback address used for TCP/IP configuration testing.

Table D-2. Network IP Addressing by Class

a part of a network. On a network, this allows for traffic to be isolated and managed, and not be seen on the external Internet. This also enables an internal network to be managed more effectively and does not require additional IP addresses to be assigned for nodes. In the subnet mask, all bits that correspond to the host ID are assigned as 0; those that correspond to the network ID are assigned to 1 and displayed as IP addresses in binary notation. Some online resources for methods used in subnetting can be found here:

- ▼ **RFC 950** http://www.tcp-ip.nu/tcp-ip/subpages/subnetting/rfc950.txt

- ■ **Ezine: Subnetting** http://www.ezine.com/EZInternet.SubNet.html

- ■ **Subnet Mask Calculator** http://www.telusplanet.net/public/sparkman/netcalc.htm

- ▲ **CIDR Subnet Calculator** http://minnie.tuhs.org/Gateways/range_check.html

Every IP address consists of four octets. Each octet in an IP address is represented by 8 bits. For example, for 255.255.255.0, the corresponding bits are

```
11111111 11111111 11111111 00000000
```

With the introduction of *CIDR* (*Classless Inter-Domain Routing*) in 1993, assigning IP addresses for networks became easier and more effective for sizing a network than assigning by class (as noted in Table D-2). For example, for the CIDR address 205.18.11.62/24, the /24 indicates that the first 24 bits are used to identify the unique network; the remaining bits identify the specific host. CIDR uses network prefixes from 13 to 27 bits, compared to class addresses, which are limited to using network prefixes of 8, 16, or 24 bits. This allows more flexibility in assigning blocks of addresses to different sized networks. For more information on RFCs, which address the CIDR standard, refer to:

- ▼ **RFC 1517** Applicability Statement for the Implementation of CIDR
- ■ **RFC 1518** An Architecture for IP Address Allocation with CIDR
- ■ **RFC 1519** CIDR: An Address Assignment and Aggregation Strategy
- ▲ **RFC 1520** Exchanging Routing Information Across Provider Boundaries in the CIDR Environment

IP addressing also can be configured dynamically through DHCP (Dynamic Host Configuration Protocol), instead of using a static IP address for each computer. Often ISPs dynamically assign IP addresses to users who log onto the Internet through their service. All available IP addresses are stored in a main database file on a DHCP server, which also contains network specifics such as the DNS servers, gateways, and the subnet mask. When a user attempts to access the network, the DHCP server leases an available IP address to the user for a specified time frame. On a network this enables you to have a smaller pool of available IP addresses because not all of your users will be connected at once. This is the preferred method if your network is part of a *VPN* (*Virtual Private Network*) to avoid possible conflicts with the other static IP addresses of connected workstations. With Microsoft Windows 2000, DHCP has been replaced with Dynamic DNS, which works in a similar fashion as DHCP, yet allows IP addresses to be more dynamically allocated instead of being assigned by an administrator.

The current IP version 4 addressing scheme did not anticipate the tremendous demand for IP addresses that were required for Web servers and other devices; the result is a dwindling number of available IP addresses. IP version 6 (IPv6) has been proposed as a new set of standards for IP addressing by the IETF (Internet Engineering Task Force). Once it is fully implemented, this will provide enhancements in scalability, speed, and security over the Internet.

IPv6 will allow the address size to increase from 32 bits to 128 bits. This larger address size will support a larger base of Internet users and expanded architecture. Intelligent security is built in to provide sophisticated header authentication. Configuration automatically will be possible with ICMPv6 (Internet Control Messaging Protocol version 6), which allows addresses to be identified and verified. Multicast routing support is included and packets can be labeled within the header as to the type of traffic that it is intended for. Transition to and adoption of the new addressing scheme will take time, as manufacturers introduce products that can sense and support either IPv4 or IPv6.

IPv6 was first proposed in 1995 (see RFC 1884, http://www.rfc-editor.org/rfc/rfc1884.txt); there have been more than 33 additional RFCs that further define IPv6 as of this writing. Web hosts should plan now for migration to IPv6, ensure that new equipment purchases support (many routers now include support), and have staff that is knowledgeable about the new IP addressing technology. Question resellers that are partnering with hosts to provide enhanced web services about their plans to support IPv6.

At its most basic, a web server listens for a connection and client request through a port; typically the standard port 80. The initial web servers on the Internet ran an *inetd* (*Internet daemon*) as a service on Unix machines, handling HTTP (Hypertext Transfer Protocol) requests through port 80. It listened to all ports specified in the /etc/inetd.conf file and ran a server process each time a connection was made over TCP/IP. Although inetd is quite reliable, straightforward, and a standard part of most Unix servers, running inetd for each process would not make sense for today's web servers, which sometimes must handle a large number of traffic requests.

Web servers and technology has evolved to provide much more sophisticated services than was available when inetd first became available. These capabilities include being able to generate dynamic content through server-side technologies, to handle variable traffic requirements through multi-processing or load balancing techniques, and to process a much higher number of user requests (or connections) at any given time. Also contributing to this trend have been the numerous hardware advances made in overall server technology.

HTTP ERROR CODES

If a site page is not loading properly, an HTTP error code is generated. This can be used to track when a client is trying to access a password-protected area, troubleshooting to correct for a missing file, and also can indicate a problem with a script or the server itself.

The most common HTTP error codes that are returned by web servers to the browser, are shown in Table D-3.

Error Code	Explanation
000	Error undefined
201	Created
202	Accepted
203	Partial information (not from the original server)
204	No content

Table D-3.   HTTP Error Codes

Error Code	Explanation
206	Partial content (The requested file did not completely reach the client, possibly due to an unresponsive or slow server.)
300	Page redirection
301	URL permanently moved
303	Temporary relocation of URL
304	File not modified (Likely due to a file being cached)
400	Bad request (request contained a syntax error)
401	Unauthorized access (requested file requires authentication)
402	Access forbidden (Payment is required prior to accessing.)
403	Forbidden
404	File not found (Page is missing. This is one of the most common errors. See note *.)
405	Method not allowed (This could be caused by a script that is not working correctly.)
408	Request time-out (A complete request from the client was not received. This can be due to a slow server.)
500	Internet server error (This can be caused by a server configuration error or scripting problem.)
501	Not implemented (The server lacks the capability to respond to the request.)
502	Bad gateway (This can be due to an associated proxy or server experiencing an error.)
503	Service unavailable (A request is trying to access a service that is currently not available.)

* The most common error, 404, usually points to a file that has been deleted from the server but is still being requested. Through log file analysis, problem pages and files can be tracked down, as can specific pages and files (images, executables, pdfs, and so forth) that are generating the most traffic.

Table D-3. HTTP Error Codes *(continued)*

APPENDIX E

Internet Standard Specifications

RFCs (Requests for Comment) are official specifications for the Internet Protocols. RFC drafts are available for review from the IETF (Internet Engineering Task Force) at http://www.ietf.org/; anyone may submit a draft for review. If a draft becomes an official specification it is posted at the RFC Editor web site at http://www.rfc-editor.org and on the Internet FAQ Consortium at http://www.faqs.org/rfcs/. Refer to RFC 2223 for more information on submitting a draft for review from either web site. RFC standards have been issued since the first release in April 1969. From 1999 to the current date, the number of Internet standards issued has greatly increased, as is represented in Table E-1.

RFC Number	Description
3115	Mobile IP Vendor/Organization-Specific Extensions, G. Dommety, K. Leung, April 2001.
3112	LDAP Authentication Password Schema, K. Zeilenga, May 2001.
3111	Service Location Protocol Modifications for IPv6, E. Guttman, May 2001.
3110	RSA/SHA-1 SIGs and RSA KEYs in the Domain Name System (DNS), D. Eastlake III, May 2001.
3109	Request to Move STD 39 to Historic Status, R. Braden, R. Bush, J. Klensin, May 2001.
3107	Carrying Label Information in BGP-4, Y. Rekhter, E. Rosen, May 2001.
3106	ECML v1.1: Field Specifications for E-Commerce, D. Eastlake, T. Goldstein, April 2001.
3098	How to Advertise Responsibly Using E-Mail and Newsgroups, or How NOT to $$$$$ MAKE ENEMIES FAST! $$$$$, E. Gavin, D. Eastlake 3rd, S. Hambridge, April 2001.
3097	RSVP Cryptographic Authentication—Updated Message Type Value, R. Braden, L. Zhang, April 2001.
3094	Tekelec's Transport Adapter Layer Interface, D. Sprague, R. Benedyk, D. Brendes, J. Keller, April 2001.
3093	Firewall Enhancement Protocol (FEP), M. Gaynor, S. Bradner, 1 April 2001.
3092	Etymology of "Foo," D. Eastlake 3rd, C. Manros, E. Raymond, 1 April 2001.
3091	Pi Digit Generation Protocol, H. Kennedy, 1 April 2001.
3090	DNS Security Extension Clarification on Zone Status, E. Lewis, March 2001.

Table E-1. Most Recent RFC Specifications (Current—June 1999)

RFC Number	Description
3089	A SOCKS-based IPv6/IPv4 Gateway Mechanism, H. Kitamura, April 2001.
3088	Open LDAP Root Service An Experimental LDAP Referral Service, K. Zeilenga, April 2001.
3087	Control of Service Context using SIP Request-URI, B. Campbell, R. Sparks, April 2001.
3086	Definition of Differentiated Services Per Domain Behaviors and Rules for their Specification, K. Nichols, B. Carpenter, April 2001.
3085	URN Namespace for NewsML Resources, A. Coates, D. Allen, D. Rivers-Moore, March 2001.
3084	COPS Usage for Policy Provisioning (COPS-PR), K. Chan, J. Seligson, D. Durham, S. Gai, K. McCloghrie, S. Herzog, F. Reichmeyer, R. Yavatkar, A. Smith, March 2001.
3083	Baseline Privacy Interface Management Information Base for DOCSIS Compliant Cable Modems and Cable Modem Termination Systems, R. Woundy, March 2001.
3082	Notification and Subscription for SLP, J. Kempf, J. Goldschmidt, March 2001.
3081	Mapping the BEEP Core onto TCP, M. Rose, March 2001.
3080	The Blocks Extensible Exchange Protocol Core, M. Rose, March 2001.
3079	Deriving Keys for use with Microsoft Point-to-Point Encryption (MPPE), G. Zorn, March 2001.
3078	Microsoft Point-to-Point Encryption (MPPE) Protocol, G. Pall, G. Zorn, March 2001.
3077	A Link Layer Tunneling Mechanism for Unidirectional Links, E. Duros, W. Dabbous, H. Izumiyama, N. Fujii, Y. Zhang, March 2001.
3076	Canonical XML Version 1.0, J. Boyer, March 2001.
3075	XML-Signature Syntax and Processing, D. Eastlake, J. Reagle, D. Solo, March 2001.
3074	DHC Load Balancing Algorithm, B. Volz, S. Gonczi, T. Lemon, R. Stevens, February 2001.
3073	Portable Font Resource (PFR)—Application/Font-tdpfr MIME Sub-type Registration, J. Collins, March 2001.
3072	Structured Data Exchange Format (SDXF), M. Wildgrube, March 2001.
3071	Reflections on the DNS, RFC 1591, and Categories of Domains, J. Klensin, February 2001.
3070	Layer 2 Tunneling Protocol (L2TP) over Frame Relay, V. Rawat, R. Tio, S. Nanji, R. Verma, February 2001.

Table E-1.   Most Recent RFC Specifications (Current—June 1999) *(continued)*

RFC Number	Description
3069	VLAN Aggregation for Efficient IP Address Allocation, D. McPherson, B. Dykes, February 2001.
3067	TERENA'S Incident Object Description and Exchange Format Requirements, J. Arvidsson, A. Cormack, Y. Demchenko, J. Meijer, February 2001.
3066	Tags for the Identification of Languages, H. Alvestrand, January 2001.
3065	Autonomous System Confederations for BGP, P. Traina, D. McPherson, J. Scudder, February 2001.
3064	MGCP CAS Packages, B. Foster, February 2001.
3063	MPLS Loop Prevention Mechanism, Y. Ohba, Y. Katsube, E. Rosen, P. Doolan, February 2001.
3062	LDAP Password Modify Extended Operation, K. Zeilenga, February 2001.
3061	A URN Namespace of Object Identifiers, M. Mealling, February 2001.
3060	Policy Core Information Model—Version 1 Specification, B. Moore, E. Ellesson, J. Strassner, A. Westerinen, February 2001.
3059	Attribute List Extension for the Service Location Protocol, E. Guttman, February 2001.
3058	Use of the IDEA Encryption Algorithm in CMS, S. Teiwes, P. Hartmann, D. Kuenzi, February 2001.
3057	ISDN Q.921-User Adaptation Layer, K. Morneault, S. Rengasami, M. Kalla, G. Sidebottom, February 2001.
3056	Connection of IPv6 Domains via IPv4 Clouds, B. Carpenter, K. Moore, February 2001.
3055	Management Information Base for the PINT Services Architecture, M. Krishnaswamy, D. Romascanu, February 2001.
3054	Megaco IP Phone Media Gateway Application Profile, P. Blatherwick, R. Bell, P. Holland, January 2001.
3053	IPv6 Tunnel Broker, A. Durand, P. Fasano, I. Guardini, D. Lento, January 2001.
3052	Service Management Architectures Issues and Review, M. Eder, S. Nag, January 2001.
3051	IP Payload Compression Using ITU-T V.44 Packet Method, J. Heath, J. Border, January 2001.
3050	Common Gateway Interface for SIP, J. Lennox, H. Schulzrinne, J. Rosenberg, January 2001.
3049	TN3270E Service Location and Session Balancing, J. Naugle, K. Kasthurirangan, G. Ledford, January 2001.

Table E-1.   Most Recent RFC Specifications (Current—June 1999) *(continued)*

RFC Number	Description
3048	Reliable Multicast Transport Building Blocks for One-to-Many Bulk-Data Transfer, B. Whetten, L. Vicisano, R. Kermode, M. Handley, S. Floyd, M. Luby, January 2001.
3047	RTP Payload Format for ITU-T Recommendation G.722.1, P. Luthi, January 2001.
3046	DHCP Relay Agent Information Option, M. Patrick, January 2001.
3045	Storing Vendor Information in the LDAP Root DSE, M. Meredith, January 2001.
3044	Using The ISSN (International Serial Standard Number) as URN (Uniform Resource Names) within an ISSN-URN Namespace, S. Rozenfeld, January 2001.
3043	The Network Solutions Personal Internet Name (PIN): A URN Namespace for People and Organizations M. Mealling, January 2001.
3042	Enhancing TCP's Loss Recovery Using Limited Transmit, M. Allman, H. Balakrishnan, S. Floyd, January 2001.
3041	Privacy Extensions for Stateless Address Autoconfiguration in IPv6, T. Narten, R. Draves, January 2001.
3040	Internet Web Replication and Caching Taxonomy, I. Cooper, I. Melve, G. Tomlinson, January 2001.
3039	Internet X.509 Public Key Infrastructure Qualified Certificates Profile, S. Santesson, W. Polk, P. Barzin, M. Nystrom, January 2001.
3038	VCID Notification Over ATM Link for LDP, K. Nagami, Y. Katsube, N. Demizu, H. Esaki, P. Doolan, January 2001.
3037	LDP Applicability, B. Thomas, E. Gray, January 2001.
3036	LDP Specification, L. Andersson, P. Doolan, N. Feldman, A. Fredette, B. Thomas, January 2001.
3035	MPLS Using LDP and ATM VC Switching, B. Davie, J. Lawrence, K. McCloghrie, E. Rosen, G. Swallow, Y. Rekhter, P. Doolan, January 2001.
3034	Use of Label Switching on Frame Relay Networks Specification, A. Conta, P. Doolan, A. Malis, January 2001.
3033	The Assignment of the Information Field and Protocol Identifier in the Q.2941 Generic Identifier and Q.2957 User-to-user Signaling for the Internet Protocol, M. Suzuki, January 2001.
3032	MPLS Label Stack Encoding, E. Rosen, D. Tappan, G. Fedorkow, Y. Rekhter, D. Farinacci, T. Li, A. Conta, January 2001.
3031	Multiprotocol Label Switching Architecture, E. Rosen, A. Viswanathan, R. Callon, January 2001.

Table E-1.   Most Recent RFC Specifications (Current—June 1999) *(continued)*

RFC Number	Description
3030	SMTP Service Extensions for Transmission of Large and Binary MIME Messages, G. Vaudreuil, December 2000.
3029	Internet X.509 Public Key Infrastructure Data Validation and Certification Server Protocols, C. Adams, P. Sylvester, M. Zolotarev, R. Zuccherato, February 2001.
3028	Sieve: A Mail Filtering Language, T. Showalter, January 2001.
3027	Protocol Complications with the IP Network Address Translator, M. Holdrege, P. Srisuresh, January 2001.
3026	Liaison to IETF/ISOC on ENUM, R. Blane, January 2001.
3025	Mobile IP Vendor/Organization-Specific Extensions, G. Dommety, K. Leung, February 2001.
3024	Reverse Tunneling for Mobile IP, Revised, G. Montenegro, Editor, January 2001.
3023	XML Media Types, M. Murata, S. St.Laurent, D. Kohn, January 2001.
3022	Traditional IP Network Address Translator (Traditional NAT), P. Srisuresh, K. Egevang, January 2001.
3021	Using 31-bit Prefixes on IPv4 Point-to-Point Links, A. Retana, R. White, V. Fuller, D. McPherson, December 2000.
3020	Definitions of Managed Objects for Monitoring and Controlling the UNI/NNI Multilink Frame Relay Function P. Pate, B. Lynch, K. Rehbehn, December 2000.
3019	IP Version 6 Management Information Base for The Multicast Listener Discovery Protocol, B. Haberman, R. Worzella, January 2001.
3018	Unified Memory Space Protocol Specification, A. Bogdanov, December 2000.
3017	XML DTD for Roaming Access Phone Book, M. Riegel, G. Zorn, December 2000.
3016	RTP Payload Format for MPEG-4 Audio/Visual Streams, Y. Kikuchi, T. Nomura, S. Fukunaga, Y. Matsui, H. Kimata, November 2000.
3015	Megaco Protocol Version 1.0, F. Cuervo, N. Greene, A. Rayhan, C. Huitema, B. Rosen, J. Segers, November 2000.
3014	Notification Log MIB, R. Kavasseri, November 2000.
3013	Recommended Internet Service Provider Security Services and Procedures, T. Killalea, November 2000.
3012	Mobile IPv4 Challenge/Response Extensions, C. Perkins, P. Calhoun, November 2000.
3011	The IPv4 Subnet Selection Option for DHCP, G. Waters, November 2000.

Table E-1. Most Recent RFC Specifications (Current—June 1999) *(continued)*

RFC Number	Description
3010	NFS Version 4 Protocol, S. Shepler, B. Callaghan, D. Robinson, R. Thurlow, C. Beame, M. Eisler, D. Noveck, December 2000.
3009	Registration of Parityfec MIME Types, J. Rosenberg, H. Schulzrinne, November 2000.
3008	Domain Name System Security (DNSSEC) Signing Authority, B. Wellington, November 2000.
3007	Secure Domain Name System (DNS) Dynamic Update, B. Wellington, November 2000.
3006	Integrated Services in the Presence of Compressible Flows, B. Davie, S. Casner, C. Iturralde, D. Oran, J. Wroclawski, November 2000.
3005	IETF Discussion List Charter, S. Harris, November 2000.
3004	The User Class Option for DHCP, G. Stump, R. Droms, Y. Gu, R. Vyaghrapuri, A. Demirtjis, B. Beser, J. Privat, November 2000.
3003	The Audio/MPEG Media Type, M. Nilsson, November 2000.
3002	Overview of 2000 IAB Wireless Internetworking Workshop, D. Mitzel, December 2000.
3001	A URN Namespace of Object Identifiers, M. Mealling, November 2000.
2998	A Framework for Integrated Services Operation over Diffserv Networks, Y. Bernet, P. Ford, R. Yavatkar, F. Baker, L. Zhang, M. Speer, R. Braden, B. Davie, J. Wroclawski, E. Felstaine, November 2000.
2997	Specification of the Null Service Type, Y. Bernet, A. Smith, B. Davie, November 2000.
2996	Format of the RSVP DCLASS Object, Y. Bernet, November 2000.
2995	Pre-spirits Implementations of PSTN-Initiated Services, H. Lu, Editor, I. Faynberg, J. Voelker, M. Weissman, W. Zhang, S. Rhim, J. Hwang, S. Ago,. Hwang, S. Ago, S. Moeenuddin, S. Hadvani, S. Nyckelgard, J. Yoakum, L. Robart, November 2000.
2994	A Description of the MISTY1 Encryption Algorithm, H. Ohta, M. Matsui, November 2000.
2993	Architectural Implications of NAT, T. Hain, November 2000.
2992	Analysis of an Equal-Cost Multipath Algorithm, C. Hopps, November 2000.
2991	Multipath Issues in Unicast and Multicast Next-Hop Selection, D. Thaler, C. Hopps, November 2000.
2990	Next Steps for the IP QoS Architecture, G. Huston, November 2000.

Table E-1. Most Recent RFC Specifications (Current—June 1999) *(continued)*

RFC Number	Description
2989	Criteria for Evaluating AAA Protocols for Network Access, B. Aboba, P. Calhoun, S. Glass, T. Hiller, P. McCann, H. Shiino, G. Zorn, G. Dommety, C. Perkins, B. Patil, D. Mitton, S. Manning, M. Beadles, P. Walsh, X. Chen, S. Sivalingham, A. Hameed, M. Munson, S. Jacobs, B. Lim, B. Hirschman, R. Hsu, Y. Xu, E. Campbell, S. Baba, E. Jaques, November 2000.
2988	Computing TCP's Retransmission Timer, V. Paxson, M. Allman, November 2000.
2987	Registration of Charset and Languages Media Features Tags, P. Hoffman, November 2000.
2986	PKCS #10: Certification Request Syntax Specification Version 1.7, M. Nystrom, B. Kaliski, November 2000.
2985	PKCS #9: Selected Object Classes and Attribute Types Version 2.0, M. Nystrom, B. Kaliski, November 2000.
2984	Use of the CAST-128 Encryption Algorithm in CMS, C. Adams, October 2000.
2983	Differentiated Services and Tunnels, D. Black, October 2000.
2982	Distributed Management Expression MIB, R. Kavasseri (Editor), October 2000.
2981	Event MIB, R. Kavasseri (Editor), October 2000.
2980	Common NNTP Extensions, S. Barber, October 2000.
2979	Behavior of and Requirements for Internet Firewalls, N. Freed, October 2000.
2978	IANA Charset Registration Procedures, N. Freed, J. Postel, October 2000.
2977	Mobile IP Authentication, Authorization, and Accounting Requirements, S. Glass, T. Hiller, S. Jacobs, C. Perkins, October 2000.
2976	The SIP INFO Method, S. Donovan, October 2000.
2975	Introduction to Accounting Management, B. Aboba, J. Arkko, D. Harrington, October 2000.
2974	Session Announcement Protocol, M. Handley, C. Perkins, E. Whelan, October 2000.
2973	IS-IS Mesh Groups, R. Balay, D. Katz, J. Parker, October 2000.
2972	Context and Goals for Common Name Resolution, N. Popp, M. Mealling, L. Masinter, K. Sollins, October 2000.
2971	IMAP4 ID Extension, T. Showalter, October 2000.
2970	Architecture for Integrated Directory Services—Result from TISDAG, L. Daigle, T. Eklof, October 2000.

Table E-1.   Most Recent RFC Specifications (Current—June 1999) *(continued)*

RFC Number	Description
2969	Wide Area Directory Deployment—Experiences from TISDAG, T. Eklof, L. Daigle, October 2000.
2968	Mesh of Multiple DAG Servers—Results from TISDAG, L. Daigle, T. Eklof, October 2000.
2967	TISDAG - Technical Infrastructure for Swedish Directory Access Gateways, L. Daigle, R. Hedberg, October 2000.
2966	Domain-wide Prefix Distribution with Two-level IS-IS, T. Li, T. Przygienda, H. Smit, October 2000.
2965	HTTP State Management Mechanism, D. Kristol, L. Montulli, October 2000.
2964	Use of HTTP State Management, K. Moore, N. Freed, October 2000.
2963	A Rate Adaptive Shaper for Differentiated Services, O. Bonaventure, S. De Cnodder, October 2000.
2962	An SNMP Application Level Gateway for Payload Address Translation, D. Raz, J. Schoenwaelder, B. Sugla, October 2000.
2961	RSVP Refresh Overhead Reduction Extensions, L. Berger, D. Gan, G. Swallow, P. Pan, F. Tommasi, S. Molendini, April 2001.
2960	Stream Control Transmission Protocol, R. Stewart, Q. Xie, K. Morneault, C. Sharp, H. Schwarzbauer, T. Taylor, I. Rytina, M. Kalla, L. Zhang, V. Paxson, October 2000.
2959	Real-time Transport Protocol Management Information Base, M. Baugher, B. Strahm, I. Suconick, October 2000.
2958	The Application/Whoispp-Response Content Type, L. Daigle, P. Faltstrom, October 2000.
2957	The Application/Whoispp-Query Content-Type, L. Daigle, P. Faltstrom, October 2000.
2956	Overview of 1999 IAB Network Layer Workshop, M. Kaat, October 2000.
2955	Definitions of Managed Objects for Monitoring and Controlling the Frame Relay/ATM PVC Service Interworking Function, K. Rehbehn, O. Nicklass, G. Mouradian, October 2000.
2954	Definitions of Managed Objects for Frame Relay Service, K. Rehbehn, D. Fowler, October 2000.
2953	Telnet Encryption: DES 64 bit Output Feedback, T. Ts'o, September 2000.
2952	Telnet Encryption: DES 64-bit Cipher Feedback, T. Ts'o, September 2000.
2951	TELNET Authentication Using KEA and SKIPJACK, R. Housley, T. Horting, P. Yee, September 2000.

Table E-1. Most Recent RFC Specifications (Current—June 1999) *(continued)*

RFC Number	Description
2950	Telnet Encryption: CAST-128 64-bit Cipher Feedback, J. Altman, September 2000.
2949	Telnet Encryption: CAST-128 64-bit Output Feedback, J. Altman, September 2000.
2948	Telnet Encryption: DES3 64-bit Output Feedback, J. Altman, September 2000.
2947	Telnet Encryption: DES3 64-bit Cipher Feedback, J. Altman, September 2000.
2946	Telnet Data Encryption Option, T. Ts'o, September 2000.
2945	The SRP Authentication and Key Exchange System, T. Wu, September 2000.
2944	Telnet Authentication: SRP, T. Wu, September 2000.
2943	TELNET Authentication Using DSA, R. Housley, T. Horting, P. Yee, September 2000.
2942	Telnet Authentication: Kerberos Version 5, T. Ts'o, September 2000.
2941	Telnet Authentication Option, T. Ts'o, Editor, J. Altman, September 2000.
2940	Definitions of Managed Objects for Common Open Policy Service (COPS) Protocol Clients, A. Smith, D. Partain, J. Seligson, October 2000.
2939	Procedures and IANA Guidelines for Definition of New DHCP Options and Message Types, R. Droms, September 2000.
2938	Identifying Composite Media Features, G. Klyne, L. Masinter, September 2000.
2937	The Name Service Search Option for DHCP, C. Smith, September 2000.
2936	HTTP MIME Type Handler Detection, D. Eastlake, C. Smith, D. Soroka, September 2000.
2935	Internet Open Trading Protocol (IOTP) HTTP Supplement, D. Eastlake, C. Smith, September 2000.
2934	Protocol Independent Multicast MIB for IPv4, K. McCloghrie, D. Farinacci, D. Thaler, B. Fenner, October 2000.
2933	Internet Group Management Protocol MIB, K. McCloghrie, D. Farinacci, D. Thaler, October 2000.
2932	IPv4 Multicast Routing MIB, K. McCloghrie, D. Farinacci, D. Thaler, October 2000.
2931	DNS Request and Transaction Signatures (SIG(0)s, D. Eastlake, September 2000.
2930	Secret Key Establishment for DNS (TKEYRR), D. Eastlake, September 2000.

Table E-1.   Most Recent RFC Specifications (Current—June 1999) *(continued)*

RFC Number	Description
2929	Domain Name System (DNS) IANA Considerations, D. Eastlake, E. Brunner-Williams, B. Manning, September 2000.
2928	Initial IPv6 Sub-TLA ID Assignments, R. Hinden, S. Deering, R. Fink, T. Hain, September 2000.
2927	MIME Directory Profile for LDAP Schema, M. Wahl, September 2000.
2926	Conversion of LDAP Schemas to and from SLP Templates, J. Kempf, R. Moats, P. St. Pierre, September 2000.
2925	Definitions of Managed Objects for Remote Ping, Traceroute, and Lookup Operations, K. White, September 2000.
2924	Accounting Attributes and Record Formats, N. Brownlee, A. Blount, September 2000.
2923	TCP Problems with Path MTU Discovery, K. Lahey, September 2000.
2922	Physical Topology MIB, A. Bierman, K. Jones, September 2000.
2921	6BONE pTLA and pNLA Formats (pTLA), B. Fink, September 2000.
2920	SMTP Service Extension for Command Pipelining, N. Freed, September 2000.
2919	List-Id: A Structured Field and Namespace for the Identification of Mailing Lists, R. Chandhok, G. Wenger, March 2001.
2918	Route Refresh Capability for BGP-4, E. Chen, September 2000.
2917	A Core MPLS IP VPN Architecture, K. Muthukrishnan, A. Malis, September 2000.
2916	E.164 number and DNS, P. Faltstrom, September 2000.
2915	The Naming Authority Pointer (NAPTR) DNS Resource Record, M. Mealling, R. Daniel, September 2000.
2914	Congestion Control Principles, S. Floyd, September 2000.
2913	MIME Content Types in Media Feature Expressions, G. Klyne, September 2000.
2912	Indicating Media Features for MIME Content, G. Klyne, September 2000.
2911	Internet Printing Protocol/1.1: Model and Semantics, R. deBry, T. Hastings, R. Herriot, S. Isaacson, P. Powell, September 2000.
2910	Internet Printing Protocol/1.1: Encoding and Transport, R. Herriot, S. Butler, P. Moore, R. Turner, J. Wenn, September 2000.
2909	The Multicast Address-sAet Claim (MASC) Protocol, P. Radoslavov, D. Estrin, R. Govindan, M. Handley, S. Kumr, D. Thaler, September 2000.
2908	The Internet Multicast Address Allocation Architecture, D. Thaler, M. Handley, D. Estrin, September 2000.

Table E-1.   Most Recent RFC Specifications (Current—June 1999) *(continued)*

RFC Number	Description
2907	MADCAP Multicast Scope Nesting State Option, R. Kermode, September 2000.
2906	AAA Authorization Requirements, S. Farrell, J. Vollbrecht, P. Calhoun, L. Gommans, G. Gross, B. de Bruijn, C. de Laat, M. Holdrege, D. Spence, August 2000.
2905	AAA Authorization Application Examples, J. Vollbrecht, P. Calhoun, S. Farrell, L. Gommans, G. Gross, B. de Bruijn, C. de Laat, M. Holdrege, D. Spence, August 2000.
2904	AAA Authorization Framework, J. Vollbrecht, P. Calhoun, S. Farrell, L. Gommans, G. Gross, B. de Bruijn, C. de Laat, M. Holdrege, D. Spence, August 2000.
2903	Generic AAA Architecture, C. de Laat, G. Gross, L. Gommans, J. Vollbrecht, D. Spence, August 2000.
2902	Overview of the 1998 IAB Routing Workshop, S. Deering, S. Hares, C. Perkins, R. Perlman, August 2000.
2901	Guide to Administrative Procedures of the Internet Infrastructure, Z. Wenzel, J. Klensin, R. Bush, S. Huter, August 2000.
2899	Request for Comments Summary RFC Numbers 2800-2899, S. Ginoza, May 2001.
2898	PKCS #5: Password-based Cryptography Specification Version 2.0, B. Kaliski, September 2000.
2897	Proposal for an MGCP Advanced Audio Package, D. Cromwell, August 2000.
2896	Remote Network Monitoring MIB Protocol Identifier Macros, A. Bierman, C. Bucci, R. Iddon, August 2000.
2895	Remote Network Monitoring MIB Protocol Identifier Reference, A. Bierman, C. Bucci, R. Iddon, August 2000.
2894	Router Renumbering for IPv6, M. Crawford, August 2000.
2893	Transition Mechanisms for IPv6 Hosts and Routers, R. Gilligan, E. Nordmark, August 2000.
2892	The Cisco SRP MAC Layer Protocol, D. Tsiang, G. Suwala, August 2000.
2891	LDAP Control Extension for Server Side Sorting of Search Results, T. Howes, M. Wahl, A. Anantha, August 2000.
2890	Key and Sequence Number Extensions to GRE, G. Dommety, September 2000.
2889	Benchmarking Methodology for LAN Switching Devices, R. Mandeville, J. Perser, August 2000.

Table E-1. Most Recent RFC Specifications (Current—June 1999) *(continued)*

RFC Number	Description
2888	Secure Remote Access with L2TP, P. Srisuresh, August 2000.
2887	The Reliable Multicast Design Space for Bulk Data Transfer, M. Handley, S. Floyd, B. Whetten, R. Kermode, L. Vicisano, M. Luby, August 2000.
2886	Megaco Errata, T. Taylor, August 2000.
2885	Megaco Protocol version 0.8, F. Cuervo, N. Greene, C. Huitema, A. Rayhan, B. Rosen, J. Segers, August 2000.
2884	Performance Evaluation of Explicit Congestion Notification (ECN) in IP Networks, J. Hadi Salim, U. Ahmed, July 2000.
2883	An Extension to the Selective Acknowledgement (SACK) Option for TCP, S. Floyd, J. Mahdavi, M. Mathis, M. Podolsky, July 2000.
2882	Network Access Servers Requirements: Extended RADIUS Practices, D. Mitton, July 2000.
2881	Network Access Server Requirements Next Generation (NASREQNG) NAS Model, D. Mitton, M. Beadles, July 2000.
2880	Internet Fax T.30 Feature Mapping, L. McIntyre, G. Klyne, August 2000.
2879	Content Feature Schema for Internet Fax (V2), G. Klyne, L. McIntyre, August 2000.
2878	PPP Bridging Control Protocol (BCP), M. Higashiyama, F. Baker, July 2000.
2877	5250 Telnet Enhancements, T. Murphy, Jr., P. Rieth, J. Stevens, July 2000.
2876	Use of the KEA and SKIPJACK Algorithms in CMS, J. Pawling, July 2000.
2875	Diffie-Hellman Proof-of-Possession Algorithms, H. Prafullchandra, J. Schaad, July 2000.
2874	DNS Extensions to Support IPv6 Address Aggregation and Renumbering, M. Crawford, C. Huitema, July 2000.
2873	TCP Processing of the IPv4 Precedence Field, X. Xiao, A. Hannan, V. Paxson, E. Crabbe, June 2000.
2872	Application and Sub Application Identity Policy Element for Use with RSVP, Y. Bernet, R. Pabbati, June 2000.
2871	A Framework for Telephony Routing Over IP, J. Rosenberg, H. Schulzrinne, June 2000.
2870	Root Name Server Operational Requirements, R. Bush, D. Karrenberg, M. Kosters, R. Plzak, June 2000.
2869	RADIUS Extensions, C. Rigney, W. Willats, P. Calhoun, June 2000.
2868	RADIUS Attributes for Tunnel Protocol Support, G. Zorn, D. Leifer, A. Rubens, J. Shriver, M. Holdrege, I. Goyret, June 2000.
2867	RADIUS Accounting Modifications for Tunnel Protocol Support, G. Zorn, B. Aboba, D. Mitton, June 2000.

Table E-1. Most Recent RFC Specifications (Current—June 1999) *(continued)*

RFC Number	Description
2866	RADIUS Accounting C. Rigney, June 2000.
2865	Remote Authentication Dial In User Service (RADIUS), C. Rigney, S. Willens, A. Rubens, W. Simpson, June 2000.
2864	The Inverted Stack Table Extension to the Interfaces Group MIB, K. McCloghrie, G. Hanson, June 2000.
2863	The Interfaces Group MIB, K. McCloghrie, F. Kastenholz, June 2000.
2862	RTP Payload Format for Real-time Pointers, M. Civanlar, G. Cash, June 2000.
2861	TCP Congestion Window Validation, M. Handley, J. Padhye, S. Floyd, June 2000.
2860	Memorandum of Understanding Concerning the Technical Work of the Internet Assigned Numbers Authority B., Carpenter, F. Baker, M. Roberts, June 2000.
2859	A Time Sliding Window Three Colour Marker (TSWTCM), W. Fang, N. Seddigh, B. Nandy, June 2000.
2858	Multiprotocol Extensions for BGP-4, T. Bates, Y. Rekhter, R. Chandra, D. Katz, June 2000.
2857	The Use of HMAC-RIPEMD-160-96 within ESP and AH, A. Keromytis, N. Provos, June 2000.
2856	Textual Conventions for Additional High Capacity Data Types, A. Bierman, K. McCloghrie, R. Presuhn, June 2000.
2855	DHCP for IEEE 1394 K. Fujisawa, June 2000.
2854	The 'text/html' Media Type, D. Connolly, L. Masinter, June 2000.
2853	Generic Security Service API Version 2 : Java Bindings, J. Kabat, M. Upadhyay, June 2000.
2852	Deliver By SMTP Service Extension, D. Newman, June 2000.
2851	Textual Conventions for Internet Network Addresses, M. Daniele, B. Haberman, S. Routhier, J. Schoenwaelder, June 2000.
2850	Charter of the Internet Architecture Board (IAB) Internet Architecture Board, B. Carpenter, Editor, May 2000.
2849	The LDAP Data Interchange Format (LDIF)—Technical Specification, G. Good, June 2000.
2848	The PINT Service Protocol: Extensions to SIP and SDP for IP Access to Telephone Call Services, S. Petrack, L. Conroy, June 2000.
2847	LIPKEY—A Low Infrastructure Public Key Mechanism Using SPKM, M. Eisler, June 2000.

Table E-1. Most Recent RFC Specifications (Current—June 1999) *(continued)*

RFC Number	Description
2846	GSTN Address Element Extensions in E-mail Services, C. Allocchio, June 2000.
2845	Secret Key Transaction Authentication for DNS (TSIG), P. Vixie, O. Gudmundsson, D. Eastlake, B. Wellington, May 2000.
2844	OSPF over ATM and Proxy-PAR, T. Przygienda, P. Droz, R. Haas, May 2000.
2843	Proxy-PAR, P. Droz, T. Przygienda, May 2000.
2842	Capabilities Advertisement with BGP-4, R. Chandra, J. Scudder, May 2000.
2841	IP Authentication using Keyed SHA1 with Interleaved Padding (IP-MAC), P. Metzger, W. Simpson, November 2000.
2840	TELNET KERMIT OPTION, J. Altman, F. da Cruz, May 2000.
2839	Internet Kermit Service, F. da Cruz, J. Altman, May 2000.
2838	Uniform Resource Identifiers for Television Broadcasts, D. Zigmond, M. Vickers, May 2000.
2837	Definitions of Managed Objects for the Fabric Element in Fibre Channel Standard, K. Teow, May 2000.
2836	Per Hop Behavior Identification Codes, S. Brim, B. Carpenter, F. Le Faucheur, May 2000.
2835	IP and ARP over HIPPI-6400 (GSN), J.-M. Pittet, May 2000.
2834	ARP and IP Broadcast over HIPPI-800, J.-M. Pittet, May 2000.
2833	RTP Payload for DTMF Digits, Telephony Tones and Telephony Signals, H. Schulzrinne, S. Petrack, May 2000.
2832	NSI Registry Registrar Protocol (RRP) Version 1.1.0, S. Hollenbeck, M. Srivastava, May 2000.
2831	Using Digest Authentication as a SASL Mechanism, P. Leach, C. Newman, May 2000.
2830	Lightweight Directory Access Protocol (v3): Extension for Transport Layer Security, J. Hodges, R. Morgan, M. Wahl, May 2000.
2829	Authentication Methods for LDAP, M. Wahl, H. Alvestrand, J. Hodges, R. Morgan, May 2000.
2828	Internet Security Glossary, R. Shirey, May 2000.
2827	Network Ingress Filtering: Defeating Denial of Service Attacks Which Employ IP Source Address Spoofing P. Ferguson, D. Senie, May 2000.
2826	IAB Technical Comment on the Unique DNS Root, IAB, May 2000.
2825	A Tangled Web: Issues of I18N, Domain Names, and the Other Internet Protocols, IAB, L. Daigle, ed., May 2000.

Table E-1. Most Recent RFC Specifications (Current—June 1999) *(continued)*

RFC Number	Description
2824	Call Processing Language Framework and Requirements, J. Lennox, H. Schulzrinne, May 2000.
2823	PPP over Simple Data Link (SDL) using SONET/SDH with ATM-like Framing, J. Carlson, P. Langner, E. Hernandez-Valencia, J. Manchester, May 2000.
2822	Internet Message Format, P. Resnick, Editor, April 2001.
2821	Simple Mail Transfer Protocol, J. Klensin, Editor, April 2001.
2820	Access Control Requirements for LDAP, E. Stokes, D. Byrne, B. Blakley, P. Behera, May 2000.
2819	Remote Network Monitoring Management Information Base, S. Waldbusser, May 2000.
2818	HTTP Over TLS, E. Rescorla, May 2000.
2817	Upgrading to TLS Within HTTP/1.1, R. Khare, S. Lawrence, May 2000.
2816	A Framework for Integrated Services Over Shared and Switched IEEE 802 LAN Technologies, A. Ghanwani, J. Pace, V. Srinivasan, A. Smith, M. Seaman, May 2000.
2815	Integrated Service Mappings on IEEE 802 Networks, M. Seaman, A. Smith, E. Crawley, J. Wroclawski, May 2000.
2814	SBM (Subnet Bandwidth Manager): A Protocol for RSVP-based Admission Control over IEEE 802-Style Networks, R. Yavatkar, D. Hoffman, Y. Bernet, F. Baker, M. Speer, May 2000.
2813	Internet Relay Chat: Server Protocol, C. Kalt, April 2000.
2812	Internet Relay Chat: Client Protocol, C. Kalt, April 2000.
2811	Internet Relay Chat: Channel Management, C. Kalt, April 2000.
2810	Internet Relay Chat: Architecture, C. Kalt, April 2000.
2809	Implementation of L2TP Compulsory Tunneling via RADIUS, B. Aboba, G. Zorn, April 2000.
2808	The SecurID(r) SASL Mechanism, M. Nystrom, April 2000.
2807	XML Signature Requirements, J. Reagle, July 2000.
2806	URLs for Telephone Calls, A. Vaha-Sipila, April 2000.
2805	Media Gateway Control Protocol Architecture and Requirements, N. Greene, M. Ramalho, B. Rosen, April 2000.
2804	IETF Policy on Wiretapping, IAB, IESG, May 2000.
2803	Digest Values for DOM (DOMHASH), H. Maruyama, K. Tamura, N. Uramoto, April 2000.

Table E-1. Most Recent RFC Specifications (Current—June 1999) *(continued)*

RFC Number	Description
2802	Digital Signatures for the v1.0 Internet Open Trading Protocol (IOTP), K. Davidson, Y. Kawatsura, April 2000.
2801	Internet Open Trading Protocol—IOTP Version 1.0, D. Burdett, April 2000.
2800	Internet Official Protocol Standards, J. Reynolds, R. Braden, S. Ginoza, May 2001.
2799	Request for Comments Summary RFC Numbers 2700-2799, S. Ginoza, September 2000.
2798	Definition of the inetOrgPerson LDAP Object Class, M. Smith, April 2000.
2797	Certificate Management Messages over CMS, M. Myers, X. Liu, J. Schaad, J. Weinstein, April 2000.
2796	BGP Route Reflection—An Alternative to Full Mesh IBGP, T. Bates, R. Chandra, E. Chen, April 2000.
2795	The Infinite Monkey Protocol Suite (IMPS), S. Christey, April 1, 2000.
2794	Mobile IP Network Access Identifier Extension for IPv4, P. Calhoun, C. Perkins, March 2000.
2793	RTP Payload for Text Conversation, G. Hellstrom, May 2000.
2792	DSA and RSA Key and Signature Encoding for the KeyNote Trust Management System, M. Blaze, J. Ioannidis, A. Keromytis, March 2000.
2791	Scalable Routing Design Principles, J. Yu, July 2000.
2790	Host Resources MIB, S. Waldbusser, P. Grillo, March 2000.
2789	Mail Monitoring MIB, N. Freed, S. Kille, March 2000.
2788	Network Services Monitoring MIB, N. Freed, S. Kille, March 2000.
2787	Definitions of Managed Objects for the Virtual Router Redundancy Protocol, B. Jewell, D. Chuang, March 2000.
2786	Diffie-Helman USM Key Management Information Base and Textual Convention, M. St. Johns, March 2000.
2785	Methods for Avoiding the "Small-Subgroup" Attacks on the Diffie-Hellman Key Agreement Method for S/MIME, R. Zuccherato, March 2000.
2784	Generic Routing Encapsulation (GRE), D. Farinacci, T. Li, S. Hanks, D. Meyer, P. Traina, March 2000.
2783	Pulse-Per-Second API for UNIX-like Operating Systems, Version 1.0, J. Mogul, D. Mills, J. Brittenson, J. Stone, U. Windl, March 2000.
2782	A DNS RR for Specifying the Location of Services (DNS SRV), A. Gulbrandsen, P. Vixie, L. Esibov, February 2000.
2781	UTF-16, An Encoding of ISO 10646, P. Hoffman, F. Yergeau, February 2000.

Table E-1. Most Recent RFC Specifications (Current—June 1999) *(continued)*

RFC Number	Description
2780	IANA Allocation Guidelines For Values In the Internet Protocol and Related Headers, S. Bradner, V. Paxson, March 2000.
2779	Instant Messaging / Presence Protocol Requirements, M. Day, S. Aggarwal, G. Mohr, J. Vincent, February 2000.
2778	A Model for Presence and Instant Messaging, M. Day, J. Rosenberg, H. Sugano, February 2000.
2777	Publicly Verifiable Nomcom Random Selection, D. Eastlake, February 2000.
2776	Multicast-Scope Zone Announcement Protocol (MZAP), M. Handley, D. Thaler, R. Kermode, February 2000.
2775	Internet Transparency, B. Carpenter, February 2000.
2774	An HTTP Extension Framework, H. Nielsen, P. Leach, S. Lawrence, February 2000.
2773	Encryption using KEA and SKIPJACK, R. Housley, P. Yee, W. Nace, February 2000.
2772	6Bone Backbone Routing Guidelines, R. Rockell, R. Fink, February 2000.
2771	An Abstract API for Multicast Address Allocation, R. Finlayson, February 2000.
2770	GLOP Addressing in 233/8, D. Meyer, P. Lothberg, February 2000.
2769	Routing Policy System Replication, C. Villamizar, C. Alaettinoglu, R. Govindan, D. Meyer, February 2000.
2768	Network Policy and Services: A Report of a Workshop on Middleware, B. Aiken, J. Strassner, B. Carpenter, I. Foster, C. Lynch, J. Mambretti, R. Moore, B. Teitelbaum, February 2000.
2767	Dual Stack Hosts using the "Bump-In-the-Stack" Technique (BIS), K. Tsuchiya, H. Higuchi, Y. Atarashi, February 2000.
2766	Network Address Translation - Protocol Translation (NAT-PT), G. Tsirtsis, P. Srisuresh, February 2000.
2765	Stateless IP/ICMP Translation Algorithm (SIIT), E. Nordmark, February 2000.
2764	A Framework for IP Based Virtual Private Networks, B. Gleeson, A. Lin, J. Heinanen, G. Armitage, A. Malis, February 2000.
2763	Dynamic Hostname Exchange Mechanism for IS-IS, N. Shen, H. Smit, February 2000.
2762	Sampling of the Group Membership in RTP, J. Rosenberg, H. Schulzrinne, February 2000.
2761	Terminology for ATM Benchmarking, J. Dunn, C. Martín, February 2000.

Table E-1.   Most Recent RFC Specifications (Current—June 1999) *(continued)*

RFC Number	Description
2760	Ongoing TCP Research Related to Satellites, M. Allman, S. Dawkins, D. Glover, J. Griner, D. Tran, T. Henderson, J. Heidemann, J. Touch, H. Kruse, S. Ostermann, K. Scott, J. Semke, February 2000.
2759	Microsoft PPP CHAP Extensions, Version 2, G. Zorn, January 2000.
2758	Definitions of Managed Objects for Service Level Agreements Performance Monitoring, K. White, February 2000.
2757	Long Thin Networks, G. Montenegro, S. Dawkins, M. Kojo, V. Magret, N. Vaidya, January 2000.
2756	Hyper Text Caching Protocol (HTCP/0.0), P. Vixie, D. Wessels, January 2000.
2755	Security Negotiation for WebNFS, A. Chiu, M. Eisler, B. Callaghan, January 2000.
2754	RPS IANA Issues, C. Alaettinoglu, C. Villamizar, R. Govindan, January 2000.
2753	A Framework for Policy-based Admission Control, R. Yavatkar, D. Pendarakis, R. Guerin, January 2000.
2752	Identity Representation for RSVP, S. Yadav, R. Yavatkar, R. Pabbati, P. Ford, T. Moore, S. Herzog, January 2000.
2751	Signaled Preemption Priority Policy Element, S. Herzog, January 2000.
2750	RSVP Extensions for Policy Control, S. Herzog, January 2000.
2749	COPS usage for RSVP, J. Boyle, R. Cohen, D. Durham, S. Herzog, R. Rajan, A. Sastry, January 2000.
2748	The COPS (Common Open Policy Service) Protocol, J. Boyle, R. Cohen, D. Durham, S. Herzog, R. Rajan, A. Sastry, January 2000.
2747	RSVP Cryptographic Authentication, F. Baker, B. Lindell, M. Talwar, January 2000.
2746	RSVP Operation Over IP Tunnels, A. Terzis, J. Krawczyk, J. Wroclawski, L. Zhang, January 2000.
2745	RSVP Diagnostic Messages, A. Terzis, B. Braden, S. Vincent, L. Zhang, January 2000.
2744	Generic Security Service API Version 2 : C-bindings, J. Wray, January 2000.
2743	Generic Security Service Application Program Interface Version 2, Update 1, J. Linn, January 2000.
2742	Definitions of Managed Objects for Extensible SNMP Agents, L. Heintz, S. Gudur, M. Ellison, January 2000.
2741	Agent Extensibility (AgentX) Protocol Version 1, M. Daniele, B. Wijnen, M. Ellison, D. Francisco, January 2000.

Table E-1.   Most Recent RFC Specifications (Current—June 1999) *(continued)*

RFC Number	Description
2740	OSPF for IPv6, R. Coltun, D. Ferguson, J. Moy, December 1999.
2739	Calendar Attributes for vCard and LDAP, T. Small, D. Hennessy, F. Dawson, January 2000.
2738	Corrections to "A Syntax for Describing Media Feature Sets," G. Klyne, December 1999.
2737	Entity MIB (Version 2), K. McCloghrie, A. Bierman, December 1999.
2736	Guidelines for Writers of RTP Payload Format Specifications, M. Handley, C. Perkins, December 1999.
2735	NHRP Support for Virtual Private Networks, B. Fox, B. Petri, December 1999.
2734	IPv4 over IEEE 1394, P. Johansson, December 1999.
2733	An RTP Payload Format for Generic Forward Error Correction, J. Rosenberg, H. Schulzrinne, December 1999.
2732	Format for Literal IPv6 Addresses in URL's, R. Hinden, B. Carpenter, L. Masinter, December 1999.
2731	Encoding Dublin Core Metadata in HTML, J. Kunze, December 1999.
2730	Multicast Address Dynamic Client Allocation Protocol (MADCAP), S. Hanna, B. Patel, M. Shah, December 1999.
2729	Taxonomy of Communication Requirements for Large-scale Multicast Applications, P. Bagnall, R. Briscoe, A. Poppitt, December 1999.
2728	The Transmission of IP Over the Vertical Blanking Interval of a Television Signal, R. Panabaker, S. Wegerif, D. Zigmond, November 1999.
2727	IAB and IESG Selection, Confirmation, and Recall Process: Operation of the Nominating and Recall Committees, J. Galvin, February 2000.
2726	PGP Authentication for RIPE Database Updates, J. Zsako, December 1999.
2725	Routing Policy System Security, C. Villamizar, C. Alaettinoglu, D. Meyer, S. Murphy, December 1999.
2724	RTFM: New Attributes for Traffic Flow Measurement, S. Handelman, S. Stibler, N. Brownlee, G. Ruth, October 1999.
2723	SRL: A Language for Describing Traffic Flows and Specifying Actions for Flow Groups, N. Brownlee, October 1999.
2722	Traffic Flow Measurement: Architecture, N. Brownlee, C. Mills, G. Ruth, October 1999.
2721	RTFM: Applicability Statement, N. Brownlee, October 1999.
2720	Traffic Flow Measurement: Meter MIB, N. Brownlee, October 1999.

Table E-1.　Most Recent RFC Specifications (Current—June 1999) *(continued)*

RFC Number	Description
2719	Framework Architecture for Signaling Transport, L. Ong, I. Rytina, M. Garcia, H. Schwarzbauer, L. Coene, H. Lin, I. Juhasz, M. Holdrege, C. Sharp, October 1999.
2718	Guidelines for new URL Schemes, L. Masinter, H. Alvestrand, D. Zigmond, R. Petke, November 1999.
2717	Registration Procedures for URL Scheme Names, R. Petke, I. King, November 1999.
2716	PPP EAP TLS Authentication Protocol, B. Aboba, D. Simon, October 1999.
2715	Interoperability Rules for Multicast Routing Protocols, D. Thaler, October 1999.
2714	Schema for Representing CORBA Object References in an LDAP Directory, V. Ryan, S. Seligman, R. Lee, October 1999.
2713	Schema for Representing Java™ Objects in an LDAP Directory, V. Ryan, S. Seligman, R. Lee, October 1999.
2712	Addition of Kerberos Cipher Suites to Transport Layer Security (TLS), A. Medvinsky, M. Hur, October 1999.
2711	IPv6 Router Alert Option, C. Partridge, A. Jackson, October 1999.
2710	Multicast Listener Discovery (MLD) for IPv6, S. Deering, W. Fenner, B. Haberman, October 1999.
2709	Security Model with Tunnel-mode IPsec for NAT Domains, P. Srisuresh, October 1999.
2708	Job Submission Protocol Mapping Recommendations for the Job Monitoring MIB, R. Bergman, November 1999.
2707	Job Monitoring MIB—V1.0, R. Bergman, T. Hastings, S. Isaacson, H. Lewis, November 1999.
2706	ECML v1: Field Names for E-Commerce, D. Eastlake, T. Goldstein, October 1999.
2705	Media Gateway Control Protocol (MGCP) Version 1.0, M. Arango, A. Dugan, I. Elliott, C. Huitema, S. Pickett, October 1999.
2704	The KeyNote Trust Management System Version 2, M. Blaze, J. Feigenbaum, J. Ioannidis, A. Keromytis, September 1999.
2703	Protocol-independent Content Negotiation Framework, G. Klyne, September 1999.
2702	Requirements for Traffic Engineering Over MPLS, D. Awduche, J. Malcolm, J. Agogbua, M. O'Dell, J. McManus, September 1999.
2701	Nortel Networks Multi-link Multi-node PPP Bundle Discovery Protocol, G. Malkin, September 1999.

Table E-1. Most Recent RFC Specifications (Current—June 1999) *(continued)*

RFC Number	Description
2700	Internet Official Protocol Standards, J. Reynolds, R. Braden, August 2000.
2699	Request for Comments Summary RFC Numbers 2600-2699, S. Ginoza, May 2000.
2698	A Two-rate, Three-color Marker, J. Heinanen, R. Guerin, September 1999.
2697	A Single Rate Three Color Marker, J. Heinanen, R. Guerin, September 1999.
2696	LDAP Control Extension for Simple Paged Results Manipulation, C. Weider, A. Herron, A. Anantha, T. Howes, September 1999.
2695	Authentication Mechanisms for ONC RPC, A. Chiu, September 1999.
2694	DNS extensions to Network Address Translators (DNS_ALG), P. Srisuresh, G. Tsirtsis, P. Akkiraju, A. Heffernan, September 1999.
2693	SPKI Certificate Theory, C. Ellison, B. Frantz, B. Lampson, R. Rivest, B. Thomas, T. Ylonen, September 1999.
2692	SPKI Requirements, C. Ellison, September 1999.
2691	A Memorandum of Understanding for an ICANN Protocol Support Organization, S. Bradner, September 1999.
2690	A Proposal for an MOU-based ICANN Protocol Support Organization, S. Bradner, September 1999.
2689	Providing Integrated Services over Low-bitrate Links, C. Bormann, September 1999.
2688	Integrated Services Mappings for Low Speed Networks, S. Jackowski, D. Putzolu, E. Crawley, B. Davie, September 1999.
2687	PPP in a Real-time Oriented HDLC-like Framing, C. Bormann, September 1999.
2686	The Multiclass Extension to Multilink PPP, C. Bormann, September 1999.
2685	Virtual Private Networks Identifier, B. Fox, B. Gleeson, September 1999.
2684	Multiprotocol Encapsulation over ATM Adaptation Layer 5, D. Grossman, J. Heinanen, September 1999.
2683	IMAP4 Implementation Recommendations, B. Leiba, September 1999.
2682	Performance Issues in VC-Merge Capable ATM LSRs, I. Widjaja, A. Elwalid, September 1999.
2681	A Round-trip Delay Metric for IPPM, G. Almes, S. Kalidindi, M. Zekauskas, September 1999.
2680	A One-way Packet Loss Metric for IPPM, G. Almes, S. Kalidindi, M. Zekauskas, September 1999.
2679	A One-way Delay Metric for IPPM, G. Almes, S. Kalidindi, M. Zekauskas, September 1999.

Table E-1. Most Recent RFC Specifications (Current—June 1999) *(continued)*

RFC Number	Description
2678	IPPM Metrics for Measuring Connectivity, J. Mahdavi, V. Paxson, September 1999.
2677	Definitions of Managed Objects for the NBMA Next Hop Resolution Protocol (NHRP), M. Greene, J. Cucchiara, J. Luciani, August 1999.
2676	QoS Routing Mechanisms and OSPF Extensions, G. Apostolopoulos, S. Kama, D. Williams, R. Guerin, A. Orda, T. Przygienda, August 1999.
2675	IPv6 Jumbograms, D. Borman, S. Deering, R. Hinden, August 1999.
2674	Definitions of Managed Objects for Bridges with Traffic Classes, Multicast Filtering and Virtual LAN Extensions, E. Bell, A. Smith, P. Langille, A. Rijhsinghani, K. McCloghrie, August 1999.
2673	Binary Labels in the Domain Name System, M. Crawford, August 1999.
2672	Non-Terminal DNS Name Redirection, M. Crawford, August 1999.
2671	Extension Mechanisms for DNS (EDNS0), P. Vixie, August 1999.
2670	Radio Frequency (RF) Interface Management Information Base for MCNS/DOCSIS Compliant RF Interfaces, M. St. Johns, Ed., August 1999.
2669	DOCSIS Cable Device MIB Cable Device Management Information Base for DOCSIS Compliant Cable Modems and Cable Modem Termination Systems, M. St. Johns, Ed., August 1999.
2668	Definitions of Managed Objects for IEEE 802.3 Medium Attachment Units (MAUs), A. Smith, J. Flick, K. de Graaf, D. Romascanu, D. McMaster, K. McCloghrie, S. Roberts, August 1999.
2667	IP Tunnel MIB, D. Thaler, August 1999.
2666	Definitions of Object Identifiers for Identifying Ethernet Chip Sets, J. Flick, August 1999.
2665	Definitions of Managed Objects for the Ethernet-like Interface Types, J. Flick, J. Johnson, August 1999.
2664	FYI on Questions and Answers—Answers to Commonly Asked "New Internet User" Questions, R. Plzak, A. Wells, E. Krol, August 1999.
2663	IP Network Address Translator (NAT) Terminology and Considerations, P. Srisuresh, M. Holdrege, August 1999.
2662	Definitions of Managed Objects for the ADSL Lines, G. Bathrick, F. Ly, August 1999.
2661	Layer Two Tunneling Protocol "L2TP," W. Townsley, A. Valencia, A. Rubens, G. Pall, G. Zorn, B. Palter, August 1999.
2660	The Secure HyperText Transfer Protocol, E. Rescorla, A. Schiffman, August 1999.
2659	Security Extensions For HTML, E. Rescorla, A. Schiffman, August 1999.

Table E-1. Most Recent RFC Specifications (Current—June 1999) *(continued)*

RFC Number	Description
2658	RTP Payload Format for PureVoice™ Audio, K. McKay, August 1999.
2657	LDAPv2 Client vs. the Index Mesh, R. Hedberg, August 1999.
2656	Registration Procedures for SOIF Template Types, T. Hardie, August 1999.
2655	CIP Index Object Format for SOIF Objects, T. Hardie, M. Bowman, D. Hardy, M. Schwartz, D. Wessels, August 1999.
2654	A Tagged Index Object for use in the Common Indexing Protocol, R. Hedberg, B. Greenblatt, R. Moats, M. Wahl, August 1999.
2653	CIP Transport Protocols, J. Allen, P. Leach, R. Hedberg, August 1999.
2652	MIME Object Definitions for the Common Indexing Protocol (CIP), J. Allen, M. Mealling, August 1999.
2651	The Architecture of the Common Indexing Protocol (CIP), J. Allen, M. Mealling, August 1999.
2650	Using RPSL in Practice, D. Meyer, J. Schmitz, C. Orange, M. Prior, C. Alaettinoglu, August 1999.
2649	An LDAP Control and Schema for Holding Operation Signatures, B. Greenblatt, P. Richard, August 1999.
2648	A URN Namespace for IETF Documents, R. Moats, August 1999.
2647	Benchmarking Terminology for Firewall Performance, D. Newman, August 1999.
2646	The Text/Plain Format Parameter, R. Gellens, August 1999.
2645	On-demand Mail Relay (ODMR) SMTP with Dynamic IP Addresses, R. Gellens, August 1999.
2644	Changing the Default for Directed Broadcasts in Routers, D. Senie, August 1999.
2643	Cabletron's SecureFast VLAN Operational Model, D. Ruffen, T. Len, J. Yanacek, August 1999.
2642	Cabletron's VLS Protocol Specification, L. Kane, August 1999.
2641	Cabletron's VlanHello Protocol Specification Version 4, D. Hamilton, D. Ruffen, August 1999.
2640	Internationalization of the File Transfer Protocol, B. Curtin, July 1999.
2639	Internet Printing Protocol/1.0: Implementer's Guide, T. Hastings, C. Manros, July 1999.
2638	A Two-bit Differentiated Services Architecture for the Internet, K. Nichols, V. Jacobson, L. Zhang, July 1999.
2637	Point-to-Point Tunneling Protocol, K. Hamzeh, G. Pall, W. Verthein, J. Taarud, W. Little, G. Zorn, July 1999.

Table E-1. Most Recent RFC Specifications (Current—June 1999) *(continued)*

RFC Number	Description
2636	Wireless Device Configuration (OTASP/OTAPA) via ACAP, R. Gellens, July 1999.
2635	Don't Spew a Set of Guidelines for Mass Unsolicited Mailings and Postings (spam*), S. Hambridge, A. Lunde, June 1999.
2634	Enhanced Security Services for S/MIME, P. Hoffman, Ed., June 1999.
2633	S/MIME Version 3 Message Specification, B. Ramsdell, Ed., June 1999.
2632	S/MIME Version 3 Certificate Handling, B. Ramsdell, Ed., June 1999.
2631	Diffie-Hellman Key Agreement Method, E. Rescorla, June 1999.
2630	Cryptographic Message Syntax, R. Housley, June 1999.
2629	Writing IDs and RFCs Using XML, M. Rose, June 1999.
2628	Simple Cryptographic Program Interface (Crypto API), V. Smyslov, June 1999.
2627	Key Management for Multicast: Issues and Architectures, D. Wallner, E. Harder, R. Agee, June 1999.
2626	The Internet and the Millennium Problem (Year 2000), P. Nesser II, June 1999.
2625	IP and ARP over Fibre Channel, M. Rajagopal, R. Bhagwat, W. Rickard, June 1999.
2624	NFS Version 4 Design Considerations, S. Shepler, June 1999.
2623	NFS Version 2 and Version 3 Security Issues and the NFS Protocol's Use of RPCSEC_GSS and Kerberos V5, M. Eisler, June 1999.
2622	Routing Policy Specification Language (RPSL), C. Alaettinoglu, C. Villamizar, E. Gerich, D. Kessens, D. Meyer, T. Bates, D. Karrenberg, M. Terpstra, June 1999.
2621	RADIUS Accounting Server MIB, G. Zorn, B. Aboba, June 1999.
2620	RADIUS Accounting Client MIB, B. Aboba, G. Zorn, June 1999.
2619	RADIUS Authentication Server MIB, G. Zorn, B. Aboba, June 1999.
2618	RADIUS Authentication Client MIB, B. Aboba, G. Zorn, June 1999.
2617	HTTP Authentication: Basic and Digest Access Authentication, J. Franks, P. Hallam-Baker, J. Hostetler, S. Lawrence, P. Leach, A. Luotonen, L. Stewart, June 1999.
2616	Hypertext Transfer Protocol—HTTP/1.1, R. Fielding, J. Gettys, J. Mogul, H. Frystyk, L. Masinter, P. Leach, T. Berners-Lee, June 1999.
2615	PPP over SONET/SDH, A. Malis, W. Simpson, June 1999.
2614	An API for Service Location, J. Kempf, E. Guttman, June 1999.

Table E-1.   Most Recent RFC Specifications (Current—June 1999) *(continued)*

RFC Number	Description
2613	Remote Network Monitoring MIB Extensions for Switched Networks Version 1.0, R. Waterman, B. Lahaye, D. Romascanu, S. Waldbusser, June 1999.
2612	The CAST-256 Encryption Algorithm, C. Adams, J. Gilchrist, June 1999.
2611	URN Namespace Definition Mechanisms, L. Daigle, D. van Gulik, R. Iannella, P. Falstrom, June 1999.
2610	DHCP Options for Service Location Protocol, C. Perkins, E. Guttman, June 1999.
2609	Service Templates and Service: Schemes, E. Guttman, C. Perkins, J. Kempf, June 1999.
2608	Service Location Protocol, Version 2, E. Guttman, C. Perkins, J. Veizades, M. Day, June 1999.
2607	Proxy Chaining and Policy Implementation in Roaming, B. Aboba, J. Vollbrecht, June 1999.
2606	Reserved Top Level DNS Names, D. Eastlake, A. Panitz, June 1999.
2605	Directory Server Monitoring MIB, G. Mansfield, S. Kille, June 1999.
2604	Wireless Device Configuration (OTASP/OTAPA) via ACAP, R. Gellens, June 1999.
2603	ILMI-Based Server Discovery for NHRP, M. Davison, June 1999.
2602	ILMI-Based Server Discovery for MARS, M. Davison, June 1999.
2601	ILMI-Based Server Discovery for ATMARP, M. Davison, June 1999.
2600	Internet Official Protocol Standards, J. Reynolds, R. Braden, March 2000.
2599	Request for Comments Summary RFC Numbers 2500-2599, A. DeLaCruz, March 2000.
2598	An Expedited Forwarding PHB, V. Jacobson, K. Nichols, K. Poduri, June 1999.
2597	Assured Forwarding PHB Group, J. Heinanen, F. Baker, W. Weiss, J. Wroclawski, June 1999.
2596	Use of Language Codes in LDAP, M. Wahl, T. Howes, May 1999.
2595	Using TLS with IMAP, POP3 and ACAP, C. Newman, June 1999.
2594	Definitions of Managed Objects for WWW Services, H. Hazewinkel, C. Kalbfleisch, J. Schoenwaelder, May 1999.
2593	Script MIB Extensibility Protocol Version 1.0, J. Schoenwaelder, J. Quittek, May 1999.
2592	Definitions of Managed Objects for the Delegation of Management Script, D. Levi, J. Schoenwaelder, May 1999.

Table E-1.   Most Recent RFC Specifications (Current—June 1999) *(continued)*

RFC Number	Description
2591	Definitions of Managed Objects for Scheduling Management Operations, D. Levi, J. Schoenwaelder, May 1999.
2590	Transmission of IPv6 Packets over Frame Relay Networks Specification, A. Conta, A. Malis, M. Mueller, May 1999.
2589	Lightweight Directory Access Protocol (v3): Extensions for Dynamic Directory Services, Y. Yaacovi, M. Wahl, T. Genovese, May 1999.
2588	IP Multicast and Firewalls, R. Finlayson, May 1999.
2587	Internet X.509 Public Key Infrastructure LDAPv2 Schema, S. Boeyen, T. Howes, P. Richard, June 1999.
2586	The Audio/L16 MIME Content Type, J. Salsman, H. Alvestrand, May 1999.
2585	Internet X.509 Public Key Infrastructure Operational Protocols: FTP and HTTP, R. Housley, P. Hoffman, May 1999.
2584	Definitions of Managed Objects For APPN/HPR In IP Networks, B. Clouston, B. Moore, May 1999.
2583	Guidelines for Next Hop Client (NHC) Developers, R. Carlson, L. Winkler, May 1999.
2582	The NewReno Modification to TCP's Fast Recovery Algorithm, S. Floyd, T. Henderson, April 1999.
2581	TCP Congestion Control, M. Allman, V. Paxson, W. Stevens, April 1999.
2580	Conformance Statements for SMIv2, K. McCloghrie, D. Perkins, J. Schoenwaelder, April 1999.
2579	Textual Conventions for SMIv2, K. McCloghrie, D. Perkins, J. Schoenwaelder, April 1999.
2578	Structure of Management Information Version 2 (SMIv2), K. McCloghrie, D. Perkins, J. Schoenwaelder, April 1999.
2577	FTP Security Considerations, M. Allman, S. Ostermann, May 1999.
2576	Coexistence between Version 1, Version 2, and Version 3 of the Internet Standard Network Management Framework R. Frye, D. Levi, S. Routhier, B. Wijnen, March 2000.
2575	View-based Access Control Model (VACM) for the Simple Network Management Protocol (SNMP), B. Wijnen, R. Presuhn, K. McCloghrie, April 1999.
2574	User-based Security Model (USM) for version 3 of the Simple Network Management Protocol (SNMPv3), U. Blumenthal, B. Wijnen, April 1999.
2573	SNMP Applications, D. Levi, P. Meyer, B. Stewart, April 1999.

Table E-1. Most Recent RFC Specifications (Current—June 1999) *(continued)*

RFC Number	Description
2572	Message Processing and Dispatching for the Simple Network Management Protocol (SNMP), J. Case, D. Harrington, R. Presuhn, B. Wijnen, April 1999.
2571	An Architecture for Describing SNMP Management Frameworks, B. Wijnen, D. Harrington, R. Presuhn, April 1999.
2570	Introduction to Version 3 of the Internet-standard Network Management Framework, J. Case, R. Mundy, D. Partain, B. Stewart, April 1999.
2569	Mapping between LPD and IPP Protocols, R. Herriot, Ed., T. Hastings, N. Jacobs, J. Martin, April 1999.
2568	Rationale for the Structure of the Model and Protocol for the Internet Printing Protocol, S. Zilles, April 1999.
2567	Design Goals for an Internet Printing Protocol, F. Wright, April 1999.
2566	Internet Printing Protocol/1.0: Model and Semantics, R. deBry, T. Hastings, R. Herriot, S. Isaacson, P. Powell, April 1999.
2565	Internet Printing Protocol/1.0: Encoding and Transport, R. Herriot, Ed., S. Butler, P. Moore, R. Turner, April 1999.
2564	Application Management MIB, C. Kalbfleisch, C. Krupczak, R. Presuhn, J. Saperia, May 1999.
2563	DHCP Option to Disable Stateless Auto-Configuration in IPv4 Clients, R. Troll, May 1999.
2562	Definitions of Protocol and Managed Objects for TN3270E Response Time Collection Using SMIv2 (TN3270E-RT-MIB) K. White, R. Moore, April 1999.
2561	Base Definitions of Managed Objects for TN3270E Using SMIv2, K. White, R. Moore, April 1999.
2560	X.509 Internet Public Key Infrastructure Online Certificate Status Protocol - OCSP, M. Myers, R. Ankney, A. Malpani, S. Galperin, C. Adams, June 1999.
2559	Internet X.509 Public Key Infrastructure Operational Protocols - LDAPv2, S. Boeyen, T. Howes, P. Richard, April 1999.
2558	Definitions of Managed Objects for the SONET/SDH Interface Type, K. Tesink, March 1999.
2557	MIME Encapsulation of Aggregate Documents, such as HTML (MHTML), J. Palme, A. Hopmann, N. Shelness, March 1999.
2556	OSI connectionless transport services on top of UDP Applicability Statement for Historic Status, S. Bradner, March 1999.
2555	30 Years of RFCs RFC Editor, et al, April 7, 1999.
2554	SMTP Service Extension for Authentication, J. Myers, March 1999.

Table E-1. Most Recent RFC Specifications (Current—June 1999) *(continued)*

RFC Number	Description
2553	Basic Socket Interface Extensions for IPv6, R. Gilligan, S. Thomson, J. Bound, W. Stevens, March 1999.
2552	Architecture for the Information Brokerage in the ACTS Project, GAIA, M. Blinov, M. Bessonov, C. Clissmann, April 1999.
2551	The Roman Standards Process—Revision III, S. Bradner, April 1, 1999.
2550	Y10K and Beyond, S. Glassman, M. Manasse, J. Mogul, April 1, 1999.
2549	IP over Avian Carriers with Quality of Service, D. Waitzman, April 1, 1999.
2548	Microsoft Vendor-specific RADIUS Attributes, G. Zorn, March 1999.
2547	BGP/MPLS VPNs, E. Rosen, Y. Rekhter, March 1999.
2546	6Bone Routing Practice, A. Durand, B. Buclin, March 1999.
2545	Use of BGP-4 Multiprotocol Extensions for IPv6 Inter-Domain Routing, P. Marques, F. Dupont, March 1999.
2544	Benchmarking Methodology for Network Interconnect Devices, S. Bradner, J. McQuaid, March 1999.
2543	SIP: Session Initiation Protocol, M. Handley, H. Schulzrinne, E. Schooler, J. Rosenberg, March 1999.
2542	Terminology and Goals for Internet Fax, L. Masinter, March 1999.
2541	DNS Security Operational Considerations, D. Eastlake, March 1999.
2540	Detached Domain Name System (DNS) Information, D. Eastlake, March 1999.
2539	Storage of Diffie-Hellman Keys in the Domain Name System (DNS), D. Eastlake, March 1999.
2538	Storing Certificates in the Domain Name System (DNS), D. Eastlake, O. Gudmundsson, March 1999.
2537	RSA/MD5 KEYs and SIGs in the Domain Name System (DNS), D. Eastlake, March 1999.
2536	DSA KEYs and SIGs in the Domain Name System (DNS), D. Eastlake, March 1999.
2535	Domain Name System Security Extensions, D. Eastlake, March 1999.
2534	Media Features for Display, Print, and Fax, L. Masinter, D. Wing, A. Mutz, K. Holtman, March 1999.
2533	A Syntax for Describing Media Feature Sets, G. Klyne, March 1999.
2532	Extended Facsimile Using Internet Mail, L. Masinter, D. Wing, March 1999.
2531	Content Feature Schema for Internet Fax, G. Klyne, L. McIntyre, March 1999.

Table E-1.   Most Recent RFC Specifications (Current—June 1999) *(continued)*

RFC Number	Description
2530	Indicating Supported Media Features Using Extensions to DSN and MDN, D. Wing, March 1999.
2529	Transmission of IPv6 over IPv4 Domains without Explicit Tunnels, B. Carpenter, C. Jung, March 1999.
2528	Internet X.509 Public Key Infrastructure Representation of Key Exchange Algorithm (KEA) Keys in Internet X.509 Public Key Infrastructure Certificates, R. Housley, W. Polk, March 1999.
2527	Internet X.509 Public Key Infrastructure Certificate Policy and Certification Practices Framework, S. Chokhani, W. Ford, March 1999.
2526	Reserved IPv6 Subnet Anycast Addresses, D. Johnson, S. Deering, March 1999.
2525	Known TCP Implementation Problems, V. Paxson, M Allman, S. Dawson, W. Fenner, J. Griner, I. Heavens, K. Lahey, J. Semke, B. Volz, March 1999.
2524	Neda's Efficient Mail Submission and Delivery (EMSD) Protocol Specification Version 1.3, M. Banan, February 1999.
2523	Photuris: Extended Schemes and Attributes, P. Karn, W. Simpson, March 1999.
2522	Photuris: Session-key Management Protocol, P. Karn, W. Simpson, March 1999.
2521	ICMP Security Failures Messages, P. Karn, W. Simpson, March 1999.
2520	NHRP with Mobile NHCs, J. Luciani, H. Suzuki, N. Doraswamy, D. Horton, February 1999.
2519	A Framework for Inter-Domain Route Aggregation, E. Chen, J. Stewart, February 1999.
2518	HTTP Extensions for Distributed Authoring — WEBDAV, Y. Goland, E. Whitehead, A. Faizi, S. Carter, D. Jensen, February 1999.
2517	Building Directories from DNS: Experiences from WWWSeeker, R. Moats, R. Huber, February 1999.
2516	A Method for Transmitting PPP Over Ethernet (PPPoE), L. Mamakos, K. Lidl, J. Evarts, D. Carrel, D. Simone, R. Wheeler, February 1999.
2515	Definitions of Managed Objects for ATM Management, K. Tesink, Ed, February 1999.
2514	Definitions of Textual Conventions and OBJECT-IDENTITIES for ATM Management, M. Noto, E. Spiegel, K. Tesink, February 1999.
2513	Managed Objects for Controlling the Collection and Storage of Accounting Information for Connection-Oriented Networks, K. McCloghrie, J. Heinanen, W. Greene, A. Prasad, February 1999.

Table E-1. Most Recent RFC Specifications (Current—June 1999) *(continued)*

RFC Number	Description
2512	Accounting Information for ATM Networks, K. McCloghrie, J. Heinanen, W. Greene, A. Prasad, February 1999.
2511	Internet X.509 Certificate Request Message Format, M. Myers, C. Adams, D. Solo, D. Kemp, March 1999.
2510	Internet X.509 Public Key Infrastructure Certificate Management Protocols, C. Adams, S. Farrell, March 1999.
2509	IP Header Compression over PPP, M. Engan, S. Casner, C. Bormann, February 1999.
2508	Compressing IP/UDP/RTP Headers for Low-Speed Serial Links, S. Casner, V. Jacobson, February 1999.
2507	IP Header Compression, M. Degermark, B. Nordgren, S. Pink, February 1999.
2506	Media Feature Tag Registration Procedure, K. Holtman, A. Mutz, T. Hardie, March 1999.
2505	Anti-Spam Recommendations for SMTP MTAs, G. Lindberg, February 1999.
2504	Users' Security Handbook, E. Guttman, L. Leong, G. Malkin, February 1999.
2503	MIME Types for Use with the ISO ILL Protocol, R. Moulton, M. Needleman, February 1999.
2502	Limitations of Internet Protocol Suite for Distributed Simulation the Large Multicast Environment, M. Pullen, M. Myjak, C. Bouwens, February 1999.
2501	Mobile Ad Hoc Networking (MANET): Routing Protocol Performance Issues and Evaluation Considerations, S. Corson, J. Macker, January 1999.
2500	Internet Official Protocol Standards, J. Reynolds, R. Braden, June 1999.

Table E-1. Most Recent RFC Specifications (Current—June 1999) *(continued)*

Index

▼ T

▼ X

▼ Y

▼ Z

INTERNATIONAL CONTACT INFORMATION

AUSTRALIA
McGraw-Hill Book Company Australia Pty. Ltd.
TEL +61-2-9417-9899
FAX +61-2-9417-5687
http://www.mcgraw-hill.com.au
books-it_sydney@mcgraw-hill.com

CANADA
McGraw-Hill Ryerson Ltd.
TEL +905-430-5000
FAX +905-430-5020
http://www.mcgrawhill.ca

**GREECE, MIDDLE EAST,
NORTHERN AFRICA**
McGraw-Hill Hellas
TEL +30-1-656-0990-3-4
FAX +30-1-654-5525

MEXICO (Also serving Latin America)
McGraw-Hill Interamericana Editores S.A. de C.V.
TEL +525-117-1583
FAX +525-117-1589
http://www.mcgraw-hill.com.mx
fernando_castellanos@mcgraw-hill.com

SINGAPORE (Serving Asia)
McGraw-Hill Book Company
TEL +65-863-1580
FAX +65-862-3354
http://www.mcgraw-hill.com.sg
mghasia@mcgraw-hill.com

SOUTH AFRICA
McGraw-Hill South Africa
TEL +27-11-622-7512
FAX +27-11-622-9045
robyn_swanepoel@mcgraw-hill.com

**UNITED KINGDOM & EUROPE
(Excluding Southern Europe)**
McGraw-Hill Education Europe
TEL +44-1-628-502500
FAX +44-1-628-770224
http://www.mcgraw-hill.co.uk
computing_neurope@mcgraw-hill.com

ALL OTHER INQUIRIES Contact:
Osborne/McGraw-Hill
TEL +1-510-549-6600
FAX +1-510-883-7600
http://www.osborne.com
omg_international@mcgraw-hill.com